Presidential Secrecy and the Law

Presidential Secrecy and the Law

ROBERT M. PALLITTO AND WILLIAM G. WEAVER

The Johns Hopkins University Press
Baltimore

© 2007 The Johns Hopkins University Press
All rights reserved. Published 2007
Printed in the United States of America on acid-free paper

2 4 6 8 9 7 5 3 1

The Johns Hopkins University Press
2715 North Charles Street
Baltimore, Maryland 21218-4363
www.press.jhu.edu

Library of Congress Cataloging-in-Publication Data

Pallitto, Robert M., 1964–
Presidential secrecy and the law / Robert M. Pallitto and William G. Weaver.
p.   cm.
Includes bibliographical references and index.
ISBN-13: 978-0-8018-8582-2 (hardcover : alk. paper)
ISBN-10: 0-8018-8582-5 (hardcover : alk. paper)
ISBN-13: 978-0-8018-8583-9 (pbk. : alk. paper)
ISBN-10: 0-8018-8583-3 (pbk. : alk. paper)
1. Executive privilege (Government information)—United States. 2. Separation of
powers—United States. I. Weaver, William G., 1956–   . II. Title.
JK468.S4P35 2007
352.23'5—dc22

2006022814

A catalog record for this book is available from the British Library.

Portions of chapters 2 and 3 are reprinted by permission from *Political Science
Quarterly* 120 (Spring 2005): 85–112. Portions of chapter 4 are reprinted by
permission from *The Journal of Law and Border Studies* 4 (Fall 2006).

For Laura
—Robert M. Pallitto

To Judith "Dody" Roberts, my sister, for her unflagging
support for me over many years.
—William G. Weaver

CONTENTS

Acknowledgments   *ix*

Introduction: The Secret Presidency   1

1 The Secret Presidency in Historical-Theoretical Perspective   24

2 The Classified President   45

3 State Secrets and Executive Power   84

4 The Shadow President: The Attorney General, Executive Power,
and the New Anti-Terror Laws   121

5 The President and National Security Surveillance   156

6 The New Executive Privilege   193

Conclusion: A Secret Presidency for the New Millennium?   217

Notes   *227*
Index   *255*

We wish to thank Louis Fisher, the epitome of a scholar, who provided valuable insight and criticism of various draft chapters of this book. David Plotke, Patricia Williams, and Nancy Fraser provided much-needed commentary and encouragement. Jason Hungerford, Jose Medina, John Motoviloff, Kathryn Motoviloff, and Bob Murray read and commented on several chapters. Steve Aftergood, and his project on government secrecy at the Federation of American Scientists, was an invaluable resource for information and help. We also thank Sibel Edmonds for her tenacity and dedication to seeing right done. We thank our friends and families—Ana Melendez; Shelli Soto; Rachel Serrano; Danielle Escontrias; Emily Bregman; Gwyn Murray; Christina Pallitto; Elizabeth Pallitto; Ellen, Roger, and Andrew Miller; John, Daniel, and Isabel Melendez; Shay Weaver; and of course Laura Melendez and Anne Allis for everything. We express our gratitude to Martin Schneider for saving us from many errors and much embarrassment. *Political Science Quarterly* graciously allowed us to use material we published there in chapters 2 and 3. Also, *The Journal of Law and Border Studies* allowed us to use material we published there in chapter 4.

Finally, we thank editors Henry Tom and Claire McCabe Tamberino at the Johns Hopkins University Press for their encouragement and support of this project.

Presidential Secrecy and the Law

The Secret Presidency

A popular Government, without popular information, or the means
of acquiring it, is but a Prologue to a Farce or a Tragedy; or, perhaps
both. Knowledge will forever govern ignorance: and a people who
mean to be their own Governors, must arm themselves with the
power which knowledge gives.

—*James Madison*

Q: Well, what do you make . . . of the people's right to know?
A: I don't believe in that as a general principle.
—*Maxwell D. Taylor, ambassador and retired U.S. Army general, 1971*

George Bush, Richard Cheney, Donald Rumsfeld, and high-level staff from
various agencies sat in the Cabinet Room of the White House around the large
oval mahogany table, a gift from Richard Nixon to the United States. They were
assessing recent crises and the effectiveness of the intelligence community, the
problems of civil libertarians and a prying Congress, and the outdated legal strictures impeding the collection and processing of intelligence. One complained
that people do "not understand that intelligence problems must be treated in a
special category" and that present exigent circumstances require relaxing legal
standards, for "it has always been the case in history where vital interests are
involved" that the president has the power to take whatever action is necessary to
safeguard the country. Another noted, in a statement familiar since the terrorist
attacks of September 11, 2001, that "Lincoln suspended certain rights [and] we
have had emergency laws. . . . There are many examples." Speaking of civil
liberties, Bush said that "we have gone too far at this business," and claimed that
he was "extremely sensitive to possible misdeeds" of the intelligence community
but that "rights are being safeguarded." Secretary Rumsfeld agreed "entirely with
all that has been said" and lamented that because of an overly deferential attitude
toward civil liberties, "we are being forced to give up sensitive information in

order to prosecute" terrorists and people leaking information to the press and public.[1]

Surely this meeting took place since 2001, right? But it did not. This discussion occurred on January 13, 1977, during the last National Security Council meeting of President Gerald Ford's administration. It brings out the dilemma that all presidents face: how to keep as much as possible secret without risking scandal and political backlash. Presidents, of course, typically press arguments that justify maximum secrecy in their activities, and in the area of national security the attitude frequently assumed by presidents and administrators is that in order to preserve the Constitution it must on occasion be violated, or at least "stretched" to fit the exigencies at hand. The Bill of Rights, as U.S. Supreme Court Justice Robert Jackson famously claimed, is not a "suicide pact," and the president, the office mainly entrusted with national security, cannot be expected to follow the Constitution to its death.[2] "Are all the laws, but one, to go unexecuted, and the government itself to go to pieces, lest that one be violated?" asked Abraham Lincoln in an address to Congress.[3] As political scientist Clinton Rossiter starkly made the point, in times of crisis our form of "government must be temporarily altered to whatever degree is necessary to overcome the peril" lest we be "obliterated."[4]

In theory, it is easy to choose between the collapse of our political system on the one hand and the violation of the Constitution to preserve the system on the other. But the dilemma is usually invidious, for rarely is a president presented with a choice between the necessity of extra-constitutional action and the destruction of the government or a great evil perpetrated on our people. With almost all information concerning threats to the United States now controlled by the presidency and less and less of that information made available to the Congress, public, and the courts, the president is in a position to characterize threats in ways most advantageous to his or her maintenance of power and achievement of desires.

In these conditions, the language of permanent crisis enters the executive vocabulary and neither Congress nor the judiciary find themselves in a position to challenge presidential claims in the area of national security. The question of national survival is often raised to justify controversial incursion into civil liberties protections, and every acquiescence to this strategy leads to increased presidential power. The line dividing national security information that, if disclosed, would put our institutions and citizens in jeopardy and information that is innocuous or disclosable without deleterious effects is often illusory.

The idea that decisions concerning disclosure of information are based on factual conclusions about harm to United States interests is often incorrect. Frequently, such determinations are based on political considerations that have little to do with objective analyses of national security or citizen safety and arise from fear of embarrassment from disclosure and efforts to maintain presidential prerogative against congressional inquiries and judicial orders. In effect, modern presidents have given themselves additional constitutional tools to reinforce themselves against political accountability and legal scrutiny.

These tools are designed to protect U.S. interests by ensuring information security and secrecy, but they also greatly increase executive power and provide new avenues for presidents and executive branch officials to circumvent Congress and the courts. The systemic effects on the presidency of the sweep of executive secrecy are only now becoming clear, and modern secrecy is institutionalized in the executive branch to a depth and degree never before seen. More than this, secrecy has transformed into a systematized means of political control, a transformation that is most complete in the administration of George W. Bush (not his father).

Both liberals and conservatives have stories of the heroic presidency, stories that turn on presidential efforts to resist Congress and, to a lesser extent, the judiciary, and to do what is "right" or "necessary" for the well-being of the country and its citizens. The heroic president rises above partisan bickering, escaping the politics of the moment to see clearly and act on unique and seemingly intractable problems facing our nation. In this sense, the heroic president is beyond politics, has put aside the venal and banal interplay epitomized by congressional courtier politics and is in service of "that which is effective"—whatever he decides that is. The liberal version of the heroic president is one Theodore Lowi characterizes as the Domestic Necessity Model, exemplified by a president who "meets the social need in defiance of Congress and 'the interests.' "[5] This "heroism" manifests itself in elevating repression of certain segments of the population to a condition of emergency that needs immediate redress.

Conservatives also have a story of the heroic president, but instead of depending solely on defiance of Congress for the fulfilment of social needs over the greed-infested politics of Capitol Hill, it arises out of the War Model of the presidency. This model presumes "a condition of war—or constant threat of some sort to national security—that makes aggrandizement of the presidency urgently necessary."[6] In this model the heroic president must fight Congress and the courts to assure the very survival of the nation, but the president must not merely defeat Congress and the courts, he or she must *subjugate* the other two branches of government to executive desire. This subjugation comes about under the plebiscitary president, the president who directly appeals to the people unmediated by institutions. Both of these stories equate greatness in the presidency with the expansion of Article II power, with the sheer personal force of will to create new powers against the weight of traditional constitutional understanding. They both frankly claim that constitutional limitations may be overridden by exigency, by the details and contexts of crises that make constitutional formalism incompatible with the nation's survival.

But the quality of heroism is a personal quality, not transferrable from one president to the next. Much of the history of the presidency can be told as the ebb and flow of power connected to the particular personalities that inhabited the office, and Lowi criticizes the view, adopted by many presidential scholars, that there is a credible story of development of presidential power to be told for the first 150 years of the nation's history. Some scholars do not even bother with the development theory and move straight to the argument that the Constitution created an executive with immense authority and power from the beginning.

Jeffrey Tulis, for example, denigrates the idea that the post–New Deal presidency represents a "constitutional revolution," arguing that the late emergence of this executive power "signifies the development of a constitutional logic, not the repudiation of constitutional principle."[7] While there is an appealing quality to this teleological argument, it is also true that it is self-justifying and difficult to evaluate. Any "logic" to the Constitution, especially as it plays out over time in courts and politics, is logic in hindsight. Tulis's teleological view of the presidency, the idea that the modern presidential democracy is not so much a result of events and forces as the natural maturation of power originally contained in Article II of the Constitution, allows advocates of executive power to avoid difficult questions. To say that all the power available to modern presidents was available to the first presidents sets up a constitutional interpretive fiction that would be the envy of any formalist. This view has many problems, not the least of which is that it gives no place to the increasing institutional features of the presidency.

Heroism is a quality not of institutions but of people, and modern presidents who act "heroically," who distort the features of accountability and constitutional limits to respond to crises, are in a position as no presidents were in the past to fix those "heroic" actions permanently in institutional arrangements. Expanded powers of secrecy undertaken in response to particular threats to national security are now ensconced in the executive bureaucracy and are, it seems, irredeemably fixed in institutional operations. They are no longer "heroic" responses to particularized threats to national security but the daily arrangement of ordinary power in the executive branch. With each expansion of secrecy power and its institutionalization, various types and segments of information become essentially withdrawn from public access. More and more executive branch and presidential activity and information becomes unavailable, leaving the president to perform more and more of his or her actions without accountability or scrutiny.

It is important to see that the liberal Domestic Necessity Model is one for which no conditions may be created to make expanded use of executive powers permanent, and liberal thinkers are content to think of heroic presidents as sui generis, that their expanded power is not transmissible from one administration to the next. On the other hand, conservatives have sought the Holy Grail of executive power, a device that would transform the presidency into a permanent War Model office and, more importantly, something that "can be shown to be transposable from international security to internal security."[8] Time and again, Republican presidents have pressed the point that the expansive foreign affairs and military powers of the office have a significant domestic dimension that liberals unjustifiably foil.

Secrecy and Accountability

Secrecy imposes tremendous costs on elective government; it is capable of destroying or undermining the legal, political, and cultural traditions that undergird our political system. The most obvious cost of secrecy is a reduction in executive accountability. To the extent that the executive branch becomes impervious to observation, mechanisms designed to keep presidents and their administrators honest become useless. Whatever remains secret ultimately need not be justified to anyone other than the president.

The lack of accountability created by secrecy also encourages executive branch manipulation of information and experimentation that may be aimed at Congress or even citizens. The second war with Iraq is arguably the only combat action in United States history justified solely on information unavailable to the public and Congress. The United States went to war essentially on the word of the president and intelligence agencies, which ostensibly work for the president.

Finally, accountability is thwarted by cutting Congress, the public, and non-governmental organizations out of the policymaking and formulation arena.

The literature of political science and law is littered with observations about secrecy in government, but there is little sustained analysis of the subject. And there is almost no literature concerning the general development of privileges and powers of secrecy in the institutionalized presidency. Although we see this as a disciplinary oversight, perhaps a disciplinary failure, it is also easy to understand why there is little written on the subject. Most observations concerning secrecy in government are event-driven and arise only after information concerning abuse has made it to the public. Such events are usually held to be more indicative of personal wrongdoing on the part of presidents or executive branch officials and less the result of institutionalized processes. One of the underlying points of this book is that as institutionalized powers of secrecy grew, the need for abuse of secrecy power receded. Or perhaps put more precisely, the institutionalization of presidential secrecy powers redefined "abuse" as the legally justifiable results of statutorily or judicially defined processes. With "abuse" redefined as the routine result of process, the use of secrecy for political purposes or personal agendas is depersonalized against the backdrop of rules and regulations.

Once the personal link to secrecy use is severed by the façade of institutional process, it is much more difficult to accuse presidents and their advisers of acting beyond their constitutional authority. Events involving specific cases and examples of abuse are much more attractive than analyzing the secrecy process with no means to see past the process to the details of how it works in practice. What is missed by many observers is the way in which institutionalized executive secrecy has transformed the presidency and depoliticized the president's role in governmental action. Where a president may do what is desired in secret, there is no reason to withstand the ordeal of a political battle to achieve the same ends. Secrecy may still have its risks, but those risks have been greatly reduced in the last several decades by both inadvertent and explicit grants of power to the president by Congress and through judicial acquiescence to executive claims concerning "national security."

Meanwhile, as secrecy powers go undiscussed and less than fully appreciated, analysts continue to theorize about presidential power in ways that have changed little over time. In attempting to explain constitutional limits of presidential power scholars often juxtapose two U.S. Supreme Court cases. The strong extremity, exemplified by *United States v. Curtiss-Wright Export Corp.*, is read to cede near-plenary power to the president in the realm of foreign affairs and, by extension, the realm of national security. In *Curtiss-Wright*, the Court recognized "plenary and exclusive power of the President as the sole organ of the federal government in the field of international relations—a power which does not require as a basis for its exercise an act of Congress."[9]

Against this strong claim to power is posed the decision in *Youngstown Sheet and Tube v. Sawyer*, the case concerning President Harry Truman's seizure of the steel mills in support of the Korean War. The most influential opinion in the case was Justice Robert Jackson's simple but brilliant analysis of the political arrangements of power among the branches of the federal government, theorizing that the constitutionality of presidential actions ebbs and flows depending on whether or not the president acts in concert with or against the expressed desires of Congress. In his concurring opinion, Jackson started by commenting that "comprehensive and undefined presidential powers hold both practical advantages and grave dangers . . . [and these] are a more realistic influence on my views than the conventional materials of judicial decision which seem unduly to accentuate doctrine and legal fiction." Jackson smartly captured the dangers of modifying constitutional doctrine in response to emergencies or the personalities of presidents when he noted that "the opinions of judges, no less than executives and publicists, often suffer the infirmity of confusing the issue of a power's validity with the cause it is invoked to promote, of confounding the permanent executive office with its temporary occupant. The tendency is strong to emphasize transient results upon policies . . . and lose sight of enduring consequences upon the balanced power structure of our Republic."[10]

Unlike *Curtiss-Wright,* which some think envisions fixed and expansive presidential authority over national security, Jackson's opinion in *Youngstown* posits a contextually driven judicial judgment of executive power. Just which of these approaches holds sway with the courts has been the source of contention among scholars, but Harold Hongju Koh, in a thoughtful and convincing book, argues that whatever persuasive power Jackson's analysis may have had at one time, it fell apart with an increasingly institutionalized presidency. Koh claims that since the Vietnam War there has been a "subtle judicial revival of the *Curtiss-Wright* theory of the National Security Constitution [and] that *Curtiss-Wright* has not only survived *Youngstown,* but now challenges it once again."[11]

Accompanying this "subtle judicial revival" is an equally important apparatus of secrecy that underscores Koh's legal analysis. Many constitutional analyses of presidential power treat the presidency as if it were a transparent institution. But less and less of presidential machinery is observable, and we have only the processes of secrecy to refer to and explore for those disappearing portions of the institutional presidency. Through the rise of institutionalized secrecy, presidents have the source of "comprehensive and undefined" powers that Jackson feared.

Often contention over constitutional doctrine overlooks the crucial question of access to information by both Congress and the judiciary, and debates over observable uses of presidential power deflect attention from the ways secrecy has profoundly changed the presidency. If the president may operate in secret, may refuse to divulge information to coordinate branches for purposes of preventing oversight or determination of constitutional and statutory conformance, then it matters little which theory of presidential power the courts adopt. As Koh correctly points out, the story of the national security president is a "tale of three branches, not two," and the role of the courts in this story is frequently underappreciated. It is not unusual for commentators to forget about the judiciary when discussing the presidency, sharing Kenneth Collier's opinion that "how the two great branches of American government share power may be one of the most misunderstood issues in politics,"[12] the federal judiciary, of course, not counting as one of Collier's "great" branches.

Collier is right, but if the relationship between Congress and the president is misunderstood, then the relationship between presidential secrecy and the judiciary is well-nigh unexplored. While we occasionally address congressional inability to rein in presidential secrecy powers, the tale we tell here of the judiciary is one that is deeply critical of federal courts and their studied efforts to denude themselves of any power to control presidential claims over national security. Under the guise of separation of powers, the judiciary has lost control of virtually any legal means to bring the president to account for actions undertaken in furtherance of "national security" in the broadest sense of the term.

A question that is seldom explored is how much opacity in governmental activity the Constitution and our democracy will tolerate. On the one hand, we expect executive branch officials to maintain the security of the nation and its citizens, which can often be accomplished only through secret activity. On the other hand, we expect that the president and executive branch officials will be held legally accountable for their abuses of power, and accountability requires publicity of actions and policies. These two desires are often incompatible and pose difficult issues for courts and politicians.

But since the 1950s, and with increasing speed through the 1970s right up to the present, the balance has shifted decisively in favor of presidential secrecy. Before the events of 9/11, executive powers of secrecy were a set of non-interlocking privileges, powers, and policies that operated in ad hoc ways, which partially obscured the great grants of secrecy power that Congress and the courts had ceded to the president over the previous years. The events of 9/11 catalyzed these disparate powers into a set of interlocking mechanisms that have fundamentally transformed the office of president and the powers of the executive branch in a manner that is inconsistent with constitutional provisions and the functioning of our democracy.

This book is about the president's now-comprehensive power to keep information from coming out: the power to operate without scrutiny, without the obligation to bargain with parties and adverse interests. Some might object that leaks of classified information occur frequently and that this provides an important check on presidential abuse of the secrecy power. This objection has merit, but leaks are like potential news stories, and the extent to which they capture the attention of the press and the public's imagination is predicated on contextual, ephemeral, and idiosyncratic features. Many abuses of executive secrecy power will not leak; if they do, they are too complex, impossible to simplify for public appetites, and are born cold. Further, as we explain, much of the "abuse" of presidential secrecy is now so institutionalized that an extensive apparatus has grown up around it to give it the power to withstand attack and scrutiny, to clothe great expanses of secrecy with legitimacy.

Notwithstanding the perception by many people that presidents after Nixon have been hemmed in by courts and Congress and handicapped in perpetrating the kinds of abuses engaged in by Nixon and his aides, presidents now have more institutionalized powers of secrecy than at any time in history. The Iran-Contra scandal of the Reagan presidency resurfaced the concerns of the Watergate era, but these concerns receded rather quickly with no lasting damage to the presidency, and presidential acquisition of powers to shield executive branch activities from scrutiny proceeded apace.

Two Tracks

Theodore Lowi describes two tracks of presidential activities, a "Fast Track . . . of secrecy, unilateral action, energy, commitment, decisiveness, where time is always of the essence" and a "Slow Track," a "Separation of Powers Track, permitted by a longer time horizon, and desirable wherever time permits, yet highly unpredictable, uncontrollable, public, full of leaky holes, and dominated not merely by the legislature but by a large and pluralistic process fueled by greed." As grants of secrecy power to the executive branch and presidency grow, the impulse to "fast-track" as much as possible is irresistible. As Lowi notes, while the distinction between the two tracks is logical, it is "breaking down because conservative drivers on the Fast Track are like Pac-Man characters eating up the pedestrians of the Slow Track."[13]

In the choice between accountability, political danger, and interference with policy desires on the one hand and total secrecy, efficiency, and virtually unimpeded policy action on the other, it is not difficult for a president to choose secrecy over politics. And the choice *is* between secrecy and politics, for every policy, initiative, or event withdrawn from public scrutiny is a circumvention of political processes. Presidential powers of secrecy, as configured at present, are powerful means to circumvent both politics and the Constitution, for anything that may be brought under the mantle of national security is protected from exposure. And since 9/11, the already malleable term *national security* has become astonishingly ductile in its ability to cover material that previously would never have been seen as being protected by secrecy privileges and powers.

The "slow track" described by Lowi is roughly the power of persuasion through bargaining that Richard Neustadt famously described and analyzed. Neustadt argued that the president is by and large in a weak position despite an impressive array of formal powers conferred by the Constitution, Congress, and the courts. He held that the president is mainly relegated to bargaining for outcomes, a sort of high-powered Willy Loman pleading with Congress, the bureaucracy, and special interests with little more weaponry than "a shoeshine and a smile," as Arthur Miller put it. King of the mountebanks, the president must hawk his wares through charm and guile, with little resort to formal or institutional powers vested in the office. As Neustadt says, "Power is persuasion and persuasion becomes bargaining." Much of the president's power is illusory, for "command is but a method of persuasion, not a substitute, and not a method suitable for everyday employment," and "the probabilities of power do not derive from the literary theory of the Constitution." In the end, "The essence of a President's persuasive task with congressmen and everybody else, is to induce them to believe that what he wants of them is what their own appraisal of their own responsibilities requires them to do in their interest, not his."[14]

There are occasions, though, Neustadt explains, where "self-executing" orders may issue from the president, but this only occurs when certain conditions are present. Neustadt gives few examples of such orders, orders that said "'Do this, do that', and *it was done*." It is interesting that Neustadt confines his analysis of self-executing commands to controversial and highly publicized events. Indeed, he claims that one condition for a self-executing order is not only that the order be made public but that it be *widely* publicized.[15] But Neustadt overlooks presidential decisions made in secret. Virtually all efforts to justify secrecy powers are based in national security; such efforts comprise a special category of self-executing orders.

In security matters there is a rare confluence of interests between presidential and bureaucratic desires, and the combination of limited congressional powers of oversight and judicial timidity leave these desires virtually uncontested. Simply put, both the president and the federal bureaucracy have an undiluted desire to keep what they do secret, and, as we shall see, they almost without fail may now fulfill that desire. This means that in most—indeed, nearly all—cases the desires of the president and his or her advisors translate into action. As Gordon Silverstein notes, "in a cooperative environment [presidential] influence is enough" to ensure action.[16]

One might protest that Neustadt's discussion of self-executing orders was meant to deal with momentous events, not merely operational details of the secret executive bureaucracy. But over the last several years President George W. Bush, for example, has created secret military tribunals,[17] ordered court proceedings closed to the public,[18] directed massive detention of aliens without individualized suspicion of criminal behavior or criminal indictment,[19] denied detainees access to counsel and courts,[20] exercised privileges of secrecy for an astounding array of governmental material and operations,[21] conferred secrecy powers on previous presidents,[22] refused to respond to congressional inquiries,[23] ordered or sponsored intrusive investigation and surveillance of citizens,[24] and used public funds to buy seemingly legitimate journalists to propagandize government initiatives.[25] These decisions are no mere operational details; they change the complexion of power in the federal government and, we believe, have created a fundamental constitutional shift in favor of presidential power.

While aspects of these decisions are publicly known, they are largely cloaked in secrecy by the obstinate refusal of the Bush administration to make details of its policies public. In the past, when the president asserted power in reaction to crises, it was done without much of the institutional, statutory, and legal accoutrements that the presidency has now accumulated. Presidents in search of "fast track" issues naturally gravitate toward matters of foreign affairs, where Congress and the public are less apt to interfere with presidential action. But public expectations changed on 9/11, and Congress suddenly became compliant in the arena of domestic security. Presidential power expanded behind a moving wall of secrecy always already justified to the people before the fact and accepted by them as necessary to protect their lives and the wealth of the country. With no means of inspection of how such expanded power is used, the people and Congress, made malleable through fear, largely accepted presidential action without complaint. Now, because of the increasing institutionalization of the presidency, especially the institutionalization of secrecy power, when the urgency for action recedes it may well be impossible to roll back executive power, so the shift to the secret presidency may be a permanent one.

If Neustadt's analysis previously did not overstate the weakness of the presidency, it most assuredly does now. If originally one of Neustadt's main contributions was to construct the scholarly vision of the personal presidency, by now that vision is frequently both misleading and anachronistic. His engaging and convincing personalization of the presidency is from a different age, even though it remains useful in many discussions and contexts. The exercise of personal power and desires may now, through a highly developed institutional structure of secrecy, be translated into immediate action. It may be generally true, as Lynn Ragsdale observes, that "presidents have less ability to wield purely personal power now than they did earlier"; any focus on the idiosyncratic qualities of the president obscures the growing institutional continuity of the presidency across administrations.[26]

As the institutional features of the presidency increase, it is reasonable to expect that the personal desires of any one president will dissipate against the background of organizational continuity. With the White House employing thousands of people, covered by a budget of several hundred million dollars, sheer size requires that the president's personal involvement in day-to-day business is minimal. Institutional analyses rather than theories of personal style should be more efficacious now than when Neustadt first published his observations of the presidency.

As the importance of personal power in the presidency shrinks, our failure to engage in more aggressive institutional analyses of the office leads to an enormous scholarly blind spot. We agree that institutional analyses of the presidency have lagged behind fixations on personality and biography, but the events after 9/11 show that a president's personal desires concerning national security may be translated into action far more effectively by the institutions placed at the disposal of the office of the president over the last several decades. As we argue, the confluence of personal and institutional power in national security matters have transformed the presidency into a power without checks or oversight by either Congress or the judiciary. At the same time, personal presidential desire becomes more actionable in the arena of national security, the institutional features of the presidency eliminate the personal qualities of prudence, restraint, and gentility, qualities Neustadt, in his nearsighted focus on the presidential "slow track," associates with what might be termed "presidential honor."

The quaintness and present inapplicability of Neustadt's analysis of presidential power is vividly demonstrated by an article he wrote after the collapse of the Nixon presidency. The Nixon presidency failed, according to Neustadt, for lack of propriety and prudence—so "almost surely, Watergate's effect upon the presidency will be to prop up old incentives for restraint, restoring White House prudence to something like its former state." Resembling a wish more than a prediction, the return to executive prudence Neustadt expected never materialized. To be fair, he held no illusion that a return of civility would be necessarily long term, predicting that it could easily pass by the time of the 1984 election. But he also thought it possible that by the mid-1990s "the collegial constraints upon a President will be at least as strong as twenty years ago."[27] These sentiments reflect a wistfulness for a genteel presidency, one that, if it ever did exist, certainly does not now.

In contrasting the excesses of the Nixon presidency with his experiences as a White House employee in the Truman administration, Neustadt relates a story about a Republican legislator who inadvertently left an embarrassing memorandum at the White House. Neustadt recounts that he and his colleagues wanted to use the memorandum for political purposes, but that special counsel to the president, Charles Murphy, simply put it in an envelope and sent it back to the legislator's office. Neustadt writes that "Murphy's conduct showed propriety—indeed for me defines it—so that much [of Nixon's] White House staff behavior simply shocks me."[28]

This may be so, but propriety may be measured in terms other than personal interaction. The same administration Neustadt uses as an example of propriety engaged in more illegal telephone wiretaps than any other administration in history, in terms of both total wiretaps and wiretaps per year (see chapter 5). Truman also recorded the third most illegal buggings, just behind the administrations of Franklin Roosevelt and Dwight Eisenhower and apparently believed in inherent presidential power to engage in warrantless surveillance for reasons of pure domestic security.[29]

Gentility, prudence, honor, and loyalty are attributes of people, not institutions, and Neustadt helps keep alive the vision of the presidency as something dominated by personalities rather than institutional operations. Neustadt's approach remains a seductive strategy to analyze the presidency, but the presidency is far more of an "institution" than it was a few decades ago, and, as Ragsdale and others argue, an interest in the idiosyncrasies of personality must be augmented with analysis of the institutionalized features of executive power. Indeed, if we must depend on "propriety" to safeguard against presidential abuse of power, we are lost.

As George Edwards notes, "Neustadt's emphasis on relationships does not lead naturally to investigations of the president's accountability, the limitations of the institution's legal powers, or the day-to-day operation of the presidency."[30] Edwards makes the interesting and unavoidable conflation between "the president" and the "institution" of the president. It is precisely this ambiguity, the inability or unwillingness of presidential scholars to differentiate between personalities and institutions that seemingly leads us back over and over again to interest in the person of the president rather than interest in the presidency as an institution with continuity across administrations.

Neustadt's claim that a focus on relationships and personalities yields more useful information than one on law and institutional powers grew beyond its reasonable limits and ultimately helped misdirect scholarly investigation. While concentrating on the props and actors moving around the stage of our "national drama" may tell us a great deal about the office of the president—Neustadt's position—we prefer to concentrate on what transpires in the wings and backstage, out of public view.

One feature of political science scholarship that allowed Neustadt's views to overreach is that national security issues had usually been exiled to chapters and articles on the foreign affairs powers of the president. The "fast track" described by Lowi was largely one that existed in relation to foreign affairs, diplomacy, and espionage. Recent events, most notably the "war on terror," have expanded the range of national security powers of the president from those mostly confined to the conduct of foreign affairs to include what in the past had been properly domestic security matters.

In 1997, the Commission on Protecting and Reducing Government Secrecy reported that there were five sorts of information that the president and the bureaucracy may withhold from public view: (1) "national defense information, encompassing military operations and weapons technology"; (2) information concerning foreign affairs and diplomatic activity; (3) information developed by law enforcement agencies; (4) "information relevant to the maintenance of a commercial advantage (typically proprietary in nature)"; and (5) personally private information. The commission explained that (1) and (2) "together define the sphere of 'national security information.' "[31]

After 9/11 this view of secrecy became deficient. The list is no longer exhaustive of the kinds of information now withheld by the executive branch for reasons of national security. Information concerning government contracts, community emergency response plans, gasoline truck delivery routes, and many other kinds of unclassified information is routinely withheld. Since 9/11 the mission of the Federal Bureau of Investigation has gone from one mainly concerned with domestic criminal activity to one directed at the prevention of terrorism. As Attorney General John Ashcroft noted, "That day [September 11], in those early hours, the prevention of terrorist acts became the central goal of the law enforcement and national security mission of the FBI."[32] Large portions of the FBI are now given over to intelligence gathering, infiltration of organizations, and intervention of terrorist activity, functions originally a part of the president's foreign policy powers but now directed against domestic targets. The terrorist attacks of 9/11 created tremendous pressure to eradicate the differences in how domestic and external threats are managed. The presidential discretion historically used to conduct foreign operations with impunity and consideration for effectiveness rather than legality has spilled over into the domestic sphere.

National security is now as much a domestic concern as it is a foreign affairs issue, and this complicates the constitutional and political landscape to a degree encountered only rarely in our history. Not since the Red Scare of the 1950s has the government been so intent on knowing so much about the private activities of citizens and on engaging in constitutionally questionable policies. Liberals and conservatives alike have voiced concern over the secretiveness and intrusiveness of executive branch operations since 9/11. Angered by the Bush administration's unwillingness to share information and to divulge the activities it takes in the name of national security, members of both sides of the aisle object to what they regard as a "policy of secrecy."[33]

In 2001, Republican representative Dan Burton of Indiana, chairman of the Committee on Government Reform, buttonholed a deputy attorney general and told him, "You tell the president there's going to be a war between [him] and this committee. . . . We've got a dictatorial president and a Justice Department that does not want Congress involved. . . . Your guy's acting like he's king."[34] But this dissatisfaction with the Bush administration's penchant for secrecy is largely unorganized, ineffective, and frequently incoherent. The president remains largely unfazed by such criticism, and the institutionalization of mechanisms of presidential secrecy continues. The frustration evinced by Representative Burton is unlikely to recede even after the Bush presidency is over, as the tools of secrecy it institutionalized will be at hand to tempt future presidents and administrators.

Only a few years ago, a Department of Homeland Security would have been unthinkable; it is telling that the attorney general, perhaps even more than the director of central intelligence, is now identified with national security issues. The addition of the secretary of homeland security and the new powers created in the executive branch for domestic surveillance and law enforcement reflect a sea change in the public perception of safety and governmental approaches to security policy. The events of 9/11 transformed the phrase "national security" from one that conjured images of relations with nation-states to one that brings to mind suspicious fertilizer purchases, crop-duster pilots, and the capacity among our citizens to create a sealed room at home using duct tape.

In the aftermath of the terrorist attacks of 9/11, the Bush administration has made unprecedented claims of executive powers of secrecy and asserted broad powers to withhold information from Congress, the courts, and the public. In response to these claims Congress initially contributed to this expansion of executive power by rushing into effect a number of statutes either creating or extending executive authority to engage in surveillance and searches in the name of protecting the United States from both internal and external threats. Congressional members on both sides of the aisle are now concerned that these expanded powers may never be reined in and that effective oversight of their use is all but impossible. Future presidents will surely find these expanded powers appealing, and more contentious matters than ever before may be fast-tracked.

Themes and Approaches

It is the primary duty of presidents and executive branch officials to maintain the security of the nation and its citizens, a task that often can be accomplished only through secret activity. But the same powers of secrecy granted to the executive branch to accomplish these goals are also ripe for abuse. Increasingly, our governmental institutions are unable to hold the president accountable for actions undertaken in secret in the name of national security. In a subtle but sweeping way, this failure is working detrimental changes in our federal governmental institutions. The mechanisms of these changes and the effects these changes are having on our democracy are the subjects of this book.

In addition to the mechanisms of secrecy and their institutional, political, and social effects, we concentrate on several themes. First is the evolution of institutionalized executive secrecy—how massive presidential power accrued to permit a wide range of questionable activity virtually without fear of congressional oversight or judicial interference. And considering institutional development of national security apparatus in the executive branch, it is unlikely that the recent Democratic takeover in Congress will result in significant oversight successes. In the past, decisions by presidents to withhold information or engage in questionable surveillance activities were made on the basis of inherent presidential authority by the president and a close group of trusted advisors. This had the effect of placing all of the political risk for such decisions directly on the president and of guaranteeing that abusive behavior, though regrettable, would be relatively circumscribed and limited in scope out of fear of discovery by the press, the courts, Congress, and the public.

The everpresent threat of bad publicity for questionable activity acted as a delimiting force on the range of executive action. Of course, the temptations to abuse are great, and presidents and their advisors frequently overestimated their abilities to keep operations secret. Clandestine activity that violated privacy rights, compromised the sovereignty and laws of foreign nations, subjected citizens to violations of their constitutional rights, and utilized unwitting Americans in experiments eventually became public and impelled Congress to act.

The debacle of the Nixon presidency provided the final motivation needed to overcome opposition and inertia, so Congress enacted sweeping changes meant to delimit presidential power and increase legislative control of the intelligence community. Congress created structures to increase presidential accountability and decrease presidential discretion in national security matters. Paradoxically, and against all expectations, these legislative changes and their interpretation by courts have frequently institutionalized the very sorts of executive discretion they sought to eradicate. Not only have these efforts at executive control generally failed, they have in fact increased presidential power while at the same time insulating the president from political and legal liability for questionable activity. Now presidents rely on legal processes established by Congress, which often involve Article III judges and, theoretically, congressional oversight, to distance themselves from policies and decisions that formerly would have been taken only at great political risk. As we argue, congressional oversight and judicial restraint on presidential activities in these processes are largely illusory.

A second theme we pursue is the abdication of judicial responsibility for oversight of executive branch actions and the failure to maintain separation of powers in the area of national security. Whenever national security concerns are raised, time and again the courts simply capitulate to presidential and executive branch desires. Federal judges are extremely reluctant to second-guess presidential claims that exposure of information, operations, and policies may imperil the United States. Sometimes this deference reaches remarkable levels, as when courts agree with the president that the revelation of the existence of a single car battery on an Air Force base or the admission into evidence of already published bank records jeopardizes national security.[35]

And courts are often more than merely passive participants in these efforts; sometimes they actively take part in their own emasculation through the creation of legal doctrines that safeguard presidential wishes. For example, the federal judiciary often explicitly or implicitly employs a doctrine known as the "mosaic theory" to prevent the exposure of executive branch activity. The disturbing feature of the mosaic theory, discussed further in chapter 3, is that it is most often used to prevent the disclosure of information that is neither classified nor directly connected with national security concerns, with the justification that individual bits of information, though unclassified, might collectively lead to a picture of

United States activities or capabilities that would justifiably be made classified. Not surprisingly, the mosaic theory, among other legal doctrines, leads to abusive efforts by presidents to keep information secret to prevent embarrassment or the exposure of violations of the law. Courts have also shown a willingness to expand the privileges and immunities of the president based both on Article II powers and on separation of powers doctrine.

A third current is the inability of Congress to maintain oversight and control of executive national security activity. As Congress transfers massive amounts of power to the president to engage in national security operations, it becomes less and less likely that meaningful oversight of those operations will take place. Legislation in the national security area is a classic example of what Theodore Lowi calls "legiscide," where Congress grants power and then ineffectively tries to take it back, one little bit at a time.[36] Post-9/11 statutes such as the USA-PATRIOT Act and the Homeland Security Act transferred enormous power to the president without the proper consideration and contemplation.

These legislative grants of authority were rushed through without the normal hearing process, and they contained numerous provisions that raise serious civil liberties questions, issues of oversight, and concerns about the balance of power between the president and Congress. Though some of these statutes contain sundown provisions and the authority they grant to the president could theoretically end, it is unlikely that this power can or will be recalled. Large institutional changes in the executive branch have taken place in response to these statutes, and it seems likely that the grants of authority made to the president in statutes will survive in some form, sundown provisions or not.

Piecing together the statutory grants of power, expanded privileges, deference of the federal judiciary, and lack of congressional oversight and control of executive powers of secrecy, we conclude that the presidency of today is very different from that of just a few years ago. Massive amounts of power have been concentrated in the presidency, a power that has been given focus by the events of 9/11. A fundamental change has taken place in our Constitution due to both the accretion of presidential power concerning national security and the transformation of "national security" into a domestic, as well as a foreign, problem. The plenary authority presidents wield in the area of foreign relations has crept into the domestic affairs of United States citizens, and because much of the power given to the president is backed by new and increasing bureaucratic machinery and legal processes, it is unlikely that executive secrecy and clandestine operations will subside.

We investigate the three themes described above in the context of particular presidential privileges or grants of power to the president. After chapter 1, each chapter takes up a secrecy power held by the presidency and traces the history of the power concerned, how it contributed to a change in the presidency, and the effects it currently has on law, politics, and society.

In chapter 1 we address shifts in presidential power in the context of a discussion of the theoretical approaches to understanding the presidency. For example, Stephen Skowronek argues that presidents make politics within cycles of institutional order, and his work reminds us that certain typologies are inevitable in this area: for instance, the stance of a president vis-à-vis his or her predecessor. Every president must oppose or continue the order that preceded him or her, and that positioning creates the conditions under which the politics of his or her presidency will be made. As we argue throughout the book, however, the pervasiveness of presidential powers of secrecy threatens to break the constitutional strictures that have held the presidency in a dynamic, yet largely balanced, relationship with the other branches of American government. Thus, while the existing scholarship is important to understanding the contemporary presidency, we are in many ways now on new ground, and this chapter attempts to begin charting that ground through an examination of the limits of traditional approaches to understanding the presidency.

Chapter 2 concerns the presidential power to classify information, perhaps the most obvious and efficient means to promote governmental secrecy. A succession of presidents has asserted total control over all aspects of the classification process via executive order, statutes, and case law. Recently, presidents have extended this power to include kinds of information historically available to the public and courts. Even agencies and departments that have historically been prohibited from classifying material are now invested with classification authority. With this vastly expanded authority residing in the presidency, untold amounts of records of governmental activity previously available to public, judicial, and congressional scrutiny are now secret, and important democratic and intra-governmental checks on executive power have been lost. These institutional changes are exacerbated by aggressive responses to any challenges to the growth of the executive's classification power.

Chapter 3 concerns the obscure but exceptionally powerful state secrets privilege, a privilege that is little understood and little discussed in the literature of presidential studies. Richard Neustadt does not even mention it in *Presidential Power,* and Raoul Berger mentions it only once in his exhaustive work on executive privilege.[37] First adapted from British law by the United States Supreme Court in a Cold War–era case involving a military plane crash, the state secrets privilege prevents the disclosure of information in court proceedings when "there is a reasonable danger that compulsion of the evidence will expose matters which, in the interest of national security, should not be divulged."[38]

This seemingly narrow privilege soon expanded into a powerful executive branch tool to prevent judicial oversight and to conceal embarrassing or even criminal conduct from public scrutiny. The privilege even trumps constitutional rights and the courts' constitutional duty to oversee executive activities. Among other uses, the privilege has protected presidents and administrators against claims of lying to Congress, engaging in racial and sexual discrimination, violating citizens' Fourth Amendment rights, and violation of criminal and civil environmental statutes. As it becomes even more important than it has been in the past, this important tool of executive power virtually invites executive overreaching and excessive secrecy.

In chapter 4 we take up the major anti-terror initiatives since September 11. While often fulfilling legitimate national security needs, these initiatives also cede broad and largely unconsidered authority to the executive branch. This chapter illuminates the nexus covering secrecy, efficiency, and presidential power. The chief figure in these new grants of authority to the presidency is the attorney general, who is invested with enormous discretion and power both by post–September 11 legislation and by administrative changes in the executive branch. The astounding accretion of power to the office is made clear by the wide perception that the attorney general, rather than the director of central intelligence or even the secretary of homeland security, is the office most actively involved in maintaining national security. Most of these statutory grants of power are perhaps irretrievable by Congress and threaten to become permanent features of the executive branch. In many ways, the attorney general now functions as a "shadow president," wielding an unprecedented amount of executive power and often accomplishing administration goals in secret which would be more problematic if pursued directly by the White House. And of course, the Constitution does not speak directly to checking the Attorney General's power as it does vis-à-vis the president, such that the "shadow president" encounters less resistance, in this greatly strengthened role, than the president himself would face.

National security surveillance and the Foreign Intelligence Surveillance Act (FISA), discussed in chapter 5, serve as good examples of how efforts to rein in executive abuse have not only failed to achieve their goals but also expanded executive power and virtually eliminated presidential accountability for abuse of surveillance of United States citizens. The institutionalization of executive powers concerning national security and secrecy has the effect of relieving the president of political accountability for actions that are illegal or abusive, even if those actions are the result of policies established by the president. The temptation to engage in wiretapping is as old as the technology enabling presidents to do so, and presidents have consistently succumbed to this temptation.

Throughout the period when wiretapping was illegal, and even more so after FISA legalized wiretapping activity, presidents have used electronic surveillance to meet national security needs and accomplish political desires. FISA mainly sought to vitiate presidential claims to an inherent power to engage in warrantless national security surveillance of citizens, but significantly, the supervising court (Foreign Intelligence Surveillance Court) has denied only a handful of warrant applications. Requirements to acquire a warrant under FISA are far less stringent than the probable cause requirement of the Fourth Amendment and the processes established by prior law. And in 2001, Attorney General Ashcroft moved to modify FISA procedures to allow criminal prosecutors to control and direct the use of FISA warrants, thus blurring the line between law enforcement and intelligence gathering.

The result, essentially, is a means to bypass the Fourth Amendment under many circumstances. Ironically, the attempt of Congress to control presidential abuse of surveillance power through FISA has resulted in a massive grant of authority to the president to engage in exactly the sorts of actions Congress sought to prevent. Under the provisions of FISA, nothing concerning the application and issuance of warrants, the collection and processing of information, and the details of electronic surveillance need ever be disclosed to the public, Congress, or non-FISA federal judges.

But even the power under FISA is judged by presidents as insufficient to meet the needs of national security. President George W. Bush, for example, authorized warrantless surveillance by the National Security Agency shortly after 9/11, and it appears that the NSA intercepted millions, if not billions, of communications and sifted them through complex software applications designed to look for patterns of suspicious behavior. But unlike the routinized procedure provided by FISA, President Bush put his neck on the line with this program, as it was done through personal authorization under a claim of inherent Article II power to engage in national security surveillance outside of statute and the Fourth Amendment. Under FISA, process and statute protect the president from being personally attached to any abuse of surveillance power, but when the existence of Bush's order was leaked, it put the president right where he should be when such matters are disclosed: in a political fight with the Congress, the courts, and the public. It should be a matter of law, politics, and debate whether or not the president has overstepped his authority.

Executive privilege, as distinguished from the state secrets privilege discussed in chapter 4, is a qualified privilege that protects executive branch information not connected to national security. Since Watergate, executive privilege has been gradually restored to the arsenal of presidential secrecy powers, and it has been used vigorously by the Bush administration. Executive privilege is one aspect of executive secrecy power that has been studied by political scientists, and Mark Rozell, in his thorough book and several shorter works, concludes that informal mechanisms of congressional oversight prevent overuse of the privilege. We disagree. As we have seen repeatedly in the Bush administration, those mechanisms of oversight often prove unavailing, particularly when the threat of judicial involvement recedes. Thus, in chapter 6 we show that the new executive privilege complements the other secrecy powers we describe, and contrary to the beliefs of other commentators, it is not sufficiently constrained by the existing constellation of institutional forces within the American political system.

The events of September 11 changed the disparate accumulated powers of presidential secrecy into a coherent and sweeping means for presidents to close off investigation and oversight activities by Congress, the judiciary, and the public. Congress and the courts contributed greatly to this result, and in the conclusion we contend that this acquiescence helped to transform the presidency permanently into an office that now has the institutional and legal means to overreach the presidential powers contemplated by the Constitution.

The conclusion situates the specific presidential initiatives described in the individual chapters within a larger narrative of executive activity and change that has reshaped power relations through a convergence of institutional, historical, and personal factors. An awareness of all of these types of influences is necessary, as none by itself presents an adequate picture of the shifting nature of presidential power. We hope to illuminate the historical conjuncture currently faced by the United States government (and, more pressingly, by the American people) by describing presidential institutional conditions and events as well as the personal characteristics that have led us to our present situation. As a result of judicial and congressional failures, presidents are far more insulated from political acrimony and scandal for their secret activities than in the past.

The secret presidency and the recent massive increases of institutional power in the executive branch make it difficult for us to conclude other than that the presidency has become permanently deformed by the unchecked and unaccountable power it wields. As counterintuitive as it may seem, we conclude that congressional efforts to control executive abuse in areas of purported national security concerns are ill-advised. These efforts insulate the president and establish a bureaucratic machinery and process for engaging in precisely the kinds of activity that were meant to be avoided. We argue that aggressive action to control executive branch abuse of secrecy should not come from Congress but from the courts, which are in a position to provide the scrutiny necessary to discourage presidential abuse of secrecy powers.

CHAPTER ONE

The Secret Presidency in Historical-Theoretical Perspective

We depend now more than ever on the President's mind and temperament.

—*Richard Neustadt*

Introduction: Individual-Centered and Institutional Approaches to Presidency Studies

A review of the scholarship on the presidency shows that much of the work can be classified in one of two ways: as studies of presidential *character* or as studies of the presidency as an *institution*. "Character" scholars focus on the traits of individual presidents, trying to make sense of events of a particular term in office with reference to the president's formative developmental experiences, social position, worldview, temperament, leadership style, and similar factors. The general idea is that individual-specific information is the key to understanding presidential politics. "Institution" scholars, by contrast, are more concerned with the office of the chief executive itself. What norms of political practice come with the office at a given time? Where does the presidency stand with regard to other political institutions? What powers (express or implied) are available to the officeholder? Is the power of the presidency increasing or decreasing? To begin this chapter on presidency studies, we introduce one well-known, representative work from each of these two approaches in order to provide parameters for the discussion to follow.

James David Barber's book *The Presidential Character* has become a classic of presidency studies, read even by presidents themselves. Written over many years, it includes predictions of presidential performance that Barber wrote as each new president from Richard Nixon to George H. W. Bush took office. Barber stakes out a clear position from the start, telling us that "who the President is at a given time can make a profound difference in the whole thrust and direction of national politics." Moreover, character analysis facilitates comparisons: "crucial differences can be anticipated by an understanding of a potential president's character, his world view, and his style."[1]

Barber believes that presidential personality can be studied "as a dynamic package understandable in psychological terms" and that "the best way to predict a President's character, world view and style is to see how they were put together in the first place." By posing two questions, "(a) how active he is and (b) whether or not he gives the impression he enjoys his political life," Barber is able to construct a four-cell classificatory scheme by which each president is designated active or passive, positive or negative. Wilson, Hoover, and Lyndon Johnson, for example, are "active-negatives," working tremendously hard but often seeming not to enjoy it, while Truman, Kennedy, and Carter are "active-positives." Not surprisingly, there are but two "passive-negatives": Coolidge and Eisenhower, for such a combination would seem to self-select away from presidential aspirations.[2] To arrive at these classifications, Barber examines biographical material for each presidential subject, and the results are illuminating: we see, for example, how tragic Hoover's early life was, how Kennedy was pushed to excel, and how Truman grew up with abundant parental affection.

Each individual then comes up against the trials of the job. As Barber puts it, "Presidential character resonates with the political situation the President faces."[3] This interactivity between character and circumstances is crucial, for no one's political life is unalterably determined from childhood. Active-positive presidents Carter and Truman could fail: Carter made mistakes by dealing artlessly with Congress early on, and Truman's resoluteness led him to speak and act quickly without full consideration.

Predictions are just that, and in the case of Reagan, Barber predicts beforehand that Reagan might "leave the Constitution about as he found it and the nation, at peace" or, alternatively, that he might "have disaster thrust upon him."[4] The job of president is too multifaceted, and the national and international political landscape contains too many contingencies, so that it would be foolish to insist that we could know with certainty how anyone's presidential term will turn out. Nonetheless, applying the active-passive/positive-negative scheme gives Barber confidence about what the central struggles of a given president will be, at least internally. Consider, for example, what he says about the active-negative type:

> Having experienced severe deprivations of self-esteem in childhood, the person develops a deep attachment to *achievement* as a way to wring from his environment a

sense that he is worthy; progressively, this driving force is translated into a search for independent *power* over others, pursued with intense dedication, and justified idealistically. Whatever style brings success in domination is adopted and rigorously adhered to; but success does not produce joy—the person is frequently depressed—and therefore ever more striving is required.[5]

This description fits Richard Nixon well, and Barber's presentation of Nixon's negativity and suspicion is one of the most powerful passages in the book. Again, what is crucial here is the way that Nixon fits into the active-negative type the author constructs. Personality shapes presidential behavior, and personality comes in a "dynamic package," which gives the observer material to construct a good prediction.[6]

The Decline and Resurgence of Congress by James R. Sundquist examines the presidency from the institutional perspective, which contrasts sharply with Barber's character study approach.[7] Interestingly, Sundquist's account pivots around the same presidency just described—Nixon's. The "nadir" of Congressional power relative to the presidency occurs at the end of Nixon's first term, and the level of Congress's power increases in the months following. Rather than personality, Sundquist is concerned about what was happening to the presidential office during that time and about what powers Congress was able to exercise in response. The institutional approach asks about the relative power of governmental institutions over time.

At the pivotal point of October 1972, the Nixon administration challenged Congress on budget matters and impoundment of funds and won. Two years later, Nixon was gone, and legislation was passed to redress several of his excesses. That legislation signals, in Sundquist's view, a resurgence of congressional power and a corresponding decline in the power of the executive. There had been other ebbs and flows of institutional power in the history of the American political system, so the events of 1972 through 1978 were simply a continuation of what Sundquist calls "the unending conflict" between the political branches.[8] The picture that emerges here is one of a *system* that adjusts itself to threat and change, in which the power of Congress is understood in relative terms to the power of the president.

Scholars of political institutions examine forces that affect institutional behavior. In the context of American politics, party organizations are one force that is likely to exert influence on institutions. As the strength of political parties declined after midcentury, though, the strength of the presidency grew. Sundquist explains that "the bonds of party . . . engender impulses toward harmony to offset the natural tendencies toward dissension." The stronger the bonds of party, the more constrained the president will be when he shares the same party identification with the majority party in Congress. This feature of institutional behavior leads one to expect that in a period of party decline, the executive will seek to consolidate power because he feels the absence of party-organizational constraints.[9]

In view of this dynamic, Sundquist asks whether a "responsible party" model would be helpful in stabilizing congress-president relations, and he suggests some reforms that would give the party more influence over those relations.[10] Political parties, then, play a part in narratives of institutions, and their influence transcends individual presidencies, following longer-term trends. Of course, one could argue that weak parties make the character traits of individual presidents more important by giving presidents more room to exert their influence. Our purpose here, though, is simply to give a sense of what comes into focus when one uses an institutional or an individual lens to study the presidency. In the institutional paradigm, one sees a play of forces that shape the office, and any snapshot in time shows the temporary state of those forces. To look at a particular presidency this way is to see how opportunities are structured in that political moment.

In this introduction to presidency studies, we briefly mention a theory that has been discussed frequently during the George W. Bush administration, because it allows for vast institutional power backed by constitutional sanction. The "unitary executive" has been mentioned in the confirmation hearing of a Supreme Court nominee, in the press, and even in a Supreme Court opinion.[11] Its proponents consistently suggest that certain presidential emergency powers are unreviewable and may be exercised without prior consent of the other branches. John Yoo has argued that "the Constitution makes it clear that the process for conducting military hostilities is different from other government decision-making." War powers are limited only by "congressional appropriation and control over domestic legislation." And they should be construed broadly: "any ambiguities in the allocation of power that is executive in nature—such as the power to conduct military hostilities—must be resolved in favor of the executive branch."[12] To accept and implement the unitary executive is to change the institution significantly, and we mention the theory here because it is an example of an institutional change that would structure the office differently for future presidents, regardless of their individual characteristics. It would provide greater efficiency for the executive at the expense of balanced power.

A Closer Look at Presidency Studies: Neustadt, Lowi, and Skowronek

Having discussed briefly the broad division of presidency studies between the character and institution approaches, we can now look more closely at several important studies with a better understanding of the role of individual and institutional factors in those works. Of course, few commentators take an absolute position on the importance of individual and institutional factors; most, including those who follow here, are more nuanced, emphasizing one but not entirely discounting the other.

Modern scholarship on presidential power tells multiple stories at once. Among them are the strengthening of ties between the White House and the people and the presidency's rise in importance as an institution to the point where it eclipses party attachments.[13] To say that the president executes the people's will more directly and more effectively than the Congress would be an oversimplification, and yet there is a decided emphasis, in contemporary scholarship, on the president's ability to go "over the heads" of legislature and party and appeal directly to the voters.[14]

Stephen Skowronek argues that presidents make politics within cycles of institutional order, and his work reminds us that certain typologies are inevitable in this area: for instance, the stance of a president vis-à-vis his predecessor is something that each presidential administration must negotiate.[15] Every president must continue or oppose the order that preceded him; that positioning, in turn, creates the conditions under which the politics of his presidency will be made. As we argue throughout this book, however, some of the changes in the presidency we have seen recently, produced when historical events and individual actions arose against the institutional framework of the modern (or postmodern) presidency, seem to take us into an entirely new realm of political power relations. Recent presidential action threatens to break the constitutional strictures that have held the presidency in a dynamic yet largely balanced relationship with the other branches of American government. For example, changes that have been institutionalized by the Bush administration, especially those implemented following the unprecedented events of 9/11, reorder the institution in ways never before seen. Thus, while the existing scholarship is important to understanding the contemporary presidency, we are in many ways on new ground with the retreat of party influence, the advance of a permanent or semi-permanent "war" presidency, and a judiciary clearly sympathetic to the expansion of presidential power.

We begin this section with a discussion of Richard Neustadt's landmark work on the presidency. *Presidential Power* treats the presidency generally rather than with respect to secrecy or executive privilege alone—in fact, he mentions executive privilege only once in the book.[16] Neustadt sees the modern presidency as a sharp break with the past. He depicts a gentlemanly president who operates according to shared rules of presidential conduct and who resolves problems of executive branch management and interbranch conflict through diplomacy and tact. It is impossible to escape the influence of Neustadt's work, which has shaped the field of presidential studies for five decades. But as we indicated in the introduction, we hold that the gentlemanly president has been eclipsed by a presidency that relies on a stronger institutional framework. These institutional features enable presidents to accomplish more and render the rules of Neustadt's bargaining paradigm less applicable, if not completely obsolete. In our evaluation, it is more useful to study the increased institutional capabilities first and only then to consider the relevance of any surviving rules and norms of presidential conduct.

Theodore Lowi's work shows the plebiscitary character of the modern presidency, focusing more than Neustadt on the rather direct and unmediated relationship between the presidency and the American people.[17] So while Neustadt is concerned with the way the president manages governmental conflict, Lowi sees the president's relationship with the *people* as paramount: the president replaces the two major political parties as the object of the voters' affective attachment. Once again, though, the institutional changes wrought over the past three decades complicate Lowi's story of the plebiscitary presidency, and we explore that tension here.

Stephen Skowronek's work on the presidency, which is historicist in orientation, fits our investigation best. Skowronek manages to draw parallels between presidential administrations separated by a century while keeping in sight the historical trends that change the institution over time, such as the rise of mass media. He maintains this dual focus by measuring the recurring patterns of presidential leadership in *political time* and American historical events in *secular time*. He argues that presidents make politics within cycles of institutional order and that certain typologies are useful in highlighting those cycles: for instance, the stance of a president vis-à-vis his predecessor. Every president must oppose or continue the order that preceded him, and that positioning creates the conditions under which the politics of his presidency will be made. It is easy to see the increased secrecy practiced by the Bush administration, for example, as part of Bush's repudiation of the preceding Democratic regime of Bill Clinton.

Despite our affinity with Skowronek's methodology, however, we part company with him to some extent when we emphasize the lasting institutional changes threatened by the secrecy initiatives of various recent presidents. The presidency in the new millennium appears changed in ways that will be difficult to reverse; although there is unquestionably a strong historical orientation in Skowronek's work, we focus even more than he does on the break with established patterns of institutional power dynamics. Thus, although we follow Skowronek more than we rely on the other leading contemporary scholars of the presidency, we see the need for a shift in emphasis as we survey the politics of secrecy generally in this chapter and executive privilege specifically in chapter 6.

By discussing only three major currents in presidential studies in this chapter, we do not purport to offer a complete—or even representative—survey of the works in the field. Rather, we see each of the three scholars discussed in this chapter advancing the study of the presidency in ways that matter most for our purposes: understanding the changes in the presidency after Watergate and gauging the effect of those changes on the possibilities for presidential action, both now and in the future. Neustadt, Lowi, and Skowronek ask the kinds of questions that are most relevant for our inquiry, so it is critical for us to consider their answers from within our framework; it is to their work that we turn, in chronological order.

Neustadt's Gentlemanly President

Richard Neustadt's monumental scholarly work on the presidency was shaped entirely by his experience working in the Truman administration. He brought the lessons and understanding he gained by watching and participating in presidential politics to the academy, where his landmark *Presidential Power* has influenced generations of scholars up to and beyond his death in 2003. For Neustadt, the "modern" presidency, which began with Franklin Delano Roosevelt, was defined by the emergence of a new set of presidential leadership skills. Starting with FDR's presidency, Neustadt sees a different institution from the one that came before, exhibiting differences that make the "modern" period incommensurable with what came immediately before. One distinctive feature is a certain kind of individual skill: "We depend now more than ever," he tells us, "on the President's mind and temperament." In particular, he notes the importance of expertise in negotiating the complex political landscape of the mid–twentieth century: dealing effectively with Congress, the executive bureaucracy, and powerful state government officials, among other groups, had become crucial to presidential power—indeed, marking the difference between an administration's success and failure. In a typically aphoristic formulation, Neustadt asserts that a president must convince all politically relevant parties of his "right to everybody's information."[18] By doing so, he can gain and preserve a power advantage within the executive and in relation to the other branches. This example of Neustadt's presidential prescriptions is telling because it indicates what kind of resource the president needs most (information) and what the informal processes are to get it (persuasion and management of individuals).

Neustadt recounts a specific incident wherein one of President Truman's senior aides, Charles S. Murphy, accidentally obtained an incriminating document written and left behind by a congressional adversary.[19] While we might have expected Murphy to provide the document to the press, Neustadt tells us that Murphy actually managed to let his adversary know that the president had seen the document; Truman did nothing more with the document after that. Such an indirect and informal move by Truman (through his aide) could be seen as gentlemanly and dignified, but Neustadt sees more in it than that.

He explains that Truman's aide saw at once what less adept observers would not notice on their own: that it was far more effective to proceed subtly and indirectly, that nothing additional would have been gained by the more heavy-handed responses of getting the press involved or confronting the document's author. This incident is important because it is an example of the use of a certain kind of leadership skill to maximize power. As we shall see, Neustadt conceptualized power in a way that became important and influential for students of the presidency.

Neustadt draws a key distinction between the formal powers of the president, which are specified in Article II of the Constitution (for example, the veto power, the appointment power), and power in the form of "influence on governmental action." He wants us to see that power conceptualized as "influence" is more important in analyzing the presidency and that the effective use of even the enumerated powers depends on the president's skill in gaining and using influence. The president has the power to carry out "self-executing" orders (even though, as Neustadt points out, someone else is *actually* executing those orders in most cases): seizure of steel mills or deployment of the National Guard, to take two of Neustadt's historical examples.[20] While the president can proceed with self-executing orders and can usually accomplish what he seeks to do in such cases, the injudicious use of that available power over the long term can be damaging.

The key question—one that the president must ask in advance when considering whether or not to deploy power—is what resources he will expend when he uses self-executing orders. Sometimes the cost is too great, and the result is a

Pyrrhic victory or a weakened administration in a poorer position to fight and win the next political conflict. Neustadt's discussion of self-executing orders and the costs of issuing them has found its way into our contemporary political lexicon in the term *political capital*: that phrase, while it did not originate with him, captures the kind of interpersonal, transactional, and diplomacy-based understanding of the presidency that Neustadt pioneered. George W. Bush's statement after the 2004 election ("I earned capital in the campaign, political capital, and I intend to use it") implicitly invokes Neustadt and his notion of persuasive power.[21]

What determines or influences the result of a successfully deployed self-executing order? Neustadt tells us that in successful instances such as the steel seizure, the following factors were present: "The President's involvement was unambiguous. So were his words. His order was widely publicized. The men who received it had control of everything needed to carry it out. And they had no apparent doubt of his authority to issue it to them."[22]

Some appraisal of these factors (involvement, words, publicity, control, authority) must be done in advance by the president so that the contemplated use of power will be successful and not too costly. A prudent executive will analyze the situation with something like this five-part test in mind. One reason why such close, careful analysis is necessary is that the self-executing order is a last resort: other, less costly means are usually tried first—or at least they should be. This was certainly true in the desegregation context: "There were few things [Eisenhower] wanted *less*," Neustadt assures us, "than federal troops enforcing desegregation of a southern school."[23]

Thus, the five factors were clearly present at the time the president decided to send the National Guard to Little Rock, so the president could act with confidence that his self-executing order would be accomplished. But it was equally significant that the president had reached a juncture where such a decision was needed— indeed, where it was unavoidable. Neustadt hints that the constitutional show-down in Little Rock was produced in part by the slightly deferential manner in which Eisenhower had approached earlier discussions with segregationist governor Orval Faubus.[24] This makes the point about earlier choices structuring full-blown crises down the road, but it also conveys Neustadt's belief that adept maneuvering early on can eliminate the need for the riskier course of self-executing orders.

At any given decision-making juncture, then, a president will consider whether these factors are present. However, the "institutional thickening" that has occurred in the years since 1960 problematizes the making of such a straightforward calculation based on the assumption of a thinly populated institutional field.[25] Is it really the case that a president can always, or even usually, avoid major conflict by using diplomatic skill alone? What about institutional change over nearly half a century? Even if we focus on the straightforward question of the size of the White House staff, we can readily see a difference in institutional complexity. We quote Neustadt's prescription above that the president must convince the government of his "right to everybody's information," but what use is that "right" when the volume of information is unmanageably large? Indeed, Bush administration supporters raised just that defense when pressed on the administration's failure to act on terror alerts in the months before 9/11.[26]

Some scholars have criticized Neustadt for overemphasizing individual traits of presidents at the expense of the institutional features of the modern presidency.[27] While this point is well taken, he can scarcely be faulted for taking such an approach. First, it was personal experience that informed and even shaped his scholarly style: his own involvement in executive affairs positioned him to provide just that sort of insider's perspective. Moreover, he sought to show us that the modern presidency presented a new set of conditions against which each successive officeholder's skills would be tested. He presented his account of these political phenomena by way of case studies involving certain presidents and particular events.

Harvey Mansfield's *Taming the Prince* explores the tension between an executive situated within a constitutional scheme of balanced powers and an executive defined by its ability to get things done.[28] After reconstructing the constitutional executive using materials from the modern political philosophy of Machiavelli (obviously), Montesquieu, Locke, and others, he ends with the Reagan presidency and argues that Reagan navigated the constitutional separation of powers effectively while maintaining an active and efficacious executive branch. In the end, Mansfield uses the Reagan administration to show that it is individual virtue, as conceptualized by Aristotle and Hamilton, that the modern executive both calls for and develops in its leaders. Virtue is the element that resolves the tension between legality and effectiveness and cements the modern executive branch into a potent political force.

Mansfield's work resonates with Neustadt's conception of modern presidential power in that both rely heavily on virtue and conceptualize it similarly. For Neustadt, presidential power is *performative*: we know it in its instancing, and we evaluate it according to what it does. Diplomacy and the ability to control information are the virtues disclosed in Neustadt's stories of presidential success and failure. Moreover, what matters in the evaluation of the gentlemanly president is the effective utilization of managerial skills, so that virtue for both Neustadt and

Mansfield draws on a Machiavellian conception: the gentlemanly president is an ideal to strive for not because gentlemanly comportment is valuable in itself, but because it is instrumental to success in the modern context.

It is difficult to forgo all other categories of normative analysis of the presidency (such as constitutional and democratic values), especially when one has lived through Watergate, the Iran-Contra scandal, and the Supreme Court's *Bush v. Gore* decision.[29] Neustadt cautions that "the probabilities of power do not derive from a literary theory of the Constitution," and while this aphorism is often cited as a helpful plea for realism in presidential studies, it also underscores the overreliance on individual virtue (conceptualized narrowly) in Neustadt's account of things.[30] By dismissing constitutional interpretation as "literary theory," he manages to disparage normative inquiry into political practice (and literary theory too), leaving to one side anything that does not help to predict success or failure. While descriptive, instrumentalist political analysis is obviously an accepted variety of political science scholarship, we submit that such analysis shortchanges normative concerns, and anyone who employs it must be aware of the tradeoff.

Skowronek's criticisms of Neustadt are even more penetrating. While he credits Neustadt with "introduc[ing] a sense of coherence into the relentless succession of incumbents and rais[ing] the study of leadership efforts above the idiosyncrasies of the case at hand," he sharply questions whether "modern" presidents are as different from their earlier counterparts as Neustadt insists they are. He suggests that Neustadt renders premodern presidents as nothing more than "caricatures" of actual historical figures when in fact they shaped the developing institution, negotiated interbranch relations, and practiced constitutional interpretation. Nineteenth- and early twentieth-century presidencies were far more than "mere clerkships," and the tendency to view them as such is "nothing more than a conceit of modern times."[31] Thus does he dispose of the "modern" demarcation point with which Neustadt begins his theorizations on presidential power.

Skowronek turns next to the unidirectional relationship between the officeholders and the office that is implicit throughout *Presidential Power*. While Truman and Eisenhower certainly influenced *events,* they worked within the institution of the modern presidency, which for Neustadt has remained static from its inception. The office comes with certain constraints, and individual presidents are successful, in Neustadt's view, to the extent that they can negotiate those constraints: obtaining information from cabinet heads, to take one example. Thus, great presidents may influence history in a larger sense, but they leave the office as they found it. Skowronek, by contrast, points out that presidents shape the institution just as much as they are shaped by it; they structure, to a significant

extent, the possibilities that the succeeding president faces. This criticism is useful: a recursive conception of the officeholder's relationship with the office serves
to enliven theorizing about presidential politics.

Where, then, do these criticisms leave us with regard to the relevancy of
Neustadt's work? Is there anything worth preserving beyond the initial ordering it
brought to presidential studies? The obvious, continuing relevancy of *Presidential
Power* is shown by the influence this single, short work has had on political
scientists for decades. All of the criticism we cite here was written in the last ten
years: discussion of Neustadt's work continues today, over forty years after the
work first emerged.

One interesting speculation emerges when one applies Neustadt's work to the
Bush administration: a sort of inverse corollary to his rule of presidential expertise.
Neustadt predicts that "our need will be greater for a presidential expert in the
Presidency," and by "expert" he means someone who can skillfully negotiate
institutional constraints and individual personalities in government to his or her
advantage. Looking forward from the end of the 1950s, Neustadt predicts that
racial integration and organized labor will pose great political challenges for
presidents in the 1960s. To depend upon one man to see the nation through such
challenges is acceptable, Neustadt tells us, so long as that man is an expert, because
his expertise will "naturally [commit] him to proceed within the system."[32]

The corollary to this rule of expertise is the following: leaders who lack the
expertise that Neustadt finds so crucial will have to compensate for that shortcom-
ing by using other means to achieve their political goals. Perhaps this corollary
explains the unprecedented reliance by George W. Bush on secrecy. Bush has not
been comfortable with the press; he does not address the public often but frequently commits gaffes when he does so. When asked on July 4, 2003, about the
death toll on American soldiers in Iraq and the possibility of continued Iraqi
resistance, Bush famously remarked, "Bring it on."[33] What would Neustadt have
made of this callous, thoughtless, and flippant retort—and its cost? The error,
moreover, is a typical rather than an isolated one.

The infrequency of Bush's contact with the press is highly unusual, and his
solo news conferences as president are by far the lowest number held by any
recent president.[34] The administration has acknowledged, moreover, that press
events in the Bush White House have on occasion been staged affairs.[35] Journalist
Ken Auletta notes that Bush maintains a suspicion of the media that originated
with the president's father, and to some extent, with his mother. Auletta suggests
that for Bush the media are not a part of the public that helps to keep the government accountable but rather a group with selfish motives, a personal threat.[36] It is

difficult to say whether such an attitude generates a hostile and guarded relationship with the press, or whether the relationship generates more of the same—or both—but in any event the Bush administration has shown itself unable to deal with the press in the "virtuous" manner that Kennedy did and has chosen instead to veil its actions from the public scrutiny offered by the conventional and accepted method of media reporting.[37]

The evident hostility in President Bush's relations with Congress has been noted by members of his own party as well as by Democrats (see chapter 5). It is clear that Bush does not fare well when his record is juxtaposed with the "modern" presidencies Neustadt surveys: not in terms of his statecraft or his political virtue. What sort of anecdotes would Neustadt have gleaned from the first four years of the Bush administration? While major world events have occurred on Bush's watch (the 9/11 attacks, wars in Iraq and Afghanistan) and while serious allegations of misconduct requiring response have arisen during his first term (alleged intentional misuse of false intelligence on Iraq, torture of Iraqi prisoners, questions about desertion of his own military duty), none of them brought forth presidential action in response that exhibited the skills Neustadt noted in Truman, Roosevelt, Kennedy, or even Eisenhower, of whom Neustadt was more critical. What, then, for example, is the relationship between such shortcomings and the politics of George W. Bush's presidency? It may well be that Bush's disdain for proceeding "within the system"—and by "system" we take Neustadt to refer to such things as the give-and-take of interbranch relations and the norms of media interaction—is fully explained by his lack of precisely those skills Neustadt found to be so important to a modern president. So we see a reliance on secrecy and a frequent circumvention of accepted rules for practicing presidential politics as a default position to which Bush has resorted.

As we shall see in chapter 6, the Bush administration sought to make major advances in the scope and nature of executive privilege. These advances demonstrate both an attempt to build secrecy-related institutional structures that increase executive power and a means of operating when constructing them that relies on secrecy as well. Thus, this corollary—that lack of expertise in controlling information access and practicing diplomacy generates a politics of secrecy—goes quite far in explaining the institutional changes in the presidency under Bush.

Lowi: The Personal Presidency

Theodore Lowi's concern about the growth of the institutional presidency is captured particularly well in one of his comments about the direction of executive

reform: it would, he said, "have to deal effectively with the excessive personification of American government in the presidency." Lowi coined the terms *plebiscitary presidency* and *personal presidency* to describe what happened to the institution
in the mid– to late twentieth century, as political parties declined in power and
influence and the legislative and judicial branches helped the presidency to grow.
He explains that the presidency has become "an office of tremendous personal
power drawn from the people—directly and through Congress and the Supreme
Court—and based on the new democratic theory that the presidency with all
powers is the necessary condition for governing a large, democratic nation."[38]

Lowi lays blame with Congress for what he calls "legiscide": when "Congress
delegates broadly and then tries to take it back in bits and pieces." By giving broad
grants of discretionary authority to the president, Congress fostered the growth of
the presidency—and then found itself unable to check the ever-increasing powers
of the office. Referring to the War Powers Resolution as a specific example, Lowi
notes, "Even when Americans looked to Congress to . . . get out of Vietnam,
Congress was delegating new legislative powers to the presidency—some of the
broadest powers ever delegated by Congress to the executive branch."[39] We will
discuss in greater detail just how legiscide works, but first it is necessary to flesh
out the processes by which American government reached that juncture in the
first place.

Lowi ties the growing congressional acquiescence evident in legiscide to a
political theory emphasizing managerial competence: government administration had to be rethought "in order to cope with the politicization of administrative
agencies." But this very politicization of the agencies, he explains, "result[ed]
from the delegation of broad policy-making powers to them" in the first place.[40]
For Lowi, the evident circularity of this thinking points up the fact that the impetus for the changes that led to the plebiscitary presidency lacked theoretical
grounding. Theory looked to satisfy needs of the emerging institutional presidency as if those needs were pre-given and inevitable, when in fact it was only
theory itself that made them seem so.

At the same time that Congress was helping to create the plebiscitary presidency, the Supreme Court contributed to that result as well. Lowi notes that the
Court's ruling in its *Schechter* decision (a New Deal–era case), enunciated a rule
that could constrain the executive significantly: broad, vague delegations of congressional power to the executive are unconstitutional. However, the Court did
not subsequently enforce its ruling in other cases, and that potential constraint
lay unused for decades, right up to the present day.[41] And even when the Court
denied Truman's claim of constitutional authority for seizure of the steel mills

during the Korean conflict, Lowi argues, it suggested that statutory authority might be found elsewhere; Truman had merely relied on the wrong source of law.[42] These two landmark cases, then, leave open more than is commonly supposed.

Lowi warns that the decline of political parties, the investiture of greater political power within the executive, and the identification of the state with the president lead us to what he calls the "homogenized regime." Democracies "tend to impose a single value on all institutions and practices." The homogenized regime is the opposite, Lowi tells us, of the "mixed regime," in which different branches share powers and functions. The regime breeds vagueness in legislation, in the sense that the real work of "substantiat[ing] statutes is left to the president and the agencies."[43] Deceit is inherent and unavoidable in this scheme of things, Lowi tells us, because the plebiscitary presidency creates unfulfillable expectations about that office—no one person or branch of government can do all that has been left for the executive to do, so the executive began to resort to deceit in the face of impossible tasks.[44]

As we discuss in chapter 5, the Foreign Intelligence Surveillance Act (FISA) is another example of legiscide, right alongside the War Powers Act. In both cases, in response to recent threats of executive overreaching, Congress ostensibly acted to constrain the president. The national experience of Vietnam, and the national experience of a president who had (among other things) vastly overused domestic surveillance created an awareness of presidential power run amok, and both these crises generated reformist impulses. However, what resulted in both cases was not a constrained executive but rather an executive cloaked with legality, free to pursue the same activities as before, but acting now within a legitimating statutory framework.

Nixon's suspicion-fueled bugging and snooping stood out as deviant, unseemly, and impeachable in part because the president made no attempt to legitimate or legalize it. Forced to defend himself against allegations in court, Nixon claimed an overbroad privilege to protect information within his possession, and that privilege claim, as we will show, was rejected by the Supreme Court. However, the surveillance activities themselves could hardly be justified legally—in fact, their very illegality was the reason Nixon fought so vigorously to keep them secret in the first place; for what trial judge, after seeing the things Nixon wanted to keep secret, would agree that the public's interest to see those materials was trumped by Nixon's secrecy claim? But the FISA framework, in contrast, gives to the president a space to pursue surveillance that is cordoned off and legitimized by congressional act. To put it slightly differently, the space where the "dirty business" of wiretapping now takes place is an adjudicated space, a bureaucratized space. It is more difficult to find fault with a president operating according to a process Congress gave him.

It is even easier to see legiscide at work in the War Powers example. Since the passage of that measure, presidents Reagan, George H. W. Bush, Clinton, and George W. Bush have had little trouble committing forces overseas. Congress, by contrast, finds itself in sticky situations where exercising its statutory authority to call back already deployed troops will likely be seen as failing to support those soldiers or even as endangering them. Moreover, another of Lowi's observations about the plebiscitary presidency applies here: when the government is personified in the president (as it is in the plebiscitary presidency), dissent from presidential action comes to be seen as anti-state and even disloyal, because the president is the state.[45]

So the tendency to see president-as-state consummates the act of legiscide in the War Powers case, as it is nearly impossible to constrain the president when military action is imminent (and even harder once hostilities have commenced). The Iraq War vote has been analyzed in just these terms by the constitutional scholar Louis Fisher. Fisher has argued that the vote on the use of force in Iraq did damage to the republic. Citing Lincoln for the proposition that the decision to go to war is a "voluntary act of sovereignty," Fisher notes that it became a "mere endorsement" of a presidential decision—in a season of Congressional elections. The blame laid with Congress here is double: first, passage of the War Powers Act enables presidential overreaching in the military context, and second, Congress in late 2002 abdicated its most serious legislative responsibility for the short-term gain of its individual members. The 2002 vote resembled the Gulf of Tonkin Resolution nearly forty years earlier, even though a statute purporting to regulate the president's military command power had been passed in the intervening time.[46]

Skowronek: Temporalizing Presidential Studies

Writing in the early 1990s, Stephen Skowronek brought a "new historicist" orientation to the study of presidential leadership in *The Politics Presidents Make*.[47] Skowronek's work represents an important advance in presidential scholarship in at least two ways. First, he brings more nuanced conceptions of *time* into play. Rather than a simple and absolute measurement for political and historical events, for Skowronek time is articulated in two interactive dimensions, which we describe below. In his conceptions of time, he reveals and transmits the influence of J. G. A. Pocock's *Politics, Language, and Time,* in which the perception of time by political actors reflects differing worldviews and, ultimately, different political situations and orders.[48] Second, Skowronek moves beyond the paralyzing structure/action polarity that often characterizes scholarly debates over presidential politics to offer a model that includes both structure *and* agency, as presidents act within the space created by institutional and, more broadly, social development.

Skowronek's first conceptual move is to posit two notions of time: he charts recurring patterns of presidential leadership in *political time* and extra-political events in *secular time.* He argues that presidents make politics within cycles of institutional order, while broader historical events bear on those politics as well. As he puts it, "We are no longer isolating segments of history to posit a stable system in which institutions mark order and routine; we are dividing the history up in several ways . . . to juxtapose contending forces of order and change. Institutions become the arenas in which these forces converge, collide and fold back on one another."[49] Institutions are not stable or static in this conception: as the situs of political practice, they cannot remain unaffected by what happens in and around them.

Skowronek goes a step further when he posits an "institutional logic of political disruption." It is not merely that institutions change in response to political and historical forces. There is something about political institutions, the presidency in particular, that allows their occupants to make changes both without and within. This more fluid understanding of the structure/action dynamic in presidential politics is exemplified by Skowronek's statement that the presidency contains "order-shattering," "order-creating," and "order-affirming impulses." Presidential politics are "order-shattering" because the office "prompts each incumbent to take charge of the independent powers of his office and to exercise them in his own right."[50]

Here, he implicitly recalls Harvey Mansfield's description of the executive as a moving force in government: what defines and distinguishes the modern executive is the ability to exercise power, to get things done. But the executive is also "order-creating" in that he engineers "political arrangements that can stand the test of legitimacy within the other institutions of government as well as the nation at large." With a skillful executive, all of these changes can be accomplished. Finally, Skowronek suggests that "the power to recreate order hinges on the authority to repudiate it." Here, he reminds us that a destructive or reconstructive project will succeed only if the president can articulate "his own definition of the moment at hand" in a "coherent public discourse"—only then will the president's vision of change take hold.[51]

Skowronek notes a paradoxical trend in the modern presidency wherein the "rise" of the institution has favored *weaker,* rather than stronger, individual presidents—weaker, that is, in terms of personal authority. He notes that a "progressive proliferation of organized interests and independent authorities has redounded to greater reliance on the president for central management and coordination of the affairs of state." This trend has "bolstered those incumbents whose feeble political warrants might in earlier times have stymied their possibilities for independent action quite quickly."[52] The president as manager/coordinator gains a certain institutional authority that outstrips his personal authority.

But the openness of Skowronek's model rescues it from a rigid determinism. First, he notes that "classic claims of leadership authority . . . have endured despite their growing irrelevance."[53] This observation underlines a very real pattern in American public political discourse: "institutional thickening" has not extinguished what Lowi calls "the excessive personification of American government in the presidency."[54] The people still look to the president—whoever holds the office at any given time—for leadership; while weak leaders still generate expectations, people with strong classical leadership traits will be able to convey those traits to the public whether the institutional space allows those skills to flourish or not.

The second freeing move within Skowronek's argument is his positing of an "opposed/affiliated" framework for successive administrations. This element of the model allows him to point to a space that opens when a president seeks to reconstruct political order: at those junctures, classical leadership thrives and the potential for a strong leader to make change is greatest.

We argue that George W. Bush started with weak leadership claims and has not measurably improved them, despite the occurrence of galvanizing events during his first term. So Skowronek's point about institutional thickness favoring weaker individual leaders is proven true in the present case. Moreover, the office has certainly made the individual seem bigger. A certain amount of legitimacy is inevitably conferred on anyone who occupies the White House. Public statements become press conferences, and every word of them is scrutinized. An earnest facial expression or a strongly worded response becomes "presidential" behavior. Executive orders, bill signings, and campaign stops are facets of institutional behavior in which the president is a role player; it matters more that these things get done than it matters what individual does them.

Skowronek implies a certain fungibility of individuals in this sense that is often overlooked by the public—and just as much, if not more so, by news commentators who make a living interpreting presidential behavior and whose jobs would become very strange indeed if they pointed out how "unpresidential" leaders sometimes are. The media critic Mark Crispin Miller points out that constructing our leaders for us, so that we do not rely on our own reading of their body language, has become an obligatory task for TV news reporters.[55]

NOTHING NEW UNDER THE SUN—OR IS THERE?

"Nothing is new under the sun," Ecclesiastes assures us: "Even the thing of which we say, 'See, this is new!' has already existed in the ages that preceded us."[56] But if something new *did* show up, would presidential scholars recognize it? We think that despite the theoretical richness and nuance of Skowronek's conceptual framework, he is unable to account, in the end, for the truly new features of the secret presidency. Institutional change is not the same thing as bursting the boundaries of an institutional arrangement structured and defined by separated governmental powers, and we are, now, quite close to the latter. We have argued that institutional changes since Watergate have increased power and secrecy in the executive, correspondingly *decreasing* the accountability of the president to the other branches and to the people. In the state secrets privilege, in the expanded use of FISA, in the new executive privilege and in the broad array of anti-terror capabilities, the presidency is poised, at the start of this new century, to redefine fundamentally its status as a locus of power among equal power sources.

Lowi tells us that legiscide is a feature of the contemporary presidency in which Congress willingly and irretrievably cedes power to the president, and we have documented the repeated capitulation of the courts to ever bolder power bids by the executive as well. Recent presidents, especially George W. Bush, have sought aggressively to continue these trends, and while Skowronek's structure/agency problematic helps us to see how existing features of the office combined with what he calls "secular" phenomena (like increased terror threats) to bring about the secret presidency, we submit that it is necessary to move beyond Skowronek's model if we want to understand and appreciate just how close we are to a new governing arrangement. If we are indeed witnessing a transition to government by an executive that is unconstrained, unaccountable, and reliant on secrecy as the most basic tool of governing, a cyclical model of presidential history cannot take us all the way there. The model remains useful genealogically, but a new analysis is needed to map out the new terrain on which we find ourselves.

To be sure, Skowronek is aware of the possibility that the end of the twentieth century is indeed a departure point in presidential history like the one Neustadt perceived as beginning between the two world wars. In the closing chapter of *The Politics Presidents Make*, he looks at the administrations of Reagan and

George H. W. Bush and considers the possibility of the "waning of political time." As possible evidence of such an event, he recalls the "fact that Bush could manipulate so many different identities [which] suggests something of the plasticity of ascribed leadership roles in contemporary American politics."[57]

At first it seems as though Skowronek might be employing a postmodern trope here, acknowledging that political time is receding in favor of a featureless and fungible authority position for the postmodern executive, but a closer look at the chapter reveals that he sees Reagan and G. H. W. Bush replaying, almost in caricature, the "reconstructive repudiator" and "faithful son," respectively.[58] Thus, when claims of a new presidential politics—or, for that matter, the *end* of presidential politics—are being pressed most strongly, the typological roles occupied by Jefferson and Adams, dating back to the early years of the republic, seem to fit most strongly, suggesting to Skowronek that his model still applies to the American presidency.

Summary: Lessons Learned

It would be foolish indeed to ignore the presidential scholarship of the past half-century simply because recent events are not fully explained by it. We have noted Skowronek's freely acknowledged debt to Richard Neustadt and his recognition of the revolutionary role Neustadt has played in presidential studies. Scholarship progresses by testing existing work and modifying or abandoning what no longer repays close study. Moreover, it makes little sense to hold theorists responsible for failing to foresee future historical developments. One might as well fault Marx for neglecting to theorize global capitalism or the rise of commodified information. Instead, scholars recognize that they are participants in an ongoing conversation that is perpetually complicated by historical events and emerging phenomena—so the conversation never ends.

Presidential Power still has insights to contribute; the need for attunement to the persuasive activities of the executive is one lesson that reminds us repeatedly of the ongoing relevancy of the work. And we have found within the George W. Bush presidency—which began long after Neustadt wrote his landmark work—an inverse truth about the informal power processes of the executive: when the president lacks diplomatic or interpersonal skill, he is likely to compensate by shielding his activities—even shielding his very self—from the public within and without government, relying on secrecy rather than diplomacy. This insight is bequeathed to us via Neustadt, and only becomes possible to articulate as we live through the secret presidency of George W. Bush.

Just as Neustadt's insights remain useful despite a vastly changed historical and political landscape, so does Lowi's depiction of a plebiscitary president. We see that Congress and the courts have been willing to give away their own power to help the presidency grow institutionally, and we appreciate Lowi's concerns about a plebiscitary/personal president who brooks no dissent (for dissent is anti-state) and who must resort to deceit in order to manage and negotiate the public's expectations of him. It would be imprudent, certainly, to dismiss the possibility of direct links between president and people when studying an administration—that is, the present one—that prides itself on direct, plain-spoken communication with the American people. Further, Lowi's notion of legiscide is absolutely crucial to understanding the growth of the institutional presidency, and we refer to the concept throughout this book.

Finally, Skowronek's historically informed and theoretically robust scheme for reckoning political and secular time in the presidency shows us that regimes change against a backdrop of wider historical events. Seeing political time as cyclical becomes a crucial reminder of the institutional resiliency, for one thing, of the American presidency. Commitments and presidential behavior resemble moments in the distant presidential past, and a strictly linear conception of time causes us to miss such resemblances. Moreover, the interactivity of political and secular time makes Skowronek's model even more useful as we see that both kinds of time movement happen at once. Bush seeks to repudiate his predecessor, Bill Clinton (cyclical), even as we apprehend an unprecedented growth in institutional secrecy that both Clinton and Bush have fostered (linear).

Thus, rather than a stark choice between wholesale rejection of the models offered by Neustadt, Lowi, or Skowronek on the one hand and the uncritical choice of one of them on the other, we have proceeded critically, seeking to apply insights from all three where possible and questioning when later events fail to fit within their schemes.

CHAPTER TWO

The Classified President

Secrecy is a mode of regulation. In truth, it is the ultimate mode, for
the citizen does not even know that he or she is being regulated.

—Daniel Patrick Moynihan

Disclosure of Government information is particularly important today because Government is becoming involved in more and more
aspects of every citizen's personal and business life, and so the access to information about how Government is exercising its trust
becomes increasingly important. The growing complexity of
Government . . . makes it extremely difficult for a citizen to become
and remain knowledgeable enough to exercise his responsibilities
as a citizen; without government secrecy it is difficult, with Government secrecy it is impossible.

—Representative Donald Rumsfeld, 1966

Presidents have virtually unfettered power to classify executive branch material, thereby making it presumptively, and usually conclusively, beyond the reach
of the public, courts, and Congress. Congress has aided the president in these
matters by enacting laws that inure to executive powers of classification, but
presidents claim to depend on no external power to safeguard information that
could damage national security if disclosed publicly or passed to our enemies.
The lure of classification is strong, beguiling presidents and executive branch
officials with the expediency of secrecy. Recall that in the introduction we discussed Lowi's two tracks, an idea Lowi fashioned from a discussion by Louis
Koenig. The fast track "is the track of secrecy, unilateral action, energy, commitment, decisiveness, where time is always of the essence."[1]

On the other hand, the slow track is "a Separation of Powers Track, permitted
by a longer time horizon, and desirable wherever time permits, yet highly unpre-

dictable, uncontrollable, public, full of leaky holes, and dominated not merely by the legislature but by a large and pluralistic process fueled by greed, otherwise called the pursuit of happiness." Of course the fast track may also be "fueled by greed" and full of "leaky holes." But Lowi's distinction is worth pointing out. The events of 9/11 and the "global war on terrorism" presented the Bush administration with an enormous opportunity—some might say necessity—to transfer vast amounts of slow track material to the fast track. By 2003, the United States was involved in two shooting wars and one metaphorical war—the war on terror; as Lowi notes, "under assumptions of the War Model, the president needs access to, if not control over, increasing numbers and types of resources in the domestic part of society that ought to be operating under the Slow Track, and control over those types of people and groups and political actors capable of effective political obstruction."[2]

By fast-tracking as much in the domestic sphere as possible, the president is "in as strong a position as possible to alarm and morally to rearm Americans against external and internal threats."[3] But at no point in our history has an administration been so consciously and deliberately committed to the idea of secrecy as has the Bush administration. Fast-tracking information and programs by classification and secrecy obviates the need to justify actions in public or engage in debate about the wisdom of decisions or policies. The fast track is a lure, a promise of escape from exposing important decisions to criticism; it is also an end run around democracy and accountability.

The chief means to fast-tracking information, policy, and action is through classification authority, and information and documents previously unclassified are now removed from public access through a complex system that pursues secrecy for both political and national security purposes. Disclosure of frank communications confirm the impulse of the executive branch to fast-track items to avoid public debate. For example, Admiral John Poindexter wrote in a 1986 memorandum that "the purpose of keeping a particular covert action covert was to enable intelligence operatives to embark on a particular course of action 'without having to endure further domestic partisan political debate.' "[4]

Virtually all classified documents, rules concerning classification, and declassification decisions are controlled by the executive branch through authority under executive orders, statutes, and case law. Each year, millions of files, reports, computer programs, intercept tapes, pieces of equipment, and a host of other items are generated and classified by White House staff and the executive bureaucracy. Most observers acknowledge that overclassification is a significant problem, and this has led to some embarrassing moments for the executive branch. In

1995, for example, the Federation of American Scientists discovered that a report written in 1917, before America entered World War I, was still unavailable due to classification. The report and five other documents from 1917 and 1918 still remain classified, and not even legal action could force their disclosure.[5]

And, rather infamously, administrators reasserted classification of the Pentagon Papers after large portions of the papers had already been published in the *New York Times* and after the entire document was placed in the public record at a hearing by U.S. Senator Mike Gravel.[6] Even a memo from one member of the Joint Chiefs of Staff to another member claiming that too many documents were being classified, was itself classified.[7] As Senator Daniel Moynihan noted, "The classification system . . . is used too often to deny the public an understanding of the policymaking process, rather than for the necessary protection of intelligence activities and other highly sensitive matters."[8]

Perplexing controls over information also exist under statutes such as the Arms Export Control Act and exemptions to the Freedom of Information Act (FOIA). For example, the users of service manuals for naval laundry washers and dryers are confronted with the warning "This document contains technical data whose export is restricted by the Arms Export Control Act" and are commanded to destroy the document "by any method that will prevent disclosure of contents or reconstruction of the document."[9] The manuals contain no sensitive technical information—since they were posted on the Internet by the U.S. military along with a myriad of other such documents also containing similar warnings, it would seem that the warnings are misplaced. Additionally, the administration of George W. Bush has made it much more difficult to obtain information under the Freedom of Information Act (FOIA) and has been zealous in pursuing agency exemptions for compliance with FOIA.[10] In a 2003 example of secrecy overreach under FOIA, a Department of Defense training video on how to handle FOIA requests was itself denied release under FOIA.[11]

These examples point to the innate bureaucratic discomfort with releasing information to the public, concrete instances of Max Weber's well-known observation that the "concept of the official secret is the specific invention of bureaucracy, and nothing is so fanatically defended by the bureaucracy."[12] Bureaucratic officials "almost reflexively reach out to the classification system."[13] And, as former solicitor general Erwin Griswold noted, it is apparent "to any person who has considerable experience with classified material that there is massive over-classification and that the principal concern of the classifiers is not with national security, but rather with governmental embarrassment of one sort or another."[14] Accordingly, the Commission on Protecting and Reducing Government Secrecy began their final report with the observation that "secrecy is a form of government regulation" and that like any other form of regulation, it is subject to abuse.[15] This abuse derives from a number of motivations.

First, in deciding whether or not to classify a document, administrators know that there are no risks in shielding from view material that represents no danger to United States interests if made public. So there are no disincentives to classify unclassified material, but there are enormous disincentives for the reverse. Any administrator who underclassifies a document that is released to the public or even to the intelligence community at a wider level of distribution than is wise is risking his or her career. The safest route in any questionable circumstance is simply to classify the material at hand to the highest level feasible. The action with the least number of possible adverse consequences for the administrator is to put his or her chips on secrecy. As one report notes, "Organizations within a culture of secrecy will opt for classifying as much as possible, and for as long as possible."[16] This is perhaps exemplified by the fact that most classifiers appear to compromise, with consistently two-thirds of all classification decisions made at the "secret" level, rather than at "confidential" or "top secret."[17]

Second, classification power may be used to prevent dissemination of embarrassing material or even material that is evidence of criminal activity. Solicitor General Griswold greatly overstates the point when he says that the "principal concern" in classification is avoiding embarrassment, but there are of course times when the classification power is used for exactly that reason. The case of whistleblower Sibel Edmonds, discussed in greater detail in the next chapter, is a rather stark example of such an action. Edmonds made damaging allegations concerning the FBI's translation department, allegations that were found to be substantially supported by a bipartisan group of members of Congress and an investigation by an inspector general for the Department of Justice.[18] In that case the Department of Justice, under orders from Attorney General John Ashcroft, retroactively classified documents that it had already supplied to Congress and that had already been in the public realm and on the Internet for two years. The effect of this retroactive reclassification was to dare Congress to use the documents in public hearings in spite of their classification. Congress proved weak, as it often does in the face of executive claims of national security, and did not publicly use the documents. Congress shrank from confronting a transparent attempt to limit the amount of executive branch embarrassment in the case.

Third, the agency that historically generates classified material feels a proprietary right to that material and makes calculations of classification with the idea of interagency rivalries in mind. It is a truism that knowledge is power, and agencies often simply do not wish to give away their hard-earned intelligence to rival agencies that will then use it to aggrandize their own positions within government or use it for purposes at odds with the generating agency's goals. Further, once the information has left an agency's hands, the generating agency no longer has control over dissemination of the information, and the material becomes subject to forces, such as motivations for leaks, that the agency cannot foresee.

Every day, material is classified in such a way as to cover the activity of one agency against the prying eyes of another or to prevent access to potentially embarrassing information by the intelligence agencies of our allies. Bureaucrats acknowledge this even to congressional investigators, expressing concern "about the protection and handling of their agencies' information by other agencies" and admitting to "classifying information inappropriately to ensure its protection."[19] And, as William Arkin observes, "The sad truth is that code names are not just used to confuse and confound the enemy, but to build power inside various bureaucracies and keep prying eyes . . . from understanding what is really going on."[20]

There is a complicated scheme of classification that can allow dissemination of material as broadly as the entire intelligence community, including agencies of allied nations, or as narrowly as one office within one division of one agency. But the impulse to secrecy is universal in the bureaucracy, and since it is often difficult to predict what sorts of information could become an embarrassment or detriment to an administrator's agency or bosses, it is always wise simply to attempt to keep as much secret as possible.

While the motivations discussed above are not central to this study, it is important to see that the culture of secrecy is highly nuanced and is not merely directed at preventing exposure to the public, Congress, and the courts. Much discussion over relations between the presidency and the bureaucracy focuses on the animosity, prevarication, and contumaciousness of bureaucrats in their dealings with presidential advisors and appointees. As Louis Fisher noted, the separation of powers between the president and Congress may be less than between the president and the bureaucracy.[21] The inability to undermine, erode, and rechannel established paths of power and process limits presidential efforts to effectuate policy and frequently renders agencies nearly impervious to White House influence. But to the extent that presidents follow policies of secrecy and resistance to efforts by Congress, the public, and courts to force disclosure of information, they can almost without exception count on cooperation by law enforcement and intelligence agencies.

Policies of secrecy are readily accepted by the bureaucracy because they empower administrators by giving them greater discretion over how information under their control may be handled. They increase discretion by diminishing congressional oversight power, judicial power to compel production of information, and the public's power to gain access to information through FOIA and other disclosure statutes.

From the point of view of intelligence and law enforcement agencies, every request or order for information is an assault, a potential disaster, either because it could lead to exposure of investigations or sources and methods of intelligence gathering or to exposure of illegal activity by administrators or embarrassing information. As the policies, privileges, reasons, and authority underlying powers of secrecy proliferate in the institution of the presidency, they concomitantly increase bureaucratic power, since many presidential powers of secrecy by necessity penetrate deep into the bureaucracy to safeguard information.

Secrecy may increase certain administrators' status or opportunities for promotion, as it helps to define who is part of the "club" and who is not. As Richard Gid Powers put it, "Official secrecy during the Cold War took on overtones of ritual, that is, a performance intended to demonstrate who was in and who was out, who could be trusted and who could not—in other words, who should have the power and who should be powerless."[22] In no other context are the president and administrators so like-minded. As Mark Zaid, an attorney who almost exclusively handles plaintiff national security cases, commented, "When [agencies] have an administration that is willing to cater [to secrecy], they go for it."[23]

And increased classification authority gives the president greater control over agencies, as it provides an institutional means for managing information. For example, President George W. Bush has granted original classification authority to several agencies that heretofore have not had the power to classify information. This newly created power provides presidential appointees in those agencies with the power to segment off information that may be embarrassing or damaging to the president's administration. Historically, bureaucrats have used information in their own agencies against administrations that run afoul of agency desires. But if the information to be used is classified, it becomes a far more complicated matter to disclose it to non-agency actors.

Of course, leaks frequently occur, but this activity is often dangerous and usually requires a serious risk analysis on the part of the person contemplating the leak. And leaks of information hardly act as an effective means of accountability for presidential and executive excesses, since they are idiosyncratic, driven by the desires of the leaker, and usually only deal with limited types of information that may be easily comprehended by the general public. Also, leaks may even lead to greater executive branch excesses to keep even more information from the public. As we will see, it is more dangerous than ever for those who would leak classified information.

It is now routine for extravagant claims of power to be made on behalf of the president, claims that not long ago would have been difficult to comprehend. The stance of every president since Eisenhower is that he has "ultimate and unimpeded authority over the collection, retention and dissemination of intelligence and other national security information. . . . There is no exception to this principle for those disseminations that would be made to Congress or its Members."[24] This is an extraordinary claim to power that channels against balancing of powers, accountability, and oversight. But, as we discuss, while this claim may be extravagant as a matter of history and theory, it is fairly routine now, the operating principle of courts and bureaucrats.

We need to know how we reached this point, for it is important to understand how the presidency obtained a monopoly of secrecy power when the only power of secrecy mentioned in the Constitution is given to Congress. The executive monopoly on secrecy is an extra-constitutional power unabated by mechanisms of accountability. Whatever the exigencies that gird executive powers of secrecy, there are also exigencies that warn that there must be legally defined limits to such powers and mechanisms of oversight. Congress may provide some oversight of this largely uncontrolled power, but, as we argue throughout this book, the judiciary has virtually abdicated authority over these matters, even though it is equipped with well-established processes to check executive abuse of secrecy.

Classification Authority
Making Secrets

Executive orders limit classification of material to just three categories, "confidential," "secret," and "top secret," but this does not do justice to the dense nature of the world of classification. Even though classification is restricted to these three categories, there are dozens of special handling caveats and special access codewords that limit information access to particular offices and personnel. But the decisive feature in determining whether or not information is to be classified under executive order is based on the damage its unauthorized release would do to national security.

The unauthorized release of the three levels of classified information—"top secret," "secret," or "confidential"—would "reasonably . . . be expected to cause," respectively, exceptionally grave, serious, or mere damage to national security.

But beyond these simple markings, the control of information can become quite convoluted. For example, one classified affidavit to a judge was marked "TOP SECRET UMBRA GAMMA ORCON US/UK ONLY," meaning that its unauthorized disclosure would cause exceptionally grave damage to national security, that it was generated by a signals intelligence source, that it concerned information about the Soviet Union, that the originating agency asserted continuing control, and that it may not be distributed to foreign agencies beyond the United Kingdom.[25]

Most of what is classified are not "secrets" in the normal sense of the term. In fact, if someone unfamiliar with the intelligence field were to rummage through National Security Agency information classified "top secret," he or she would alternately be bored by its tedious nature, unable to comprehend the information, and perplexed, but he or she would very likely not learn anything obviously identifiable as "important."[26] The idea of "the Big Secret" is mainly one of fiction and Hollywood, for most classified information is on the order of detail and would have very little meaning to the non-expert. Of course, there are occasionally discrete and important secrets, for example the design of a nuclear weapon. But even such a clear "secret" is so complex and detailed, implicates so much other information and expertise, that it is a stretch to categorize it as a discrete item.

Most of what could be fairly called "Big Secrets" have at least a strong political flavor to them, and the reason for their secrecy is often almost purely political. We do not mean to suggest that "political secrets" are necessarily abuses of authority, for there is plenty of political activity, especially in the realm of foreign affairs, that is wisely and correctly classified. But the proper classification of political material must be done in the service of national needs, not in the service of a party or a president's personal desires or in contravention of law. The range in this category of secrets is large, and it includes examples such as tapping underwater Soviet communication lines, covering up aspects of the Israeli attack on the USS *Liberty* in 1967, and the Nixon administration bombing of Cambodia in 1969.

Some of these Big Secrets are more politically risky than others, such as Eisenhower's personal direction of U2 overflights of the Soviet Union and his subsequent suborning of subordinates to lie about the matter to Congress.[27] Here too fits President Ronald Reagan's Iran-Contra debacle, and President George W. Bush's warrantless electronic surveillance of U.S. citizens. But Big Secrets are rare, and while they are frequently utilized to cover illegal or embarrassing activity, their damage to our democracy is equaled by the habitual overclassification of workaday material throughout the government and the recent expansion of classification authority.

It is traditional for analysts and commentators to assert that there are two kinds of secret information: objective secrets and subjective secrets. Objective secrets are ones that our adversaries may discover independently, through research, experimentation, due diligence in analysis of open sources, or other means of investigation. Technological or scientific secrets are in this category, and this type of information is perhaps best thought of as temporary—though sometimes of long duration; they are advantages over adversaries, not true secrets. As L. N. Ridenour testified before Congress in 1945: "The use of the word 'secret' for the results of scientific investigation or the findings of engineering is genuinely misleading. . . . The word secret [does] not [mean] that you cannot find out what I know, but that you must find it out for yourself, without my help."[28]

Subjective secrets, on the other hand, are those that cannot be found out through diligent investigation or experimentation. The classic example used to illustrate this sort of information is a Big Secret, the government's secret plans to invade a foreign country on a particular date. As Arvin Quist, perhaps the most thoughtful commentator on secrecy policy, describes this type of secret: "The adversary cannot independently generate that information. Subjective information, if properly controlled and protected, cannot be obtained by another country except through espionage or through unauthorized (either inadvertent or deliberate) disclosures of that information." Frequently, the implication of scholars in describing subjective secrets is that they are relatively few in number and closely held among a small number of people. Quist defines other characteristics of subjective secrets: they are compact, easily understandable by the average person, and perishable.[29] Because subjective secrets are not discoverable by others but may only be revealed by events (the invasion takes place) or by disclosure by one of their holders, subjective secrets are often called "true" secrets.

But the characterization of subjective secrets as rare and shared by a small number of people is not an accurate reflection of practice. For example, virtually everything we know about our adversaries, terrorists or otherwise, are subjective secrets, in that our enemies cannot find out what we know about them without the information coming from us. This uncertainty is in itself a deterrent to action by our adversaries and an incentive for them to engage in costly and cumbersome efforts to shield information and activity; our enemies not knowing what we know is a cost inflicted on them. And instantiations of the ubiquitous reasoning for classifying or refusing to disclose information, the protection of "sources and methods" as contained in the National Security Act of 1947, are also usually subjective secrets.[30] Sources and methods of gathering intelligence may be guessed at or glimpsed by enemies, but intelligence-gathering methods are extremely complex and integrated in almost unimaginable ways.

So the range and number of subjective secrets is not as limited as the literature would suggest, and this informs our investigation because the president has virtually unfettered authority to create and maintain subjective secrets in special ways that evade even the minimal accountability that exists otherwise. Abuse of power is most effectively concealed by means associated with the protection of subjective secrets.

Of course, there are situations where illegal activity also would result in a compromise of national security if it were made public. As one prominent government report on secrecy put it, "One persistent problem . . . has been the intermingling of secrecy used to protect carefully defined national interests with secrecy used primarily to enhance such political or bureaucratic power."[31] This motivation to resistance of disclosure is the one that is most likely to be the closest to the office of the president. And recent presidents have raised the level of secrecy to new constitutional ground that excludes congressional oversight and prevents external accountability.

Exclusive executive control of classified information represents a great expansion in presidential authority, but there is also a classification scheme within the classification scheme available to the president that provides an even greater forum for abuse than normal classification activities. Special Access Programs (SAPs) provide the government with tools to engage in extremely important activities for national security under the most secure of conditions, but they also provide means for abuse. Operation Green Copper, for example, an SAP, is alleged to have been behind the abuse of Iraqi prisoners at Abu Ghraib prison, an example of information escaping presidential clutches in spite of aggressive safeguards.

Congress has attempted to provide some measure of control and oversight of SAPs through its appropriation powers, but presidents have repeatedly asserted they have no duty to comply with these provisions. For example, George W. Bush, in a statement typical of his position concerning SAPs, noted, "The U.S. Supreme Court has stated that the President's authority to classify and control access to information bearing on national security flows from the Constitution and does not depend upon a legislative grant of authority"; he further observed that "especially in wartime," the president may not be able to comply with statutory requirements.[32] But it is rather telling—indeed, disconcerting—that Bush did not cite a single U.S. Supreme Court case to support this proposition. There are no cases that have directly held what Bush claimed—the truth is that the national security area abounds in such nebulous statements.

Information Security Oversight Office and Classification Actions

Modern classification and security of information is an enormous and complex enterprise. While executive orders provide the guidelines and authority for the classification of material, the process is lacking in oversight, and the result is that all parties agree that overclassification of material is commonplace. Such overclassification means that the public has less access to governmental activity than it should, and it also creates a great amount of unnecessary expense. The costs to secure and store material that is incorrectly classified are impossible to estimate with any accuracy, but total government costs to secure information run to seven billion dollars a year. But this figure does not include the Central Intelligence Agency, which—naturally—keeps its costs to keep its secrets secret.[33] There is also reason to believe that security costs are underreported.

The Information Security Oversight Office (ISOO), the agency responsible for policy oversight of the government's classification system, admits that "in the past, the costs for the security classification program were deemed nonquantifiable, intertwined with other overhead expenses . . . many of the program's costs remain ambiguous." And since requiring "agencies to provide exact responses to the cost collection efforts would be cost prohibitive," the ISOO "relies on the agencies to estimate the costs of the security classification system."[34] The ISOO's dependence on self-reporting to accomplish its oversight function yields questionable results. Agencies have incentives not to report the full costs of their information security measures, as high reported costs may attract the attention of Congress or even the Executive Office of the President, bringing about either investigation or embarrassment or both.

Further, ISOO's lack of oversight power is evident in even its own reports, where frustration over its weakness is sometimes barely concealed. Noting years of difficulty in coordinating information collection with the Department of Defense, the ISOO wearily reports that it "will continue to work with DOD to develop a system whereby we can report meaningful data."[35] The ISOO does the best with what it has, but it is understaffed and overcommitted, and it lacks any real authority to undertake key elements of its mission. It has a total of twenty-five staff members to oversee seventy or more agencies and departments containing four thousand original classifying authorities and three million derivative classifiers. It also is charged with oversight of the National Industrial Security Program for the National Security Council, which oversees the classification activity of government contractors.

With a tone of exasperation, a 2003 ISOO report to the president notes that "some individual agencies . . . have no real idea how much of the information they generate is classified; whether the overall quantity is increasing or decreasing; what the explanations are for such changes; which elements within their organizations are most responsible for the changes; and, most important, whether the changes are appropriate, i.e., whether too much or too little information is being classified and whether it is for too long or too short a period of time."[36]

The ISOO has little ability to force agency compliance or production of accurate information concerning the classification of material. Created by Executive Order 12065 in 1978, the ISOO replaced the Interagency Classification Review Committee, established by President Nixon in 1972. The ISOO was part of important efforts to increase executive branch accountability in the aftermath of the Watergate affair. To this end, it is charged with conducting on-site reviews of agency security programs, reviewing all agency implementing regulations and guidelines concerning classified information, overseeing agency actions to ensure compliance with executive orders, creating policy concerning classification procedure, reviewing requests for new original classifiers, and responding to complaints.[37]

But it has little power to force agency compliance with these matters except to appeal to the National Security Council. Agencies are understandably more concerned with performing their direct missions than with expending substantial resources on compliance with classification authorities. They will do what is convenient, but it is likely they are suspicious of ISOO involvement with their operations.

Under these conditions, the ISOO must tread very lightly, for it may find itself substantially shut out by intransigent and uncooperative agencies and personnel if it engages in sharp criticism or attempts to force reform or change of classification practices too rapidly. Since it has so few resources, it is dependent on agency goodwill for compliance, living off of the amity of bureaucrats. Further, executive branch officials see it as a creation of the president that reports to the president, and one that is not authorized or expected to aid Congress in investigations or report violations of policy or law to congressional committees. When the ISOO discovers violations of security policy, it is directed to report those violations to the appropriate agency head or designated senior member for action but cannot undertake sanctions itself.[38] The only real power the ISOO has is in forcing uniformity of policy and process in classification determinations, which is an appreciable power but does not reach the deep problems of overclassification and abuse that have historically plagued the executive branch.[39]

Additionally, the ISOO is administratively located in the National Archives and

Records Administration (NARA), a venerable institution but not one placed to have a profound effect on current security operations. This placement continues a history of questionable actions concerning the agency, for prior to 1994 it was funded out of the General Services Administration (GSA), even though the GSA had no control over ISOO operations. In 1994 Congress threatened to cut off funding for the ISOO unless the NSC accepted funding responsibility for it, and a committee report in 1994 expressed "concern . . . that ISOO, which exclusively performs National Security Council functions, is funded by the General Services Administration" and that it "appears that by funding its operation in GSA, the true costs of the Council are not accurately reflected in the President's budget request."[40] In the end, Congress accepted the ISOO's relocation to NARA, where this chief watchdog for classification abuse often appears toothless. For example, Attorney General Ashcroft classified information in the Sibel Edmonds case that had been available to Congress and the public for two years, and the ISOO was powerless to do anything about it.

Since 1996, by the ISOO's own estimate, the number of classifications of material has almost tripled. Between 2001 and 2005, the number of such decisions increased nearly 65 percent.[41] No doubt this increase is a result of greater concern for information security in the wake of the 9/11 attacks and also reflects an increase in intelligence collection activity and the increased number of personnel involved in classification decisions. But this increase also raises the question of whether or not information is being hastily classified to keep as much as possible from public exposure or availability to citizens.

There are two kinds of classification decisions that take place: original and derivative. Original classification is performed by agency heads or other highly placed personnel, and they are the policymakers for each agency concerning what information should be classified. Derivative classifiers, amounting to some three million personnel, are only authorized to classify material in accordance with guidelines approved by original classifiers, and it is common to hear the claim that derivative classification is nondiscretionary or "determined" by policy.

Compared to derivative classifiers, the number of original classifiers is relatively small; there are fewer than one thousand original classifiers for "top secret" material. These administrators make very few classification determinations, with each "top secret" classifier making around ten decisions per year on average for the most recent years with reported data.[42] This amounts to less than four tenths of one percent of all recorded decisions, both original and derivative, in the "top secret" category. As for the categories themselves, on average 12 percent of all classification decisions yield a "top secret" determination, with about two-thirds and one-fifth for "secret" and "confidential" classifications, respectively. Original "top secret" classifiers are disproportionately unlikely to make classification determinations compared to other original classifiers: they account for less than three percent of all original classification determinations but make up about 20 percent of original classifiers.

Overall, less than two percent of all classification decisions are made by original classifiers. But even these numbers are misleading, since large amounts of material are presumptively classified simply by virtue of the computer system or office in which it resides or is generated. In many cases there is never a formal determination made for this material; it is simply classified by context and location. For example, when electronic documents are generated on a system designed to handle classified information, then they are deemed classified without reference to content. It would be extremely dangerous and expensive to require administrators to parse systems into classified and unclassified areas. Since many documents never exist in paper form, they are shifted around, deleted, relocated within offices, and so forth, which makes it extremely difficult to determine just how they fit in to the classification determination schemes developed by ISOO.

The real world of classification is simply the world of contextually driven decisions, not the policy world of original classifiers. Derivative classifiers—the analysts, intelligence collection operators, translators, investigators and other operational personnel—comprise the real engines of classification, not the policies adopted by senior agency personnel. But they most certainly take their cues as to how far to go from senior agency personnel.

J. William Leonard, the head of the ISOO, is remarkably frank in expressing his unhappiness with some of that culture and with problems in the classification system. Recently he noted, "I have become increasingly concerned with respect to how [classification decisions] are being implemented in some quarters. . . . Unfortunately, I have lately found some to use war as an excuse to disregard the basics of the security classification system. Yet, the classification system is not self-directing . . . the security classification system works, and its integrity is preserved, only when agency leadership demonstrates personal commitment and commits senior management to make it work." He goes on to say that "many agencies are excelling at fulfilling [classification system] requirements; others are not," and he expresses concern that recent "disclosure of classified reports . . . feed the perception that the security classification system is used to conceal violations of law."[43] Leonard may have been referring to the *Taguba Report* on the abuse of Iraqi prisoners at Abu Ghraib prison, a report that seems to have been classified to prevent its public distribution.[44] The report was classified as "secret," but it was nevertheless widely distributed, and there seems to be nothing in it to warrant classification. But we can only guess that Leonard was referring to the *Taguba Report*, for he may have had in mind other abuses of classification authority to conceal violations of law.

Classification decisions can be terribly difficult, at least as an intellectual matter. In terms of policy, "every act of classifying information must be able to trace its origin to an explicit decision by a responsible official who has been specifically delegated original classification authority."[45] But just as in applying rules in law, interpretation reigns supreme in classification decisions.

Take the example of a published novel that is found in a signals intelligence facility and is classified "top secret." The first impulse of someone unfamiliar with classification decisions might be to scoff at the very idea that a widely distributed document such as a novel could or should ever be classified. But what if the novel is the Cold War–era thriller *The Fourth Protocol* by Frederick Forsyth, and it is being analyzed for a very specific intelligence reason. In that novel, Forsyth writes about an attempt by the Soviet Union to smuggle a nuclear weapon into Great Britain and detonate it near an American air base, making it look as if a nuclear accident had occurred, thus creating strong feeling against the American military presence in Europe.

Suppose also that the Americans suspect that some of the information in the novel was supplied to Forsyth by British intelligence agencies to help promote the novel and to influence its plot development. This might be to the benefit of both the Americans and the British, since the publication of such a hypothetical scenario might foreclose the possibility that the Soviets would indeed undertake such an action. After publication of the novel and its attendant publicity, it may preempt or discourage any Soviet plans designed along similar lines.

So the Americans, not receiving any confirmation from the British, find themselves in the position of trying to determine if Forsyth's novel contains information that could only have come from British intelligence sources. Under those circumstances, should or could the novel be properly classified, since the association of the novel with the intelligence agency could provide useful information to our adversaries? The person making such a decision will almost certainly be a derivative classifier, not an original classifier, and will look less to policy than to practicality and, of course, an overabundance of caution. Indeed, one of the authors of this book engaged in precisely this sort of decision on a number of occasions.[46]

The vast majority of classification determinations are made by derivative classifiers, people who generate or analyze material in the course of their work. These determinations account for more than 98 percent of the nearly fifteen million classification decisions made each year by federal employees. The claim that derivative classification is nondiscretionary or merely an application of policy ignores the fact that almost all classification decisions are made in virtual anonymity with no oversight. It is true that executive orders prohibit the classification of material in order to "conceal violations of law, inefficiency, or administrative error" or to "prevent embarrassment to a person, organization, or agency."[47] But any violation of this prohibition is at most subject to administrative sanction, and it is so unlikely that someone will be sanctioned for overclassification that it never enters a classifier's mind when making decisions. Indeed, a diligent search has found no case in which a classifier was sanctioned for overclassification of material. And in e-mail communication with Leonard, neither he nor ISOO staff could recall an instance in which a federal employee was sanctioned for overclassifying or improperly classifying material.[48]

Regardless of what executive orders or policies may dictate, it is quite obvious that classifiers are well-advised to err on the side of secrecy and that they will not be punished for such action even if it is done for illegal purposes. As Senator Moynihan noted, "Too often, there is a tendency to use the sources and methods language contained in the National Security Act of 1947 to automatically classify virtually anything that is collected by an intelligence agency—including information collected from open sources." Moynihan calls this "classification by rote" and holds that the "secrecy system has developed into one in which accountability barely exists."[49] The story of how this power accrued in the president is an important one, and we now turn to the development of presidential powers of classification authority.

Creating the Classified President

The impulse to secrecy is one that has always resonated with presidents, but only in recent decades have the technical, political, and institutional means converged to create astoundingly broad powers of secrecy in the presidency. We now trace the history of the bases for the modern claim that presidents have exclusive control over national security information. A parallel line of investigation would trace the history of bureaucratic and military withholding of information; Arvin Quist has already written a fine history on that subject.[50]

In the early part of the last century, military and bureaucratic secrecy merged under uniform classification systems and orders, blossoming into the "national security state" in the 1940s. Presidents, of course, even from the beginnings of the republic, have often refused to disclose information on various grounds. These grounds were, for the first 140 years of the United States, generally left undifferentiated, with the incipient beginnings of executive privilege, the state secrets privilege, and the classification power collapsed under the general claim of separation of powers as a justification for refusal of disclosure. There was little urgent need to differentiate the grounds of these claims, since the presidency was a modest office with a limited need for secrecy. It is impossible to tease out the exact early provenance of the president's power to control national security information, but a path toward this end can be traced from presidential action in specific events to the modern constitutional and statutory bases for such control.

Governmental concern for mechanisms of secrecy is nothing new, evident even in the structure and actions of the Continental Congress. On November 9, 1775, the Congress adopted a resolution "That every member of this Congress considers himself under the ties of virtue, honour, and love of his country, not to divulge, directly or indirectly, any matter or thing agitated or debated in Congress . . . without leave of the Congress."[51] Members who violated "this agreement . . . shall be expelled this Congress, and deemed an enemy to the liberties of America."[52] Less than a year later, the Committee of Secret Correspondence refused to transmit information to the rest of the Congress because they found by "fatal experience, that the Congress consists of too many members to keep secrets."[53]

And the Framers of the Constitution debated the need for secrecy in certain cases. In discussing whether or not to allow one or both houses of Congress to withhold information from the public, Elbridge Gerry and Roger Sherman proposed a constraint that would allow for the secrecy of material relating to "treaties & military operations." Contrary to this view, James Wilson thought "the people have the right to know what their Agents are doing or have done, and it should not be in the option of the Legislature to conceal their proceedings."[54]

This debate yielded what became Article I, Section 5, Clause 3, of the U.S. Constitution, which explicitly gives Congress discretion to keep secrets: "Each House shall keep a Journal of its Proceedings, and from time to time publish the same, excepting such Parts as may in their Judgment require Secrecy." This is the only constitutional provision conferring a power of secrecy on a government body or official, and nothing in the language of the Constitution can fairly be said to imply a power of secrecy in the president.

Nevertheless, concerning the power of presidents to engage in secrecy, John Jay held in *Federalist No. 64* that "it seldom happens in the negotiation of treaties . . . but that perfect *secrecy* and immediate *dispatch* are sometimes requisite . . . and there doubtless are many [people] who would rely on the secrecy of the president, but who would not confide in that of the Senate, and still less in that of a large popular assembly."[55] It was not long until Jay's observations were put to the test. In 1792, President George Washington was negotiating an agreement with Algiers that he certainly did not want the French to learn about, yet Senator Ralph Izard, at a dinner party, brought up the negotiations. Thomas Jefferson reported that Izard, "sitting next to [Washington] at table on one hand, while a lady . . . was on his other hand and the Fr[ench] minister next to her . . . got on with his communication, his voice kept rising, and his stutter bolting the words out loudly at intervals, so that the minister might hear if he would."[56]

Three weeks later, with Izard's breach fresh in his mind, Washington called his closest advisors together to discuss efforts by members of the House to investigate the decimation of General St. Clair's army by the Indians. At the meeting, Washington gave no opinion about the power or limits of Congress to investigate executive branch activities, "for he had not thought upon it, nor was acquainted with subjects of this kind. . . . [But he] could readily conceive there might be papers of so secret a nature as they ought not to be given up."[57] Washington at the time did not locate this right of refusal in constitutional or other legal considerations, and after his advisors discussed the matter, they too advanced political, rather than legal, reasons for the power of the president to withhold information.

Jefferson reports that the advisors concluded that "the Executive ought to communicate such papers as the public good would permit, and ought to refuse those the disclosure of which would injure the public," but asserted no authority for this position.[58] Interestingly, a not-so-subtle shift is present in this case, since it was more of a domestic problem than an issue of foreign affairs. Jefferson's account seems to suggest that the basis for an executive power to withhold information is not located in specific constitutional provisions but in the separation of powers and in the practical need to prevent some matters from becoming public.

Washington's first significant refusal to disclose information to Congress did not come until 1796, when he resisted a request from the House of Representatives for instructions given to the United States minister to Great Britain concerning the Jay Treaty. He prefaced his refusal with the remark that he had a "constant endeavor to harmonize with the other branches" but went on to say that since the House has no constitutionally defined function in the making of treaties, the "boundaries fixed by the Constitution between the different departments should be preserved . . . [and] forbid . . . compliance with your request."[59] The precedent thus established, virtually every president since has justified withholding information from Congress on the same separation of powers grounds. The instance prompting Washington's refusal is squarely in line with situations contemplated by Jay in *Federalist No. 64*, but subsequent presidents broadened this power.

Other presidents, such as John Tyler, were recalcitrant with Congress, claiming that the notion that Congress may compel production of information from the executive branch "would render [the President] dependent upon [Congress] in the performance of a duty purely executive."[60] Tyler's position was no less hard-edged than that of President Andrew Jackson, who often refused congressional requests for information, once saying that "as the representative and trustee of the American people [I have] the painful but imperious duty of resisting to the utmost . . . encroachment on the rights of the Executive."[61] But these were political claims that were not based on well-founded doctrines.

Nothing like policy or trans-administration principles began to develop before the administration of James Polk. Indeed, Polk is the first president of the nineteenth century not merely to articulate publicly idiosyncratic reasons for the denial of information requests in particular circumstances but to outline principles concerning disclosure of information that should fix in the presidency as an institution. In 1846, the House of Representatives passed a resolution demanding from Polk "all payments made on President's certificates from the fund appropriated by law" during the Tyler administration. Monies to this fund were appropriated for expenses incurred by diplomatic activity and, presumably, the hiring of spies, and "may in [the President's] judgment be made public."[62]

Tyler "solemnly determined that the objects and items of these expenditures should not be made public," and Polk faced the "important question . . . whether a subsequent President, either voluntarily or at the request of . . . Congress, can without a violation of the spirit of the law revise the acts of his predecessor and expose to public view that which he had determined should not be 'made public.'" Polk thought that "if not a matter of strict duty, it would certainly be a safe general rule that this should not be done." He claimed he was "fully aware of the strong and correct public feeling which exists throughout the country against secrecy of any kind in the administration of the Government" but that "foreign negotiations are wisely and properly confined to the knowledge of the Executive."[63]

He observed that "in time of war or impending danger" it may be necessary to "employ individuals for the purpose of obtaining information or rendering other important services who could never be prevailed upon to act if they entertained the least apprehension that their names or their agency would in any contingency be divulged."[64] By this reasoning, the claims of secrecy in one administration must, absent exigent circumstances, be honored by subsequent administrations. Even though this is an example of statutory interpretation and not a claim to inherent presidential power, Polk was the first to articulate and advance the principle of maintaining secrecy within the *presidency*, not merely within the administration of a particular president or for a particular ad hoc purpose. This is a step toward institutionalized presidential secrecy that ventured beyond mere assertion of separation of powers grounds. It is unclear if he grasped the idea that an institutionalized power of secrecy in the presidency would have the potential effect of greatly expanding presidential power, but it is clear that Polk had a broader vision of such power than did his predecessors.

From these beginnings, the presidential power to withhold information began to migrate to the legal realm, as theories in law evolved in support of executive claims. As time elapsed, doctrinal positions asserting executive power to withhold information remained stable across various presidential administrations; efforts to fix these doctrines in law began in earnest in the last half of the nineteenth century. In 1865, Attorney General James Speed asserted in an official analysis of presidential power that "the President . . . [is] not bound to produce papers or disclose information . . . where, in [his] own judgment, the disclosures would, on public considerations, be inexpedient."[65]

In Abraham Lincoln's administration, issues of presidential refusal to comply with congressional and judicial requests for information took on a more overtly legal dimension. For example, in refusing to release information concerning the arrest of General Charles P. Stone for the debacle of the battle of Ball's Bluff, Lincoln stated that the general "was arrested and imprisoned under my general authority, and upon evidence . . . I deem it incompatible with the public interest . . . to make a more particular statement about the evidence."[66] Never charged and eventually released, the evidence against Stone was never disclosed. Lincoln's immediate justification for Stone's arrest and surrounding the case in secrecy was that the "public safety" required such extraordinary measures.

What makes this incident remarkable is that the motivation for the arrest of Stone may be located in the fact that the fiasco of Ball's Bluff resulted in the death of Lincoln's close friend Edward Baker. It is easy to view the arrest of Stone as an abuse of presidential power for personal reasons, and this event points up what historically has frequently been the case—that exercises of power taken in the name of national security are entangled with personal and political considerations of the president and his cabinet.

All administrations engage in secrecy for partisan advantage or to prevent congressional enemies from acquiring useful information, but the trajectory of presidential secrecy power has been on an uninterrupted upward course since the beginning of the last century. The early attempts described above to shield executive branch information became increasingly awkward as the federal government grew and the national security environment burgeoned with complexity. More formalized mechanisms were needed, and these could only be created with the help of Congress.

At the end of the nineteenth century, there existed two broad bases for withholding information, one based on the separation of powers and the other on the consideration of bad consequences that would flow from release of information. The separation of powers argument is designed to protect the functioning of the presidency and to prevent overreaching by Congress and the courts. The concern under this argument is for a preservation of constitutional divisions of authority. On the other hand, the protective power argument flows from nothing more than the purely pragmatic and functional necessity to prevent damage to the nation and its citizens. While these powers were not insignificant, they were exercised on an ad hoc basis—it was the press of technology and the entanglement in large-scale war in the twentieth century that provided the fulcrum allowing the presidency to lay claim to unlimited control over all national security information. Through statutory intervention just before and during World War I, the separation of powers and the protective power arguments merged into the single claim that the Constitution commits to the president sole authority over control of national security information.

The Legal Origins of Classification Power

In 1911, Congress passed the first statute criminalizing the unauthorized acquisition and disclosure of national security information.[67] Entitled "An act to prevent disclosure of national defense secrets," the statute applied to the obtaining and transfer of "knowledge" as well as renderings and depictions of national defense facilities. It also contained an extraterritoriality clause, subjecting people to prosecution for acts done outside United States jurisdiction. While this statute was repealed by the Espionage Act of 1917, to this day the principal criminal statute governing the unauthorized disclosure of classified materials, it was an important first step toward the classified president. Without criminal statutory provisions, the president and administrators were severely handicapped in their ability to control the dispersal of information and protect national security. Often their enforcement power was limited to termination of government employees, with virtually no recourse in the case of nongovernment employees.

The 1911 statute is one of the very few times that Congress has acted to criminalize espionage activity, and Congress is historically consistent in its refusal to expand the criminal grounds on which a president may act against those divulging classified information to unauthorized personnel. It is important to see that the statute is a framework of a grant of power to the presidency, since it is the executive branch that will determine what "information respecting the national defense" means.

The 1911 statute was a move toward a massive transfer of power to the executive branch in the form of discretion to mold the meanings of terms such as *national defense* and *national security*. Notably, there were no provisions in the statute for determining what information is covered by its criminal sections, though it was clearly oriented toward the protection of physical facilities such as navy yards, vessels, and government buildings, examples specifically covered in the law. But the statute also prohibited the unauthorized acquisition of "knowledge of anything connected with the national defense" at these facilities and any agreement to receive such knowledge. The statute both provided a means and the necessity for determining classes of information protected under its provisions. Since the term *national defense* was left undefined, the executive branch, in order to prevent the statute from being unconstitutionally vague in its operation, needed to identify the types of information that could trigger criminal provisions. But the main motivation for the administrative organization of national security information under the statute was that it provided the president with enormous power to shield information from disclosure. This represented the beginnings of a sea change in presidential power, one overlooked by all but a few scholars.

For the first time, the president had the means to a fully integrated apparatus of secrecy, from the determination of what should be protected from disclosure to the power to imprison or execute those who collect and transfer protected information to third parties. Secrets in the federal government became, as one 1997 government report memorably put it, "whatever anyone with a stamp decides to stamp secret."[68] But the 1911 statute was only in short operation, as it was displaced by the Espionage Act of 1917, which is still the chief criminal statute governing unauthorized disclosure of national security information. The Espionage Act extended the inchoate features of the 1911 act and provided for harsher penalties for espionage activity. The Espionage Act is one of the most important pieces of legislation ever created, not merely because of the subject matter but also, again, because of the enormous transfer of power to the executive branch it represented.

There are good reasons why the Espionage Act, nearly a century later, is largely unchanged and unaugmented by companion acts concerning similar matters. Congress is well aware of what it did in 1917, and it is quite unwilling to repeat itself. So, for example, there still is no general legislation criminalizing the leaking of classified information. As many have noted, if such legislation existed, much of the senior bureaucracy would be locked up. But with the advent of the Espionage Act, according to the same 1997 report, "the Executive Branch . . . assumed the authority both for structuring the classification system and for deciding the grounds upon which secrets should be created and maintained."[69]

Nor has there been any congressional effort to govern classified information in general. The Atomic Energy Act is one of the few exceptions to congressional unwillingness to classify material by statute. There, Congress classified all information as "Restricted Data" that concerns "(1) design, manufacture, or utilization of atomic weapons; (2) the production of special nuclear material; or (3) the use of special nuclear material in the production of energy."[70] But less than two percent of all classification is made pursuant to statute; the rest is classified in accordance with executive orders and administrative guidelines.[71] Thus, "what commonly is referred to as 'government secrecy' more properly could be termed 'administrative secrecy' or 'secrecy by regulation.' "[72]

Congress has simply failed to exercise oversight or control over general classification authority, and the "absence of adequate oversight across the Executive Branch by the Congress has resulted in little accountability for decisions and little incentive to reduce the scope of government secrecy."[73] This failure by Congress to assume control of the use of classification authority has left the modern president in a position of power that is devoid of accountability. The failure to delineate classification powers and to define appropriate uses of classification authority have also placed the judiciary in an awkward position. The judiciary, if it wishes to challenge executive decisions concerning classification, must second-guess intelligence experts and professionals on matters of national security, since there are few statutes to rely on in examining classification decisions. Further, deference to the executive branch over matters of national security is a powerful impulse in the federal judiciary for reasons addressed throughout this book. And, as we discuss later in this chapter, these conditions make the judiciary tentative—overly tentative—when they handle cases involving classified material.

The Espionage Act criminalized the disclosure of national security information "to any foreign government, or to any faction or party or military or naval force within a foreign country, whether recognized or unrecognized by the United States" and provided for lengthy prison sentences or, for certain offenses committed in time of war, a penalty of death.[74] Although the Act provided examples of national security information, determination of what qualifies as national security information and is thus covered by the Act is left undefined. Section 6 of the Act further provided that the president "in time of war or in case of national emergency may by proclamation designate any place . . . in which anything for the use of the Army or Navy is being prepared or constructed or stored as a prohibited place for the purpose of this title. . . . [The President] shall determine that information with respect thereto would be prejudicial to the national defense."

The chief application of the Espionage Act at its beginnings was to suppress speech that was nonconformist or opposed United States involvement in World War I. Extravagant uses of the statute abound. For example, in *Goldstein v. United States* the defendant was convicted for, among other things, violating the Act's prohibitions against any attempt "to cause insubordination, disloyalty, mutiny or refusal of duty in the military or naval forces of the United States" or to "willfully obstruct the recruiting or enlistment service of the United States." Goldstein had made a movie depicting aspects of the Revolutionary War and was convicted under the Espionage Act because the depiction put our British allies in a bad light.[75] And in *United States v. Nagler,* the defendant was convicted because he had spoken against the Red Cross and the Y.M.C.A., organizations, the court held, that were part of the war effort.[76] These uses of the statute tend to overshadow the features of the Act that shift enormous powers of secrecy to the president.

Even as Congress debated and passed the Espionage Act in the midst of a war, it realized that transparency in government was necessary for democracy to function and so rejected provisions that would have given the president a ranging power to censor material discussing issues of national security. But the Act perforce created in the president the capacity to define matters that must be excluded from the public debate by providing the means to classify information and to buttress that classification with prosecutorial threats.

Up to this point, decisions to withhold information were made largely on an ad hoc basis, governed by the contexts of each particular case. With the advent of the Espionage Act, the president now had the power to "class" information into types, types that contained information that is presumptively nondisclosable. Section 2(a) of the statute, the provision with the harshest penalties, criminalizes the transfer to foreign entities of "any document, writing, code book, signal book, sketch, photograph, photographic negative, blue print, plan, map, model, note, instrument, appliance, or information relating to the national defense." The phrase "information relating to the national defense" is left undefined; it provided the basis for the presidential establishment of a system for classifying information. It is true that sections 1(a) and 1(b) of the statute contain a lengthy list of examples of material and sites that are protected under the statute, but there is no evidence that the provisions of section 1 are meant to delimit the language of section 2.

National Security Information

"National security" is a notoriously vague term, and most definitions do little to make its meaning any clearer. For example, former presidential advisor Frank Press testified before Congress that "we have to take a broad view of what constitutes national security" and that "we have to define it in terms of economic growth in the country, of the cultural life in the country, the quality of life for our citizens, and the example we portray to other nations."[77] And Sidney W. Souers, the first director of central intelligence, wrote that "'national security' can perhaps best be understood as a point of view rather than a distinct area of governmental responsibility."[78] Under this view, almost everything implicates national security. Over the years, "national security" has justified the redirection of cotton seed cake to feed privately owned cattle, limits on the importation of oil and petroleum products, the purchase of oats, the training of British pilots in the United States, and countless other actions. More recently, President George W. Bush asserted that national security "means economic security for every single citizen,"[79] used the term to justify termination of government employee union participation,[80] and used it to justify exploration of energy independence.

It is generally claimed and admitted that the term "national security," in the sense that it is used now, did not come into being until after World War II. But this understanding is debatable. In a convincing article, Mark Shulman traces the origin of "national security" much further back in our history, arguing that the "National Security League of the World War I era framed the discourse of national security for the Cold War and today."[81] Souers gives some support for this claim in asserting that before World War II, "a few far-sighted men were seeking for a means of correlating our foreign policy with our military and economic capabilities." These "far-sighted men" saw that national security meant much more than mere physical safety or military superiority, and it became apparent during World War II that the war "involved more than a purely military campaign to defeat the enemy's armed forces."[82]

Whatever the origins, this point of view emerged most fully after World War II, and presidential advisors moved quickly to consolidate powers over security matters in the presidency. The national security acts of 1947 and 1949 provided the reorganization and statutory framework necessary to achieve this goal. As Shulman notes, in a few short years the "national security state would build a highway network crisscrossing the continent to facilitate the movement of troops and supplies in case of war. In the cause of national security, the armed forces, the intelligence apparatus, national resources, and even domestic transportation were drawn into the expanding federal government's control and coordination . . . at the start of the Cold War."[83]

National security required the correlation of "foreign policy with . . . military and economic capabilities."[84] In an era of atomic weapons and the accelerated rapidity at which world events could unfold, the pressure for centralization and uniform authority over security information broke the traditional practice of military control of classified material. The presidency was the only institution situated to take over control of classified information and manage it in integration with nonmilitary information.

Despite having authority since World War I to manage the classification and safeguarding of information, presidents chiefly left this activity to the various military services because the need for executive control of information was either not recognized or only inchoately understood and out of a desire to avoid conflict with the military. The consolidation of power in the president and the recognition of the multivalent nature of modern security during World War II pressed presidents into new claims over control of information.

Classification authority has been explicitly controlled by presidents and handled through executive order since 1940, when Franklin Roosevelt claimed the power to authorize and designate the classifications for material concerning military bases. Prior to this time, the vast majority of classification was undertaken at the direction of the military, and the center of authority for classification activity was clearly in military hands. In Executive Order 8381, Roosevelt, relying on a 1938 statute, engaged in some sleight of hand to shift the center of classification of information from the secretaries of war and the navy to the president.[85]

In E.O. 8381, Roosevelt protected "all military or naval installations and equipment which are now classified . . . under the authority . . . of the Secretary of War or the Secretary of the Navy . . . and all military or naval installations . . . which may hereafter be so classified . . . at the direction of the President." As Quist notes, "This EO also apparently gave governmental civilian employees the authority to classify information. . . . Until this time, Army and Navy personnel and civilian employees of those services had been the only recipients of governmental classification directives."[86]

To be sure, this was a small step, as the president as commander-in-chief no doubt had the authority to control the classification of material in that capacity, if no other. But the effect of the E.O. 8381 was also to begin the transfer of classification authority away from military hands and into civilian control. It is worth noting that nowhere in the order does Roosevelt claim to be exercising power other than that granted in the 1938 statute.

Likewise, President Harry Truman issued Executive Order 10104,[87] which protected certain bases from surveillance and depiction, solely on the statutory power granted to the president in a 1948 revised version of the 1938 statute used by Roosevelt.[88] In Order E.O. 8381, Roosevelt claimed his authority "by virtue of the authority vested in me by the . . . statutory provisions," but Truman, in E.O. 10104, takes a step outside of this narrow justification. He claims authority to act not only by virtue of statute but also "in the interests of national defense." It is a small addition, but it is telling, for it implies that there is presidential authority to act outside the scope of—or independent of—statutory authorization. Once it is claimed that presidential authority to classify information exists independently of statutory authority and once the other parties implicitly acquiesce to that justification—there is no way for Congress to close off the resort of the president to the use of secrecy to shield information.

But the language of E.O. 10104 was merely preparation for that found in E.O. 10290, the first order dealing comprehensively with the classification of information.[89] Not to sound overly dramatic, but one could say that the "national security president" was born on paper at 10:57 a.m., September 26, 1951. That is when E.O. 10290 was submitted for publication in the Federal Register. That order represents the maturity of the transition from military classification of information to civilian control of classification. This important shift highlights the expansion of the term *national security* from merely a military consideration to a broader and more inclusive definition that implicates many activities outside of military control or concern.

Parallel changes in reference also began to occur in the area of secrecy privileges. For example, the "military and state secrets privilege" discussed in chapter 3 has gradually come to be known as simply the "state secrets privilege." And President Truman took action immediately following World War II to "civilianize" and expand presidential control over national security information. He created the National Intelligence Authority (NIA), the Intelligence Advisory Board, and the Central Intelligence Group (CIG), the immediate forerunner of the Central Intelligence Agency. These organizations were designed to increase the efficient executive use and control of intelligence information and weaken military control of information by including key civilian members. Congress followed this trend by adopting the National Security Act of 1947, which abolished the NIA and the CIG and established the National Security Council and the CIA in their place. The mission of the NSC "was to serve in an advisory capacity to the president in matters concerning the integration of domestic, foreign and military policy."[90] In other words, the term *national security* had clearly outgrown any military connotation it had once had. The permanent members of the NSC at its inception were all civilian, and though the membership of the council has changed over the years, it is still completely governed by civilians.

Under Truman, the U.S. Communications Intelligence Board (USCIB) also expanded its membership from purely military participants to include the FBI, the CIA, and the Department of State, though this expansion did little to wrest power over communications intelligence policy from the military. In 1948, Secretary of Defense James Forrestal insisted that the USCIB should be subordinate to the NSC, but the military managed to avoid this result. But the military hold on communications intelligence would not last. On October 24, 1952, Truman "stated that the communications intelligence function was a national responsibility rather than one of purely military orientation"; through a national security directive, Truman reconstituted the USCIB into the basis for the present-day National Security Agency.[91] Truman's directive took power over communication intelligence away from the Joint Chiefs of Staff and placed it under the control of the Department of Defense.

In form and wording, E.O. 10290 is prosaic, but it tracks the changes discussed above by shifting the center of gravity for the control of information to civilian hands, resulting in an expanded understanding of presidential power. Just a year before E.O. 10290, in E.O. 10104, the most recent previous order concerning classification of information, President Truman based his authority on "statutory provisions, and in the interests of national defense."[92] But E.O. 10290, issued during the Korean War, which makes the emphasis of civilian control of classification even more remarkable, abandons the presidential tradition of relying chiefly on statutory authority as the basis for usurping classification power. The order holds that "in order to protect national security . . . [and] by virtue of the authority vested in me by the Constitution and statutes, and as President of the United States, the regulations attached hereto . . . are hereby prescribed for application throughout the Executive Branch of the Government."[93] This is the first time the term "national security" appears in an executive order concerning classification orders, which itself provides insight into contemporaneous thinking about the transition of classification authority from the military to civilian control and new thinking about the bases of executive power.

For example, it implies that there is a source of authority that derives from the presidency that may be independent of the Constitution and statutes, since it lists

"President of the United States" as a third source of power for issuing the order. Perhaps the language is evidence of an abundance of caution in undertaking a new ground for executive classification authority, but it sounds suspiciously like a claim that there is a power in the presidency that does not arise from the Constitution. This idea of extra-constitutional authority is never far from executive thinking concerning national security matters. At least one privilege, the state secrets privilege discussed in chapter 3, rests on implied assumptions that there is an extra-constitutional power to prevent disclosure of information when national security is at stake, even in the face of constitutional claims to the affected information. The language of E.O. 10290 coaxes this idea into the realm of classification authority. Most recently, presidents have claimed inherent authority to act unilaterally and secretly in the name of national security, even when such action appears to be constitutionally questionable or even a clear violation of criminal law.

Clearly, E.O. 10290 no longer relies on statutory authority for the executive power to classify information. Once this claim was made, the expansion of presidential authority to include control over classified information independent of congressional approval, no future president would ever take it back. Indeed, in E.O. 10501, President Eisenhower's chief order concerning classification of material, he cited the same sources that Truman did in E.O. 10290, but Eisenhower added the phrase "deeming such action necessary in the best interests of the national security."[94] In Truman's order, the term *national security* appears in the first paragraph of the order, a "whereas" paragraph, as a justification for the need to rework classification procedure. It is not invoked as a source of presidential power, but as a source of need. In Eisenhower's order, the term is dropped from a "whereas" paragraph and relocated to the "therefore" paragraph that contains enumeration of the powers available to the president to issue the order. In other words, "national security" is no longer a *justification* or a description of some need for action, it is now a *source* of executive power in its own right. The difference is subtle but important. In the first case, "national security information" is the result of classification authority; in the second it is the source of classification power. By simply defining information, policies, actions, programs, and so forth as critical to national security, the president may unilaterally withdraw such items from public scrutiny.

Just what was meant by "national security" is unclear, but it is clear that the concept had outstripped the military connotation it had traditionally held. Various subsequent executive orders used different language in justifying presidential authority. For example, Eisenhower's E.O. 10865 on rules concerning the handling of classified information by industry dropped the "deemed" language described above but cited "Commander in Chief" as a separate authority for acting, along with statutory and constitutional authorization as well as powers as president.[95] So between 1940 and 1960, the claimed presidential authority to determine classification of information went from one based solely in statute to one that was based in inherent constitutional powers—and perhaps even extraconstitutional power.

By the 1960s, the term *national security* was freely cited to withhold material the disclosure of which not only could jeopardize military preparedness or success but also could harm the economy or even the confidence and happiness of the American people. "National security information," a subset of material under the concept of "national security," is not so amorphous but is still often nebulous. National security information is defined in various places in the Code of Federal Regulations and other statutory material as "information that has been determined pursuant to [executive order] to require protection against unauthorized disclosure and that is so designated."[96] But this tautological definition goes too far; national security information requires protection because it is classified. It is also under-inclusive, for there is information that may be protected as "national security information" that is not classified pursuant to executive order.

Information generated entirely privately may even be suppressed in the interests of national security. The Invention Secrecy Act, for example, requires the U.S. Patent and Trademark Office (USPTO) to withhold patents when the patent application or invention would compromise national security. In those circumstances, the USPTO "shall order that the invention be kept secret and shall withhold the publication of the application or the grant of a patent." Such withholding must be renewed yearly, except that an "order in effect, or issued, during a time when the United States is at war, shall remain in effect for the duration of hostilities [and an] order in effect, or issued, during a national emergency declared by the President shall remain in effect for the duration of the national emergency."[97]

Where the patent application is made by a private citizen or corporation and the government has no property interest in the application, the protective orders are called "John Doe Orders." These orders, for reasons of national security, deny access to, publication of, or use of inventions that come solely from the minds of civilian inventors. From a constitutional perspective, this is an astonishing power. An invention or process generated solely from the imagination of a citizen may be suppressed—and the inventor subject to imprisonment and fine for divulging the content of his or her own thoughts.

The Invention Secrecy Act is not alone in this regard, though, as the government has claimed that certain information is "born classified." In the famous 1979 case of *United States v. Progressive,* the Department of Energy successfully claimed in federal district court that an article written by a nonscientist journalist describing the theory and design of thermonuclear weapons was "restricted data"—without any action or determination of that fact by the government. In the words of the court in granting an injunction prohibiting publication of the article, "What is involved here is information dealing with the most destructive weapon in the history of mankind, information of sufficient destructive potential to nullify the right to free speech and to endanger the right to life itself."[98] But the article was published in another forum, and in a later issue of *The Progressive* itself, without apparent damage to national security.

The Atomic Energy Act,[99] as the government has argued vigorously, results in automatic classification of certain information concerning nuclear weapons design, means of materials production for nuclear weapons, and other privately generated material that could be used to aid other nations or groups in developing military uses of nuclear material.[100] In a legal and technical sense, information classified under the Inventions Secrecy Act and the Atomic Energy Act is not national security information, and it is represented that classification actions under these statutes are required by law and are not open to executive branch discretion. But, of course, executive branch officials interpret these statutes in light of national security needs as defined by the president and his staff.

Finally, as we discuss in the next chapter, the executive branch may assert the state secrets privilege to block the disclosure of information that may be detrimental to national security, even if the information is wholly in the hands of private parties. So the term *national security information* is even broader than it is often defined in regulations and executive branch documents, and it includes not only material classifiable under executive order or statute but also material that may be restricted by executive fiat.

The first instance of the term *national security information* in the Federal Register came in 1967, and President Nixon used the term in the title of a 1972 executive order.[101] Since that time the use of the term has grown greatly. The year 2003 saw the greatest use of that term in the Federal Register, where it appears in sixty-eight separate entries. Statutes and judicially adopted rules govern the disclosability of national security information under statutes such as the Freedom of Information Act or at trial or discovery. All of these statutes and rules pay great deference to presidential authority and virtually mandate judicial hesitancy in matters concerning classified information. We turn now to the judicial response to the growth of the classified president, to the expansion of presidential power under the aegis of national security.

The Judicial Deference to Claims of National Security: An Overview

The legal power of the executive branch to maintain secrecy is based on executive order, seven chief statutes, and two common-law doctrines. The chief statutes are the Espionage Act, the National Security Act of 1947, the Atomic Energy Act, the Freedom of Information Act,[102] the Foreign Intelligence Surveillance Act,[103] the USA-PATRIOT Act,[104] and the Inventions Secrecy Act. The applicable common-law doctrines, the state secrets privilege and executive privilege, are generalized concepts providing the president with wide, nonstatutory-based discretion to keep information secret. As we shall see, judicial behavior toward all of these items is uniformly deferential, even in the face of evidence of prevarication, manipulation of law, and abuse of authority. When it comes to determining the possible damage of classified information, most judges find themselves adrift in rough seas. Judges rely disproportionately on the advice of government representatives in these matters, even if they recognize the zealous nature of government claims concerning national security. And even in the rare instance that a judge admits that governmental abuse may be behind claims of secrecy, he or she is often hesitant to order disclosure of material where evidence of abuse is mixed with material that is protected legitimately under national security concerns. Judges normally see the task of determining whether or not information is properly classified as beyond their ken and an encroachment on executive authority. In this context, courts err on the side of government. But the costs are high—and often unwarranted.

The federal judiciary assiduously avoids confrontation with the president concerning the classification and handling of information. Courts that do not hesitate to invade the spheres of executive action in other contexts shrink at the invocation of national security. Often, courts simply seem confused about how to proceed when secrecy privileges are asserted. For example, in the case of Sibel Edmonds, a whistleblower who sued for retaliatory termination, an appeals court removed Edmonds and her counsel from the court without providing them an opportunity to make their scheduled oral argument. In that case, the government had asserted the state secrets privilege, but the oral argument ended up being an *ex parte* hearing with only government representatives present. No classified information was discussed at the impromptu *ex parte* hearing, and the government's counsel were not cleared to hear or present such information even if it had come up. The three-judge panel was simply uncertain how to proceed in the face of relentless assertions on the part of the government that virtually every aspect of the Edmonds case was classified, so an overabundance of caution resulted in a perversion of the legal process. This judicial confusion, uncertainty, and hesitancy is not unusual in litigation concerning national security matters; time and again plaintiffs see their access to courts and legal processes cut off or seriously denuded.

The main evolution of judicial doctrine in connection with classified material occurred during the height of the Cold War, when the chief concerns for national security were focused on the Soviet Union, an adversary with enormous resources and a large variety of technicians dedicated to gathering information about our capabilities and weaknesses. In the face of such an enterprise, courts were reluctant to second-guess claims of national security or to examine classification decisions. As courts are fond of saying or implying, judges are not suited to making important decisions concerning the national security of the United States.

But this wise caution threatens to swallow the judicial enterprise, for many judges conclude that deference is the only legitimate response to claims of national security by the executive branch. Secrecy is not merely a deprivation of information, a passive act, it is often a means to cover up and hide egregious governmental behavior that merits extensive public and judicial attention. As former representative Larry Combest noted, "The growing fear of government secrecy is linked directly to the growth of government power and intrusiveness."[105] The judiciary has a legitimate and crucial goal of providing accountability for presidential and executive actions, but it has prostrated itself before the altar of national security and, through its neglect of duty, has allowed a substantial and unchecked increase in presidential power. This increase threatens the balance of power among the branches of government and puts citizens' constitutional rights and civil liberties at risk.

The U.S. Supreme Court has greatly bolstered presidential claims of constitutional power to control classified information exclusively. The Court has repeatedly implied, though not directly held, that the president has an undiluted power to control access to classified information. In one case that many commentators cite in support of the proposition that the executive has unchecked control of classified information, *Dept. of the Navy v. Egan*, the Court wrote, "The President, after all, is the 'Commander in Chief of the Army and Navy of the United States.' . . . His authority to classify and control access to information bearing on national security and to determine whether an individual is sufficiently trustworthy to occupy a position in the Executive Branch that will give that person access to such information flows primarily from this constitutional investment of power in the President and exists quite apart from any explicit congressional grant." The protection of classified information is committed to the judgment of the president and various agencies, and "it is not reasonably possible for an outside nonexpert body to review the substance of such a judgment."[106]

But all of the statements cited in *Egan* are dicta, since the case was not decided on constitutional grounds and all of the Court's comments are qualified by the statement "unless Congress specifically has provided otherwise."[107] In other words, where Congress has not acted the president has plenary authority to control and manage classified information. Despite the common interpretation of *Egan*, it is not reasonable to conclude from the case that the president has sole, inherent power over classification and classified information. Louis Fisher makes this point with his usual clarity and crispness when he writes, "The conflict in Egan was solely within the executive branch (Navy versus MSPB), not between Congress and the executive branch"; the case "decided merely the 'narrow question' of whether the MSPB had *statutory* authority to review the substance of a decision to deny a security clearance."[108]

This unchecked power is perhaps reasonable in principle, but in practice it is a different matter. The Whistleblower Protection Act is designed to prevent retaliation against federal employees for disclosing to appropriate offices (such as inspectors general) evidence of malfeasance, waste, fraud, or abuse.[109] The WPA itself is notoriously ineffective. The offices of inspectors general are often filled with employees loyal to management and they are not independent watchdogs but enforcers to prevent reporting of illegal and unethical activity that might damage the current hierarchy in the particular agency.[110] Further, the Office of Special Counsel (OSC), which is supposed to be the chief source of protection and means of investigation for whistleblowers, has long been politicized and is now ineffective and is itself now subject to investigation that it wrongfully retaliated against its own employees.

Appeals from adverse decisions of WPA complaints made through the administrative process—virtually every decision is adverse to the employee—are taken to the Merit Systems Protection Board and then to the U.S. Court of Appeals for the Federal Circuit. According to a Project on Government Oversight analysis, in only one out of more than a hundred cases considered on the merits did a whistleblower prevail at the Federal Circuit.[111] Congress has been forced to amend the WPA twice in apparently futile attempts to get the Federal Circuit to apply the

WPA as intended. For example, the WPA requires only that the disclosing employee have a reasonable belief that the disclosure evinces gross mismanagement, waste, fraud, or abuse in order to gain statutory protection. But in *Lachance v. MSPB* the court held that in reviewing the matter, it was proper to make the "presumption that public officers perform their duties correctly, fairly, in good faith, and in accordance with the law and governing regulations. . . . And this presumption stands unless there is 'irrefragable proof to the contrary.' "[112] The standard of "irrefragable truth" seems to vitiate completely the reasonable person standard, and the result is that disclosing employees must present incontestable evidence of wrongful behavior to avail themselves of protection under the WPA.

And the WPA is unavailable to employees working with national security information, which means that these employees are completely unprotected when they make disclosures of malfeasance. Since the courts and Congress have yielded to the president and agency heads complete discretion concerning access to national security information, whistleblowers are often subjected to revocation of their security clearances. This is tantamount to termination, since clearances and codeword access are necessary for employment with agencies involved in national security. These reflexive responses to embarrassment over disclosure need not even take place as a result of public exposure of information; internal complaints are often enough to trigger efforts to punish complaining employees. This means that employees are often unnecessarily forced to choose between conscience and career.[113]

In the rare circumstances that an executive branch agency or the president relents and restores a security clearance, the employee is still usually subject to retaliation. Clearance officers comprise a small and interconnected group of people who between them control almost every security clearance granted in the United States. Once an employee becomes known for his or her uncomfortable revelations about an agency engaged in national security matters, that employee may suffer continuing problems in securing access to national security information. This can limit an employee's ability to advance in rank, for while the employee may have clearance, codeword access for a specific position may be denied the applicant, thus making him or her ineligible for the promotion or new job.

The failure to extend the WPA to national security employees is paradoxical, for waste, fraud, abuse, and malfeasance in this arena may have a disproportionately greater effect on citizen safety than similar activities in other agencies. But national security agencies are addicted to the lack of accountability and the freedom from scrutiny that other agencies must endure, and their opacity contributes to the perception—indeed the fact—that there is little that can be done about people who use classification to cloak illegal, wrong, ill-conceived, or irrational activities.

Likewise, because of the common perception that presidents exercise unimpeded control over matters touching foreign relations, presidents have an incentive to tie activity to the foreign relations power to maximize their authority to keep information secret. For example, George W. Bush argued that certain operations in Iraq and Afghanistan were "defense actions" rather than "intelligence activities." Through such recategorization, Bush hoped to avoid statutory triggers for reporting activities to the congressional intelligence oversight committees.[114] The Supreme Court has found that in the foreign relations area, "if there is to be judicial enquiry, it will raise concerns for the separation of powers in trenching on matters committed to the other branches"[115] and that "the generally accepted view [is] that foreign policy [is] the province and responsibility of the Executive."[116] Indeed, as the Court has stated quite bluntly, "The very nature of executive decisions as to foreign policy is political, not judicial." Further:

> The President, both as Commander-in-Chief and as the Nation's organ for foreign affairs, has available intelligence services whose reports are not and ought not to be published to the world. It would be intolerable that courts, without the relevant information, should review and perhaps nullify actions of the Executive taken on information properly held secret. Nor can courts sit *in camera* in order to be taken into executive confidences. . . [National security] decisions [are] of a kind for which the Judiciary has neither aptitude, facilities nor responsibility and which [have] long been held to belong in the domain of political power not subject to judicial intrusion or inquiry.[117]

As implied here, the absolute authority of the president to control classified information does not rest exclusively on his power over foreign affairs, and even information that is classified but without connection to foreign relations will receive no more searching review from the courts. For "the protection of classified information must be committed to the broad discretion of the agency responsible. . . . it is not reasonably possible for an outside nonexpert body to review [such discretionary decisions] and to decide . . . what constitutes an acceptable margin of error in assessing the potential risk." As the Court has accordingly acknowledged, "As to these areas of Art. II duties the courts have traditionally shown the utmost deference to Presidential responsibilities."[118] "Utmost deference" means almost universal judicial refusal to second-guess agency and presidential decisions and actions justified by national security claims, even when such decisions and actions give rise to reasonable concerns that they were made in furtherance of illegitimate goals.

In matters concerning the production of allegedly classified information under the Freedom of Information Act, the courts have again been the friends of the executive branch. FOIA allows the withholding of information "specifically authorized under criteria established by an executive order to be kept secret in the interest of national defense or foreign policy."[119] Legal history is replete with examples of courts giving the executive branch and presidents great latitude concerning claims of national security under Exemption 1, the national security exemption, in FOIA litigation. In *EPA v. Mink*, the first time that the Supreme Court considered Exemption 1 of FOIA, it reached the conclusion that the statute did not authorize courts to examine contested material *in camera* to determine if classification decisions by agencies were made to defeat release of material for reasons other than national security.[120] This "see no evil" interpretation is typical of the approach of federal courts in the entire area of national security; after *Mink*, Congress amended FOIA to provide courts with "jurisdiction to enjoin the agency from withholding agency records and to order the production of any agency records improperly withheld. . . . In such a case the court shall determine the matter de novo and the burden is on the agency to sustain its action."[121]

Courts, though, are as forgiving as ever toward executive claims of national security. As the Circuit Court of Appeals for the District of Columbia recently noted, "We have consistently reiterated the principle of deference to the executive in the FOIA context when national security concerns are implicated. . . . Moreover, in the FOIA context, we have consistently deferred to executive affidavits predicting harm to the national security, and have found it unwise to undertake searching judicial review." And while the Cold War necessities for deference to the presidential national security claims are no more, "America faces an enemy just as real as its former Cold War foes, with capabilities beyond the capacity of the judiciary to explore." The lone dissent in the case noted that the decision "eviscerates both FOIA itself and the principles of openness in government that FOIA embodies."[122]

Another court also recently found that classified information that revealed and documented criminal or tortious activity need not be revealed. The court held that E.O. 12958 only "prohibits an agency from classifying documents as a ruse when they could not otherwise be withheld from public disclosure. It does not prevent the classification of national security information merely because it might *reveal* criminal or tortious acts."[123] It is difficult to read this statement as anything but an invitation to use classification to hide criminal activity. Determining what is "a ruse" and what is not is precisely the sort of review and judgment courts refuse to undertake in cases involving national security claims.

Courts will even accept a lack of response as acceptable under FOIA in a rather strange device known as a Glomar response. Built under the guise of a private vessel designed to mine manganese nodules from the ocean floor, the *Glomar Explorer* was actually designed to recover nuclear weapons and other material from a sunken Soviet submarine. An FOIA request for information concerning the relationship between the CIA and the *Glomar Explorer* was met with rejection and an explanation that "the fact of the existence or non-existence of the records . . . request[ed] would relate to information pertaining to intelligence sources and methods which the Director of Central Intelligence has the responsibility to protect from unauthorized disclosure in accordance with section 102(d)(3) of the National Security Act of 1947."[124]

The Glomar response was designed to permit the CIA to remain silent in the face of requests for information when the very fact of possession or lack of possession of the requested materials would provide sensitive information about intelligence collection sources and methods. Although the government eventually abandoned its position in the original case, it is now accepted by every court that has ruled on the issue that the CIA is entitled to make Glomar responses. As one all-star appellate panel claimed in justifying judicial timidity, "When a pattern of responses itself reveals classified information, the only way to keep secrets is to maintain silence uniformly. And this is what the CIA has done."[125] With complete predictability, the doctrine, which obviously is consistent with increased secrecy and bureaucratic discretion, was seized on by other government departments. Since the mid-1990s, the FBI, the Department of Justice, the U.S. Marshals Service, the Department of State, and even the U.S. Customs Service have all used the Glomar response.[126]

The complete judicial deference to the executive branch in matters concerning access to classified information, control of classified information, the conduct of foreign affairs, activities undertaken in the name of national security, and efforts to thwart FOIA creates a virtually impenetrable barrier that prevents any measure of accountability for executive branch and presidential abuse of power. But, of course, these protections for the president and the executive branch are just the beginning, just the first picket in a layered defense that has yet to be breached by either courts or Congress and increasingly closes off information to the public, information that is crucial to the survival of a democratic regime. In the subsequent chapters we investigate what happens when inquiries, lawsuits, or other incursions threaten to make it past the initial picket line of executive branch secrecy.

In less than a century the presidency has changed from an institution with tenuous claims to withholding information from Congress and the courts to one with exclusive control of the talismanic term *national security* that assures the secrecy of any information it touches. There is no doubt that the great majority of classification decisions are properly undertaken and in consonance with the spirit and wording of executive orders, but it is also true that such an extensive and unchecked power as that now wielded by presidents and bureaucrats will inevitably be abused. In many ways, the presidency is an institution of our age, while Congress and the judiciary are still very much creations of the eighteenth century. There has been no concomitant change in the capacity of Congress or the courts to garner executive branch accountability similar to the changes in presidential power caused by the nature of the threats of the modern world. Secrecy in government is growing at an astounding rate, and it is difficult to see how the citizens of the United States and their representatives can make intelligent decisions about their government when much of the information they need is siphoned off into classified channels.

CHAPTER THREE

State Secrets and Executive Power

To cover with the veil of secrecy the common routine of business, is an abomination in the eyes of every intelligent man and every friend to his country.

—*Patrick Henry*

For those of us defending the government from the range of legal assaults, openness is like AIDS. . . . One brief exposure can lead to the collapse of the entire immune system. . . . [But] we can always play the trump card—state secrets—and close down the game.

—*Anonymous U.S. government attorney*

In the mid-1980s, Robert Frost, a sheet metal worker at a secret military site in Nevada popularly known as "Area 51," developed skin lesions and other physical maladies. His fellow workers also became ill, and they began to suspect that the routine burning of classified toxic chemicals used to coat "stealth" aircraft was the source of their illness.[1] In violation of numerous environmental statutes, both civil and criminal, administrators at the base illegally burned, transported, and dumped hazardous material, exposing the workers at Area 51 to extremely toxic chemicals.[2] The trenches were reported to be the size of football fields; when the workers' skin grew scaly and thick, they covered themselves with Crisco to prevent it from cracking open.[3] Two workers died, one of them Frost, assertedly as a result of the exposure, and administrators resisted all efforts by the workers to change the conditions at the base. The workers filed lawsuits to find out what chemicals they had been exposed to in order to aid their doctors in determining the best course of treatment for their illness and in order to compel government administrators to abide by federal environmental statutes.

Administrators reacted emphatically against these suits, refusing even to acknowledge that the secret base was known as Area 51. The Secretary of the Air

Force submitted an affidavit that made the rather strange assertion that "the confirmation of even publicly used names like 'Area 51' would cause 'exceptionally grave damage' to national security and place American lives in extreme jeopardy."[4] Therefore, "in addition to refusing to acknowledge the existence of this facility, the government also threatened that any worker who spoke to counsel regarding his or her employment at the facility would be subject to arrest."[5]

Nevertheless, workers came forward prepared to testify that administrators at the base had freely admitted that they were violating criminal environmental statutes and that these administrators had said that they would use claims of national security as a means to avoid responsibility for those actions. The workers' lawyer, Jonathan Turley, had to spend nights in his office to protect his case files against government attorneys seeking to have them classified and seized, and he and his clients battled almost absurd efforts to obstruct legal resolution of the suits.

Administrators argued, among other things, that acknowledgment of the existence of a single car battery or can of pesticide at the air base threatened national security. The workers lost their suit because the Secretary of the Air Force asserted an arcane governmental prerogative known as the "state secrets privilege," a privilege made no less powerful by its obscurity. The privilege affords presidents tremendous power to keep information secret and is often the weapon of last resort, the "nuclear option" of presidential secrecy powers.

Since the administration of Jimmy Carter, there has been a sharp increase in secrecy claims by executive branch officials, especially in the context of litigation. However, recent administrations have extended this penchant with even greater intensity and have been quick to raise secrecy-based objections in response to requests for information that has historically been publicly available. Currently, secrecy claims are raised so routinely and broadly that in some cases the administration officials involved do not even know what the allegedly secret documents contain.[6] Asserting secrecy privileges before finding out the contents of implicated documents demonstrates a certain cavalier approach to the use of secrecy power. Taken together, administrators' interpretations of law and blanket denials of requests for documents demonstrate an intention to expand greatly executive branch power to withhold information from the public, free from any kind of oversight.

But some federal courts have become impatient with apparent executive branch unwillingness to be diligent or accurate in its assertions of privilege: in one case, a federal district court noted that the administration had invoked the state secrets privilege 245 times, and at least one of those invocations covered a document that had already been provided in discovery by another defendant.[7]

This trend has threatening implications for the separation of powers, and executive branch officials over the last several decades have been emboldened to assert secrecy privileges because of judicial timidity and congressional ineffectiveness in reviewing the welter of substantive secrecy claims invoked by presidents and their department heads. At present, it is costless for a president to assert a secrecy privilege: the overwhelming odds are that the assertion will be successful, and even if unsuccessful the process of overturning claims of privilege is lengthy and the only potential cost of excessive claims of national security is in bad publicity. And since the legal process involved normally takes years to play out, the administration in power at the time of the invocation may no longer be in power when a final decision is rendered, so even the threat of bad publicity for abuse of the privilege may have only a negligible effect on the calculation of whether or not to invoke the privilege.

The state secrets privilege is the most powerful weapon in the presidential arsenal of secrecy, and the Supreme Court held in *United States v. Reynolds* that it is proper to prevent disclosure of information in court proceedings when "there is a reasonable danger that compulsion of the evidence will expose matters which, in the interest of national security, should not be divulged."[8] Originally justified as a means to protect the most vital secrets of the nation from exposure through litigation, the privilege has taken in much greater territory than that original justification contemplated. Despite frequent involvement by Congress in issues concerning executive secrecy, most challenges to refusals to disclose information occur in the courts, and we believe that the state secrets privilege, a judicial creation, is now judicially mishandled to the detriment of our constitutional system.

The privilege is most often used by executive branch officials in civil court cases to protect against subpoenas, discovery motions, or other judicial requests for information, and is frequently referred to as a common-law privilege, which reflects its lack of grounding in positive law. While Congress, in various statutes, recognizes the existence of the judicial doctrine concerning the state secrets privilege, it has never grounded the privilege in statutory law. Indeed, one Nixon-era effort to write the privilege into the federal rules of evidence triggered a fierce battle between Congress and the executive branch, but the effort failed.[9] In some respects the privilege indeed functions like a common-law rule; for example the head of a department of government need not rely on statutory authorization to raise the privilege and may assert it on his or her own volition. But this apparent simplicity veneers significant issues of accountability and the reach of executive authority, and the privilege creates perplexing constitutional dilemmas for the courts. These dilemmas arise in two forms.

First, it is axiomatic that the Constitution is the supreme law of the land and that the common law is conditioned by the Constitution, not the other way around. But the state secrets privilege reverses this understanding, for in virtually every case that pits the privilege against citizens' constitutional claims, it is the privilege that wins the encounter. The privilege seems to be ultra-constitutional, for courts have never forced the government to disclose classified information in any case where the privilege has been asserted, even when the basis for compulsion is the claim of plain constitutional right. For example, the case of *Halkin v. Helms* arose as a result of the National Security Agency illegally and unconstitutionally intercepting thousands of phone and electronic communications in the 1960s originating from hundreds of Americans.[10] When sued, administrators invoked the state secrets privilege, and since all of the evidence the plaintiffs needed to prove their case was in the hands of the very administrators who violated their rights and who had asserted the privilege, the plaintiffs lost the case.

The incentives to abuse the privilege are obvious, and herein lies the second dilemma with the privilege as it is now designed: how may the courts fulfill their constitutional duty of oversight of executive branch activity and still meet the legitimate goals the privilege seeks to achieve? It is often asserted that the government may invoke the privilege to prevent disclosure of any classified information. In other words, the potential use of the privilege is coextensive with all of the classified material in the possession of the United States.

In chapter 2 we discussed the extensive power of the executive branch to classify material, noting that the authority to classify material was greatly expanded during the presidency of George W. Bush. Agencies that formerly were prohibited from originally classifying records now have classification authority and are therefore able to invoke the state secrets privilege in response to judicial and congressional requests for information. The Department of Agriculture, the Department of Health and Human Services, the Environmental Protection Agency, and the Office of Science and Technology Policy now all have the power to classify information at the "secret" level or above.[11] With this authority automatically comes the power for the chief administrators of these organizations to invoke the state secrets privilege in response to judicial demands for classified information under their control. This expands the capacity of the executive branch to use the privilege to prevent embarrassing information or information of criminal wrongdoing, such as that in the Area 51 case, from coming to light.

So the dilemma for judges is how to make certain that legitimate interests are protected while trying to eliminate abuses of power in what is rapidly becoming a secret presidency. As currently formulated, the privilege is ill equipped to balance between these two goals, and it is our contention that the courts have unwisely acquiesced to executive power on this matter. As Charles Alan Wright, the distinguished commentator on federal courts and lead counsel for President Nixon in the appeal of *United States v. Nixon*, observed, "it was long a matter of dispute whether judges were entitled to overrule executive determinations that information qualified for the [state secrets] privilege and the scars of this battle are still visible in the procedures courts have devised to cover their de facto surrender on this crucial question."[12]

This "de facto surrender" has destabilizing consequences for separation of powers issues and, especially in the face of expanding presidential authority since 9/11, boxes the judiciary out of its legitimate oversight function of executive branch and presidential abuses of power. Judges frequently cite the separation of powers and lack of expertise as reasons to defer to presidential assertions of the state secrets privilege, but these judges overlook that there are separation of powers issues that counsel oversight of executive branch activity to make sure that the president is acting within his constitutional limits. The judiciary simply refuses to acknowledge that assertion of the state secrets privilege is often undertaken to denude courts of their constitutional responsibilities. By creating such a clear track record of unwillingness to tread in national security, courts invite misuse of secrecy to undercut their Article III role.

At the root of the issue over the state secrets privilege are contested views about the limits of judicial review of administrative actions and about intrusions by judges into the complex worlds of intelligence gathering and analysis and law enforcement. Although little studied, publicity, public access, and openness work to delimit the arbitrary exercise of administrative discretion. As Justice Louis Brandeis famously noted, "Sunlight is said to be the best of disinfectants; electric light the most efficient policeman."[13] Likewise, Kenneth Culp Davis held that "openness is the natural enemy of arbitrariness and a natural ally in the fight for injustice"; six out of Davis's "seven instruments" for structuring administrative discretion to avoid arbitrary use of power begin with openness as a predicate.[14] And almost half a century ago, Francis Rourke observed, "Compared to publicity . . . internal checks upon bureaucratic misbehavior . . . have but negligible value."[15] The power to expose agency misdeeds may well be the most important method of controlling executive branch activity, and the courts provide the most formal and routinized means to such control.

Courts, though, seeking to exercise such control over intelligence and law enforcement agencies inevitably confront those agencies' tendencies toward secrecy. J. Edgar Hoover, for example, claimed that if "we [are] to fully discharge the serious responsibilities imposed upon us, the confidential character of our files must be inviolate." And in support of Hoover's view, Justice Tom Clark, writing in dissent in *Jencks v. United States,* predicted that the majority decision of that case would result in disaster for the United States: "Those intelligence agencies of our Government engaged in law enforcement may as well close up shop, for the Court has opened their files to the criminal and thus afforded him a Roman holiday for rummaging through confidential information as well as vital national secrets."[16] Of course, no disaster ensued, and the dangers of disclosure are often overstated by administrators seeking to keep as much secret as possible.

But it would be wrong to say that this behavior is often calculated, for there is a deep-rooted belief in the need and efficacy of secrecy in the intelligence and law enforcement communities. Members of these communities believe that to do their jobs properly, they must be free of meddling by courts, Congress, and the public. Thus, it is unsurprising that litigation-related requests for classified documents are routinely met with refusal based on broad claims of a need for secrecy. Such refusal, though, seems to have reached new heights in recent years, where even routine requests for information by Congress and the courts are refused or stonewalled.

But even those who advocate and practice close guarding of information sometimes see the risks posed by state secrecy. Woodrow Wilson, whose own administration engaged in zealous secrecy, warned that "government ought to be all outside and no inside [for] corruption thrives in secret places, and . . . it [is] a fair presumption that secrecy means impropriety."[17] When agencies violate constitutional rights or engage in criminal activities, there are strong reasons for judicial, political, and public access to agency information. The only efficient means to such exposure is through the courts. Though Congress may indeed investigate isolated cases of abuse where privilege is claimed, unlike the federal courts it certainly cannot subject administrators to the level and frequency of scrutiny necessary to discourage abuse in a systematic way. And at present, the judicial abdication of responsibility to evaluate claims of privilege creates an incentive for presidents and administrators to use the privilege imprudently, as it all but ensures that misuse of the privilege will never be discovered, much less punished.

In the state secrets privilege, we have a profound example of the conflict between two political survival impulses. It is true that presidents and their advisors have always advocated, and presumably always will advocate, broad powers of secrecy. Agency officials argue, and courts often agree, that judges and lay people are not competent to assess the dangers that release of information may pose to national security; the invocation of "national security" gives strong, almost talismanic, force to claims of agency expertise. After all, who wants to argue *against* national security—or even appear to be doing so? And the lack of judicial expertise in the area of national security information breeds caution, for uncertainty of the effects of the release of contested information and the necessary reliance of judges on estimates of damage by executive branch employees yields a natural prudence. But prudence, we think, has given way to surrender.

This surrender is unacceptable, for our liberal-democratic political tradition is crucially defined in part by openness in government and checks on the powers of each of its three branches, and there are powerful arguments for judicial oversight of executive branch action even when national security is involved.

First, when agencies violate the constitutional rights of citizens and commit crimes, it is perverse and antithetical to the rule of law that they may avoid judgment in court and exposure of these activities to the public by refusing to disclose inculpatory information.

Second, if the privilege protects the president and agencies from investigation and judicial oversight, then the incentive on the part of administrators is to use the privilege to avoid embarrassment, to handicap political enemies, and to prevent criminal investigation of executive branch action. In these circumstances, the privilege may have the effect of encouraging or tempting agencies to engage in illegal activity.

Third, the privilege, as now constructed, obstructs the constitutional duties of courts to oversee executive action. Oversight of executive branch activity is notoriously difficult and is even more so in areas where state secrets are claimed. The privilege, as applied by courts, is tantamount to capitulation of the oversight function.

As we will discuss, judicial intervention in activities undertaken by intelligence agencies is almost nonexistent. While the privilege is crucial to national security, it is also a bane to constitutional government, and we believe that the judiciary must carefully and selectively exercise oversight of administrators to prevent the weakening of the rule of law and the abuse of the citizenry and the Constitution.

In recent years, the privilege has protected the government from citizen litigants in a variety of cases. For example, it prevented disclosure in the following matters:

- The unconstitutional and illegal interception of thousands of telephone conversations and electronic transmissions by American citizens;[18]
- The firing of an executive branch employee and whistleblower seeking to

alert Congress that the CIA and other intelligence agencies had systematically deceived Congress in an effort to manipulate it into passing legislation
and funding particular programs;[19]

- The FBI surveillance of a twelve-year-old boy simply because the boy received mail from foreign countries;[20]
- The CIA recruitment of a banker who unknowingly became entangled in
illegal money laundering operations for the Agency; when the banker discovered the nature of the work and wanted out of the operation, the Agency
allegedly destroyed his career and threatened his family with harm;[21]
- The alleged racial and sexual discrimination by government employees
working in security agencies;[22]
- The unilateral reneging on contracts made between security agencies and
agents;[23] and
- The harassment of United States citizens, allegedly including illegal wiretapping, break-ins, threats, and psychological operations designed to cause
mental anguish and suffering.[24]

On occasion, the privilege may also serve to shield criminal defendants from
prosecution, as in the cases of some of those charged in the Iran/Contra investigation of the 1980s. The most serious charges against the defendants, as well as
all charges against one principal defendant, were dismissed when the Reagan and
G. H. W. Bush administrations refused to allow alleged national security–related
information to be introduced into evidence at trial. As the final report of the
independent counsel noted, the affair

> exposed structural problems in the . . . law when central conspiracy counts had to be
> dismissed because of the Reagan Administration's refusal to declassify information
> deemed necessary to a fair trial of the case. This raised serious questions about
> whether the Reagan Administration—which in the Iran/Contra matter had sought
> the appointment of Independent Counsel to investigate and prosecute possible
> crimes because of an appearance of conflict of interest—in fact had the final say in
> determining what crimes could be tried.[25]

Likewise, President George H. W. Bush's refusal to declassify material led to
the dismissal of all charges against the CIA Costa Rican station chief allegedly
involved in illegal Iran/Contra activity.

In a postscript to the Iran/Contra matter, a dispute arose over the outgoing
Reagan administration's plan to destroy backup e-mails that were discovered in
the course of the investigation.[26] These backup files documented communica-

tions among NSC members and key participants involved in the covert financing of the Nicaraguan Contras and the Iranian hostage matter. The original e-mails had been destroyed, so the backup files became indispensable to establishing facts helpful to the Iran/Contra prosecution insofar as they showed knowledge and participation by parties who had previously denied involvement.

Thus, when the outgoing administration sought to destroy these records, a private archival association went to court to prevent the planned destruction. They argued that the portions already made public demonstrated lying by government officials and that the remaining undisclosed records were therefore particularly important for the public to access. A protracted legal battle ensued in which the government spent seven years and millions of taxpayer dollars defending its plan to destroy the records. The litigation ended in 1996, during the Clinton administration, when the U.S. Circuit Court of Appeals for the District of Columbia accepted the government's surprising argument that the NSC was not an agency (and therefore not subject to the disclosure requirements of the Federal Records Act) but rather a group of presidential advisors. The eventual resolution of the lawsuit in favor of the executive branch demonstrated the truth of the observation, "what does not exist is de facto secret."[27] In these Iran/Contra matters, the damage to the rule of law was double: high-level criminal defendants went unprosecuted, and the independent counsel was stripped of power and left a meaningless formality, as it was left to the president to decide when and where the investigation would end.

One of the troubling features of the invocation of the privilege in the Iran/Contra cases is that much of the information withheld was already in the public domain through leaks or in the possession of the independent counsel through investigation. This points up a curious aspect of the privilege: it allows the government to withhold evidence even if that evidence is known to the public or in the possession of the litigant seeking its introduction.

So the substantive evidential basis of the privilege has been lost in the pro forma means with which courts treat executive claims of national security. The privilege exists to prevent grave damage to the U.S. government, its interests, and its citizens due to the disclosure of classified information, but courts almost never closely examine assertion of the privilege to determine if indeed exposure of the information at issue would compromise security. And, obviously, if information is already in the public realm it serves neither the spirit of the privilege nor the practical goals of its use to prevent that material from being introduced at trial.

At any event, although the Iran/Contra investigation was a criminal matter, the privilege is most often used in civil cases, where its invocation frequently spells the end of litigation.

The Origins of the State Secrets Privilege

A fundamental problem in understanding the state secrets privilege is disentangling it from the more familiar executive privilege. Executive privilege, which we take up in chapter 6, unlike the state secrets privilege, is a constitutional doctrine founded in the separation of powers. It is a *qualified* privilege designed to shield executive communication amongst the president and counselors from predation by partisan members of Congress and a prying public. Its goal is to foster frank and open discussion between a president and his advisors by removing the fear that those discussions will be made public, to the embarrassment of the discussants. In short, it prevents harassment of the executive by the coordinate branches. But, as a qualified privilege, the need for secrecy is balanced against the need for disclosure, and if a litigant demonstrates a need for information that outweighs the interests of privacy, the courts will order production.

In contrast, the state secrets privilege is universally recognized in law as an *absolute* privilege and mainly relies on practicality more than constitutional principle for its justification. Once it is determined that the privilege is asserted over properly classified information, no amount of demonstrated need on the part of a litigant will overcome the operation of the privilege; no balancing can occur, as with executive privilege.

While judges occasionally ground the privilege in the separation of powers, the ultimate reason to uphold its use is on the practical grounds that it is necessary for the survival of the state. Under this reasoning, the application of the privilege should be determined by a prediction concerning the effects that the release of the information will have on United States interests. It is reasonable to urge that courts give the executive branch deference in instances where it is claimed that information must be kept secret in the interests of national security, but this reasonable deference has become an abdication of responsibility on the part of the federal judiciary. The practical origins of the principle backing the privilege are clear enough, but the historical and legal antecedents of the *Reynolds* decision are obscure and few in number. Nevertheless, there is material that helps to clarify the political and legal origins of the principle, so we will spend some time creating a historical framework for the privilege before delving into the contemporary use of the state secrets power by executive branch officials.

Claims that the state secrets privilege derived from common law and the U.S. Constitution are only mediately plausible. Sometimes it is characterized as pre-constitutional, even pre-legal, and arises from the raw fact that countries have a responsibility to prevent becoming instruments in their own destruction. This contention is vaguely and inchoately recognized in the literature, though some commentators trouble themselves briefly to expand on this point. As one commentator explains, "The state secrets privilege is the most basic of government privileges—it protects survival of the state, from which all other institutions derive."[28] And Justice Sutherland noted in 1936 that the power to ensure national survival is not one granted by the Constitution but is a "necessary concomitant of nationality."[29]

This claim, that the power to secure the state is pre-constitutional and acquired naturally without authorization of Constitution or statute, is hardly self-evident. There are strong currents of thought in our political tradition suggesting that *all* political authority derives from the Constitution, and the Constitution, with but a single exception, says nothing about secrecy powers. Congress has never adopted the state secrets privilege in any statute granting authority to the executive branch, and a major effort to define and incorporate the privilege in the Federal Rules of Evidence failed in the early 1970s.[30]

The confusion surrounding the origins of the privilege is made worse, since historically presidents have had little incentive—indeed, great disincentive—to disentangle the state secrets privilege from executive privilege. The disincentive derives from the fact that it is in the executive's interest to infect all withheld information, where possible, with allusions to national security. Indeed, attorneys general and others frequently describe the state secrets privilege as a component of executive privilege.[31] So by keeping the lines between executive privilege and the state secrets privilege obscure, presidents have attempted to expand the reach and potency of their powers to withhold information.

In hindsight, we can tease out two major lines of provenance for the state secrets privilege that intersect in *Reynolds,* the only time the U.S. Supreme Court has substantively addressed the privilege. The first line is founded in the formulation of the Constitution and in the actions of the first several presidents and is more properly considered executive privilege rather than the state secrets privilege. But since presidents never attempted to distinguish between the two privileges, these early executive actions prepared the ground for later assertions of privilege for national security matters. The second source for the privilege is found in United Kingdom law, law that the U.S. Supreme Court explicitly adopted, if in a slightly modified form, in *Reynolds.*

The Political Origins of the State Secrets Privilege

As with assertions of power to withhold information from Congress, presidential claims of immunity to judicial orders came early in the republic. The first time this issue arose was in the trial of Aaron Burr for treason, where Justice John Marshall issued a *subpoena duces tecum* against President Jefferson to produce copies of specified military orders and a letter written to Jefferson by General Wilkinson. Jefferson did not refuse to deliver the document to the court, but he objected to the publication of sensitive portions of the letter, claiming that the "letter contains matter which ought not be disclosed."[32]

Marshall agreed that information truly detrimental to the United States should not be publicly disclosed but implied that the decision over what information to withhold was one for the judge, not the executive.[33] This view comports with a robust perception of the role separation of powers must play in our constitutional structure. It would seem heedless to provide the executive with a privilege to withhold information that would prove detrimental to the public interest if released and also to allow the executive to have the sole power of determination in such matters when a judicial request for the information has been made. Principles of accountability and checks on presidential power urge that the judiciary make an independent determination of the danger posed if the material is divulged.

In the instant case, Marshall had no doubt that a subpoena could issue against the president, but he expressed concern over whether or not the president may be compelled to disclose subpoenaed documents. In Jefferson's opinion, the president "must be the sole judge of [what information] the public interests will permit publication"; Jefferson also thought that "under our Constitution, in requests of papers, from the legislative to the executive branch, an exemption is carefully expressed, as to those which he may deem the public welfare may require not to be disclosed."[34] Jefferson was more circumspect concerning judicial requests for information. In the *Burr* case he did not object to publication of parts of the Wilkinson letter based on the state secrets privilege but for reasons of irrelevancy to the issues at trial and confidentiality.[35] In any case, Jefferson never refused to disclose documents to the court.[36] Through a steady drumbeat of unstudied, self-serving opinions from executive branch officials since the 1950s, it has come to be generally accepted that the *Burr* case is a state secrets case, and that it stands for the proposition that presidents have the power to withhold information from courts in the face of a judicial order where disclosure of such information would jeopardize national security. Even though this conclusion is demonstrably incorrect, it is one that courts repeat in almost an unthinking manner.[37]

Presidents subsequent to Jefferson in the nineteenth century occasionally reflected on the subject of withholding material from courts. For example, President John Tyler asserted that "courts cannot order the President to do anything" and that "the head of a department cannot be compelled to produce any papers, or to disclose any transactions relating to the executive functions of the Government which he declares are confidential, or such as the public interest requires should not be indulged."[38] Not surprisingly, these opinions infiltrated the attorney general's office and gathered legal justification.

Over the late nineteenth century and early twentieth century various attorneys general reiterated the opinion that the president has an absolute power to withhold documents in the face of a judicial order. For example, in 1865, Attorney General James Speed stated that presidents are "not bound to produce papers or disclose information communicated to them where, in their own judgment, the disclosure would, on public considerations, be inexpedient."[39] And on the matter of compulsion, in 1905 Attorney General William Moody opined that "it seems clear that while a subpoena may be directed against the President to produce a paper, or for some other purpose, in case of his refusal to obey the subpoena, the courts would be without power to enforce process."[40] But there was nothing in law to support these assertions; they are mainly self-serving statements reflecting presidents' hopes of what they wished the law to be.

But this position gained more concrete, if somewhat indirect, support from the judiciary in the case of *Totten v. United States*, in which the Supreme Court faced the issue of whether or not secret contracts for espionage services may be sued upon by a party alleging breach of payment. Justice Stephen Field, writing for a unanimous court, noted that a "secret service, with liability to publicity . . . would be impossible" and that it "may be stated as a general principle, that public policy forbids the maintenance of any suit in a court of justice, the trial of which would inevitably lead to the disclosure of matters which the law itself regards as confidential."[41] However, this short opinion did not squarely address the issue of executive branch power to withhold information in the face of judicial requests.

A 2005 decision by the U.S. Supreme Court reaffirmed *Totten* but ended speculation among scholars and jurists that *Totten* was an early state secrets claim. In *Tenet v. Doe*, the Court firmed up the outlines of a secrecy privilege different from the state secrets privilege, one that may be even more effective in terminating cases earlier in the litigation process. In *Tenet*, a married couple who "were formerly citizens of a foreign country that at the time was considered to be an enemy of the United States" filed suit to recover money on a contract for financial support.[42] The CIA had promised to support the couple financially after they came to the United States following years of working in their home country and passing classified information to United States agencies. Eventually, the CIA cut off its support and, hoping that the *Totten* principle did not apply, the couple sued under due process and equal protection arguments rather than on contractual grounds.

The government moved the trial court to dismiss the Does' complaint on the ground that *Totten* barred the suit. The trial court refused the motion, a decision upheld by the Ninth Circuit Court of Appeals. The appellate court reasoned that *Totten* did not control in the case, because the Does' case was not based on breach of contract and that the *Reynolds* case had replaced the *Totten* decision.[43] As the court wrote, "Instead, the instant case is governed by the state secrets privilege, a separate aspect of the decision in *Totten* that has evolved into a well-articulated body of law addressing situations in which security interests preclude the revelation of factual matter in court." In other words, the government would be required to assert the state secrets privilege in response to the suit and requests for discovery and would not be able to gain dismissal before discovery under *Totten*.

In an opinion by Chief Justice William Rehnquist, a unanimous Supreme Court reversed, finding the Ninth Circuit to be "quite wrong"—*Totten* did not merely create a rule for contract cases but "precludes judicial review in cases such as respondents' where success depends upon the existence of their secret espionage relationship with the Government." *Totten*, the Court said, is meant to dispose of cases on the pleadings before they reach discovery, so "there is, in short, no basis for respondents' and the Court of Appeals' view that the *Totten* bar has been reduced to an example of the state secrets privilege."[44] This extension of *Totten* may have been justifiable under the facts of the instant case, but the Court goes on to suggest that the doctrine of *Totten* is far greater than even the facts of *Tenet v. Doe* require. Citing *Weinberger v. Catholic Action of Hawaii* for an interpretation of a "more sweeping holding" in *Totten*, the Court moved *Totten* beyond the contractual basis to which it had been confined by court and expert opinion.[45] In *Weinberger*, a group sought to force the U.S. Navy to file an environmental impact statement concerning a storage facility capable of holding nuclear weapons. United States policy is never to confirm or to deny the presence of nuclear weapons at military facilities, and the impact statement would have been, in this regard, "hypothetical."[46] The Supreme Court found that the Navy was not compelled to prepare the impact statement because the statement was not statutorily required under the circumstances. But the *Tenet v. Doe* court picked up this thread from the *Weinberger* case and extended it.

Totten, now, rather than a precursor of the state secrets privilege as defined in

Reynolds and confined to contract matters, is a potentially broad-ranging privilege to get rid of cases on secrecy grounds before litigants have an opportunity to engage in discovery. *Totten* held that "as a general principle . . . public policy forbids the maintenance of any suit in a court of justice, the trial of which would inevitably lead to the disclosure of matters which the law itself regards as confidential," but courts and commentators for well over a century have virtually unanimously agreed that this statement was confined to breaches of contract claims against the government. If this principle is unleashed from its contract law constraints, it is difficult to predict where such a potentially powerful new privilege will take the courts. But considering the unanimity of the *Tenet v. Doe* decision and the abysmal record of judicial neglect concerning executive branch secrecy claims, it is likely that the *Totten* doctrine will only expand. There seems little doubt that the state secrets privilege and the now-allied *Totten* doctrine will provide expanded powers of secrecy for the presidency.

In another tantalizing early case, *Firth v. Bethlehem Steel Co.*, a federal district court allowed attorneys for the United States to intervene in a private suit to assert the "military" privilege to have testimony stricken from the record and to prevent its reintroduction by other means.[47] After *Totten*, though, as executive branch resources and power grew, there developed a judicial impatience with frivolous administrative assertion of the state secrets privilege. But until recently courts did not undertake to disentangle executive privilege from the power to withhold military and state secrets from judicial proceedings.

Washington's and Jefferson's refusals to transmit information to disclose information are better thought of as exercises of executive privilege, while the refusal in *Totten* was arguably an example of state secrets privilege.[48] The refusal to furnish information by Washington and Jefferson concerned matters of communication directly between president and advisor and fall squarely within executive privilege. State secrets is something altogether different; it does not have as its goal the preservation of the advisory relationships to the president but rather the preservation of national security, not in the expanded sense in which it is used today but in the more basic sense that a nation cannot be made to behave suicidally by its own legal system.

Although the state secrets privilege has only been exercised by the president or his department heads, it is not a privilege that attaches only to the presidency. It is clear that the privilege applies at any point by any governmental party when disclosed information may seriously and irreparably damage U.S. interests. For example, suppose a subpoena is issued against a government contractor for information that the executive branch for political reasons decides not to contest but that members of congressional intelligence committees claim will endanger national security if exposed. While no doubt courts would look very closely at such an assertion, there is nothing in the logic underpinning the privilege that would prevent such an assertion. The goal of the privilege is to protect the government and the country's citizens, not the presidency or the executive branch.

It is crucial to see that executive privilege is a power that attaches to the presidency—it is part and parcel of the institution of the president, and it is fundamentally different from the power to shield state secrets from disclosure. Efforts by the executive branch to confuse the two doctrines are helped along by insufficiently careful legal and political analyses. Commentators, for example, discuss the "constitutionally-based executive privilege doctrine to protect executive interests, including the deliberative process, *state secrets*, law enforcement secrets, and presidential privacy."[49] Indeed, then–assistant attorney general William Rehnquist, using a title guaranteed to maximize the confusion between the two privileges, co-authored the memorandum "The President's Executive Privilege to Withhold Foreign Policy and National Security Information," asserting that "the President has the power to withhold . . . information in the field of foreign relations or national security if in his judgment disclosure would be incompatible with the public interest."[50]

The state secrets privilege simply cannot be a component of executive privilege because it is meant to protect the United States from harm from the publication of national security information regardless of who controls that information. Since the privilege is assertable against private parties for information they have acquired legally, and since it is obvious that the privilege would apply against legal efforts to obtain information from Congress or other non-executive institutions, it is not one owned by the president or the executive branch. Although, as mentioned above, it is true that all assertions of the privilege have been made through executive branch machinery, that merely clouds the fact that the privilege, as the Supreme Court held, "belongs to the *government*."[51] The impetus behind the privilege is unconcerned with separation of powers issues and is solely concerned with the effect that the release of the information will have on United States interests. It is not designed to shield the president from accountability or oversight but to shield the government and citizens from harm. Executive privilege proper *is* designed to shield the president from inquiries in order to preserve the character of the *presidency*.

An instructive parallel may be drawn between the state secrets privilege and the goals of the Invention Secrecy Act, discussed briefly in chapter 1. Under this act, whenever "the publication or disclosure of an invention by the publication of an application or by the granting of a patent [will harm national security] . . . the Commissioner of Patents shall order that the invention be kept secret and shall withhold the publication of the application or the grant of a patent for such period as the national interest requires."[52] Wholly private citizens or corporations with no connection to the government may nevertheless have their ideas and inventions classified and be prevented from using their own creations and ideas if these inventions and ideas would be classifiable if originally created by or for the government. Similarly, the state secrets privilege prevents wholly private citizens from introducing into evidence information that may be damaging to national security even if they acquired the information legally. While the Invention Secrecy Act is administered by executive branch agencies and bureaus, it is not an "executive privilege." The goals, as with the state secrets privilege, are overtly instrumental.

Of course every administrator would like to have resort to the state secrets privilege, for it is the ultimate conversation stopper; it protects against investigation and legal action. But the privilege, as historically conceived, is to be used only concerning matters of grave importance to the security of the nation, and courts in the late nineteenth century confronted and stopped bureaucratic efforts to expand the reach of the privilege. In the little-noticed cases of *District of Columbia v. Bakersmith* and *King v. United States,* courts confronted assertion of the state secrets privilege for quotidian activities of the executive branch.[53] *Bakersmith* concerned a request for inspection papers and other documents about a particular culvert in Washington, D.C., but the city, in denying the request, asserted the state secrets privilege, saying "it is laid down by the authorities as a well-established principle of law that official transactions between the heads of the departments of the government and their subordinate officers are in general treated as secrets of State."[54] This statement elides executive privilege with the state secrets privilege, even though it seems that in this case the government was trying to protect the relationship between executives and advisors. The court did not reach the claim of privilege but simply stated in the first sentence of the opinion that the right to inspect municipal public documents is undoubted.

In *King,* a criminal defendant sought to examine federal agents as to their efforts to suborn perjury and manufacture evidence. The U.S. attorney objected, asserting the state secrets privilege, to which the Fifth Circuit Court of Appeals responded, "We are clear that the conversations of government detectives and other agents with witnesses, with the purpose and effect of inducing and influencing the evidence of such witnesses, do not rise to the dignity of state secrets."[55] *King* and *Bakersmith* are the beginnings in the United States of the legal differentiation between the executive and state secrets privileges, a differentiation that has only recently gained any degree of clarity. These cases were by no means the last efforts on the part of administrators or presidents to attempt to make executive privilege legally coextensive with the state secrets privilege. These cases indicate the judiciary's incipient willingness to distinguish between the two privileges, but case law in the United States has proved too thin a resource to explain this distinction fully, so the Supreme Court turned to the law of the United Kingdom and the development of the doctrine of "crown privilege."

The Legal Origins of the State Secrets Privilege

The state secrets privilege derives from crown privilege as it developed in the law of England and Scotland. The beginnings of crown privilege in English and Scots law are unclear but are probably found in the prerogative rights of the king and queen. William Blackstone noted in his *Commentaries* that "the duty of a Privy Counselor appears from the oath of office [to require the Counselor] to keep the King's counsel secret . . . [and] to withstand all persons who would attempt the contrary."[56] Blackstone's statement highlights the lack of distinction in British law between executive privilege and the privilege to withhold state secrets; in Crown prerogative, the two are combined. The duty identified by Blackstone logically extended to the refusal to comply with judicial requests for information, and a 1775 case arising in India was one of the first to question executive authority to withhold sensitive documents from courts and the public.

In *The Trial of Maha Rajah Nundocomar* a court called in a secretary to Governor General Warren Hastings in India to produce books of the Council to the East India Company. Hastings instructed the secretary to refuse delivery of the books to the court, asserting that they contained "secrets of the utmost importance to the interest, and even to the safety of the state." Unimpressed, the court said that it would be improper to subject the books to "curious and impertinent eyes; but, at the same time . . . [h]umanity requires [evidence in the hands of the state] should be produced, when in favour of a criminal, justice when against him."[57] The court ended with a lecture to Hastings to the effect that "where justice shall require copies of the records and proceedings, from the highest court of judicature, down to the court of Pie-Powder," magistrates have the power to compel disclosure. Despite the warm rhetoric, in British courts in virtually all reported cases judges refused to compel production of the requested documents when the Crown asserted that withholding the documents was in the public interest. In what for many years was taken to be the classic phrasing of the law on this issue, Chief Baron Pollock in *Beatson v. Skene* said:

> We are of the opinion that, if the production of a state paper would be injurious to the public service, the general public interest must be considered paramount to the individual interest of a suitor in a court of justice. . . . It appears to us . . . that the question, whether the production of the documents would be injurious to the public service, must be determined not by the judge but by the head of the department having the custody of the paper.[58]

Duncan v. Cammell, Laird and Co., Ltd., which hewed to the line announced in *Beatson,* became the chief modern case on the issue of crown privilege. In that case, family members of submariners killed while putting the submarine *Thetis* through trials sued the manufacturer of the submarine and sought discovery of blueprints of the craft and other sensitive documents. The Crown asserted privilege to protect the documents, and the Lords held that "the approved [Scots law] practice . . . is to treat ministerial objections taken in proper form as conclusive."[59]

The holding of *Duncan* conferred absolute authority on the executive to withhold documents from disclosure in judicial proceedings—however, that holding was incorrect and unquestionably misstated the law of Scotland, if not the law of England. It is true that British and Commonwealth courts have shown great deference to assertions of Crown privilege, but they do compel disclosure of executive documents—and always did.[60] And there is "no doubt that there always has been and is now in the law of Scotland an inherent power of the court to override the Crown's objection to produce documents on the ground that it would injure the public interest to do so."[61] In overruling *Duncan,* the Law Lords in *Conway v. Rimmer* had "no doubt" from the case law that courts have always had the power to pass on the sufficiency of the Crown's claim of privilege, that "By a misapprehension . . . in Duncan's case the protection in Crown privilege cases . . . was held to be absolute."[62] The rule announced in *Duncan* is no longer followed by any authority in the United Kingdom.

In 1953, at the height of the McCarthy era, the U.S. Supreme Court squarely faced the state secrets privilege for the first time. In *Reynolds,* the family members of civilians who died in a plane crash while testing secret government electronic equipment sued the United States for monetary damages. The relatives sought documentation from the government relating to the flight and the crash. The government refused to produce the documents; when ordered to deliver them to the judge for *in camera* inspection to verify that their disclosure would cause harm to national security, the Secretary of the Air Force ignored the order. The court then entered judgment for the families—the Air Force appealed. The Supreme Court, in search of guidance, seized on *Duncan*. With almost no examination of the case or the precedents it relied on, the Court adopted the framework of the *Duncan* ruling nearly in toto.

Setting requirements almost verbatim from *Duncan,* the Court held that: (1) the state secrets privilege "belongs to the Government and must be asserted by it"; (2) it should not be "lightly invoked"; (3) a claim of privilege must be formally made by the head of a department after "actual personal consideration"; and (4) the judge must determine if the claim is appropriate, "yet do so without forcing a disclosure of the very thing the privilege is designed to protect."[63] Conditions (1) and (3) are merely procedural, and condition (2) is a standardless precatory statement. Only condition (4) presents substantial problems, and it is a perplexing rule for lower courts to interpret.

It is unclear, for example, why the lowliest private in the U.S. Army with a security clearance is held more trustworthy to handle classified information than federal judges. The clear message of the *Reynolds* ruling is that courts are to show utmost deference to executive assertions of privilege. The Court did write that judicial "control over the evidence in a case cannot be abdicated to the caprice of executive officers" but also that in cases where administrators make a facial showing of potential harm to national security, the "court should not jeopardize the security which the privilege is meant to protect by insisting upon an examination of the evidence."[64] The Court refused the *de jure* rule of *Duncan* that executive assertion of the privilege is conclusive on the courts but reached that result by *de facto* modeling the privilege after the procedures described in *Duncan*.

The reliance in *Reynolds* on the reasoning in *Duncan* is improvident in two important respects. First, in Great Britain there was at the time virtually no distinction between assertion of crown privilege for reasons of national security or mere political expediency. In Great Britain, the separation of powers is ill-defined and occupies a relatively less important role in the British Constitution than in that of the United States, and the Supreme Court's adoption of the *Duncan* scheme fails to recognize this difference. The structure of the U.S. Constitution gives substantial powers of oversight of the executive branch to both Congress and the courts, and the broad privilege recognized in *Duncan*—and, in turn, *Reynolds*—does not sufficiently respect oversight functions. The Third Circuit Court of Appeals understood better than the *Reynolds* Court the problems that reliance on *Duncan* could cause in the United States. Judge Albert Maris, writing for a unanimous panel hearing the *Reynolds* appeal, found that *Duncan*'s "sweeping privilege against disclosure [is] . . . contrary to a sound public policy" and that it is "but a small step to assert a privilege against any disclosure of records merely because they might prove embarrassing." The court concluded that "whatever might be true in Great Britain the Government of the United States is one of checks and balances," and that neither the Congress nor the president may encroach on the judiciary by "transferring to itself the power to decide justiciable questions."[65] These fears were nevertheless realized in *Reynolds* and subsequent lower court application of its holding.

And as it turns out, Judge Maris's concerns were warranted, since it now seems certain that the goal of the government in claiming the privilege in *Reynolds* was to expand executive power and to avoid liability and embarrassment. The material originally requested by the plaintiffs in *Reynolds* was inadvertently made public in 2000, and it contained no classified or national security information. On the basis of these materials the original plaintiffs and their relatives asked the Supreme Court to reverse its decision in *Reynolds,* at least on the question of governmental liability, since the government had perpetrated a "fraud" upon the Court by asserting the state secrets privilege without justification. The Court refused to revisit the matter, so the plaintiffs filed an action in district court to correct the alleged abuse of the privilege by the government.[66] In *In the Name of National Security: Unchecked Presidential Power and the Reynolds Case,* Louis Fisher performs a detailed analysis of the executive branch deception in the *Reynolds* case, documenting the breadth and potential motivations for government deceit.[67]

Second, both the *Duncan* and *Reynolds* courts wrestled with the issues of privilege at times of national crises, and there is reason to believe that the necessities of the moment, rather than the thought-out effects for civil liberties and constitutional arrangements of power, swayed the courts. For example, the courts in both cases refer to contemporary exigent events. In *Duncan,* a decision rendered at the height of World War II, in April 1942, the references to the war are elliptical. In *Reynolds,* notice of the current political environment is open, with the Court commenting that "we cannot escape judicial notice that this is a time of vigorous preparation for national defense" and that it "is equally apparent that [our capabilities] must be kept secret if their full military advantage is to be exploited in the national interests."[68] Under these circumstances it is possible that the courts were less concerned with civil liberties and the integrity of constitutional arrangements of power than they would have been at almost any other time.

The Supreme Court's holding in *Reynolds* fosters the same confusion presidents have repeatedly sought to promote, for after that decision executive branch personnel claimed that the *Reynolds* approach applied to a variety of requests for information. For example, in a much-maligned 1958 statement to Congress, Attorney General William Rogers reported, "Courts have uniformly held that the President and the heads of the departments have an uncontrolled discretion to withhold information and papers in the public interest."[69] This conflation of executive privilege with the state secrets privilege, of course, reached its culmination in *Nixon*, in which counsel for President Nixon desperately tried to stretch the state secrets privilege to encompass all claims of executive privilege. In their brief to Judge John J. Sirica, White House counsel unsuccessfully claimed that "the principles announced in *Reynolds* have been applied by the lower courts to all claims of executive privilege, whether dealing with military secrets or with other kinds of information."[70]

At the Supreme Court, Nixon's lawyers cited *Reynolds*, arguing that "there are some kinds of documents on which the decision of the Executive must be final, and not subject to review by the courts."[71] But the *Nixon* Court held that "neither the doctrine of separation of powers, nor the need for confidentiality of high-level communications, without more, can sustain an absolute, unqualified Presidential privilege of immunity." For the first time in United States history, the Supreme Court made explicit the distinction between the state secrets privilege and executive privilege; concerning Nixon's claim that *Reynolds* stood for the proposition that the president's power to withhold information is an absolute privilege, the Court said "no case of the Court . . . has extended [*Reynolds's*] high degree of deference to a President's generalized interest in confidentiality."[72]

Despite the narrowing of executive privilege in *Nixon*, however, the state secrets privilege retained all the scope and power it originally garnered in *Reynolds*. In less than one-third of reported cases where the privilege is invoked do courts require *in camera* inspection of documents, and in the years since the presidency of George H. W. Bush, the numbers drop to below one-quarter. Even though *Reynolds* held that "judicial control over the evidence in a case cannot be abdicated to the caprice of executive officers," the practical effect of the decision is to cause precisely that result.[73] The Court's caveat is so qualified and tempered by other language that the message cannot be but clear to lower courts that they are to avoid compelling production of documents, even for court inspection, except in extraordinary cases. As the Court put it in *Haig v. Agee*, "matters intimately related to foreign policy and national security are rarely proper subjects for judicial intervention."[74] The plain fact is that if department heads or the president know that assertion of the privilege is tantamount to conclusive on the judiciary and that federal judges rarely order documents for inspection, there is great incentive on the part of the executive branch to misuse the privilege.

Closing Down the Game

Despite presidential reference to the ancient origins of the state secrets privilege, it is only in the last several decades that it has seen extensive use. The rather clear beginning point for the increased use of the privilege occurs in the administration of President Jimmy Carter. There are nearly as many cases arising during his four years of presidency as were reported from all previous presidential history. It seems that the Supreme Court decision in *Nixon* did nothing to dampen the presidential desire for secrecy and willingness to withhold information.

Pattern of Use

Use of the state secrets privilege in courts has grown significantly over the last several decades. In the twenty-three years between the decision in *Reynolds* and the election of Jimmy Carter in 1976, there are eleven reported cases where the government invoked the privilege. Since 1977 there have been more than seventy reported cases where courts ruled on invocation of the privilege. Since reported cases only represent a fraction of the total cases where the privilege is invoked or implicated, it is unclear precisely how dramatically use of the privilege has grown. But the increase in reported cases does indicate greater willingness to assert the privilege than in the past.

In only four cases have courts ultimately rejected the government's assertion of the privilege. But even this number is misleading, for in two of those cases the privilege was obviously misused to protect unclassified information in the Department of Commerce.[75] In a third case, the court rejected assertion of the privilege for failure to follow the procedural guidelines set out in *Reynolds,* though the court allowed the government to assert the privilege in correct form and indicated that the privilege would then be upheld.[76] And the courts took a novel approach in a 1958 decision, ordering a complete trial to be held in secret to protect national security.[77] Other than the scarce exception, the privilege is invariably fatal to efforts to gain access to covered documents. It is hardly surprising that such an effective tool would tempt presidents to use it with increasing frequency.

INJUSTICE AND THE FAILURE OF OVERSIGHT: MECHANISMS OF JUDICIAL DEFERENCE

Recent events highlight limitations on congressional ability to oversee national security–related activities of the executive branch. In recognition of its limited capacities of oversight, Congress facilitates executive accountability by transferring much of its oversight function to the judiciary. These transfers pit permanent government employees against each other and so make the oversight process more enduring and comprehensive, and instances of these transfers abound. For example, the Federal Tort Claims Act, portions of the Administrative Procedure Act, the Occupational Safety and Health Act, and a host of other laws lodge substantial powers of oversight of the executive branch in the federal courts. These powers are exercised incident to criminal or civil actions and are powers the judiciary generally does not shrink from exercising. Expanded powers of oversight in non–national security areas vested in the judiciary, either through statute or judicial creation, are in striking contrast to the complete deference the judiciary affords administrators where the state secrets privilege is invoked.

This judicial timidity has not gone unnoticed; as the eminent Louis Fisher noted in one of his many appearances before Congress, "courts have traditionally shown the . . . utmost deference to [claims of privilege]. That is fine for the courts to make that judgment . . . but Congress doesn't have to defer."[78] Although generally accepting the congressional efforts to extend oversight of the executive by employing judicial process, the federal courts have notably failed to take this invitation in the area of national security. The deference emanating from *Reynolds* toward claims of national security leads to failures of oversight that threaten our constitutional arrangement of powers. Secrecy may tempt administrators to adopt activities contrary to law and the Constitution, but when those activities are suspected the courts double the damage by refusing to impose costs on the executive branch for its breaches.

The courts employ several mechanisms of deference to comply with the spirit of *Reynolds*. Although *Reynolds* located a source for deference in the separation of powers, in addition courts often advance one or both of two justifications for deference to executive branch assertion of the privilege.

THE IMPOSSIBILITY OF AVOIDING DISCLOSURE

Often, assertion of the state secrets privilege means the end of a case. If a plaintiff must obtain protected information in order to make out a prima facie case or to prove some essential element of the claim, courts will resolve the action by finding against the plaintiff. For example, in *Tilden v. Tenet* an employee of the CIA filed suit for discrimination under federal employment discrimination statutes seeking to rectify discriminatory practices of the CIA and to recover monetary damages. Filing suit under a pseudonym, "Tilden" was severely disciplined and suffered under suspicion and subsequent poor assignments because a potential recruit in a foreign country had unexpectedly kissed her. She claimed that women are perceived by agency management to be more vulnerable than male agents to subversive sexually based activity by foreigners, even though the historical record is clear that in every major case involving sexual compromise, men were the targets. This misperception led to reluctance or refusal to place single female agents in some of the most challenging and sought-after positions, thus limiting their career options and potential for advancement. In *Tilden*, the court found that, "based on a review of the Director's classified declaration the Court concludes that there is no way in which this lawsuit can proceed without disclosing state secrets [and] there are no safeguards that this Court could take that would adequately protect the state secrets in question." Judge Hilton noted that the "Court is mindful that the invocation of the state secrets privilege in this case will deny the Plaintiff a forum under Article III of the Constitution for adjudication of her claim."[79] Mindful the court might be, but as is typical in state secret cases, the government escaped scrutiny and accountability for its alleged wrongful acts.

In *Sterling v. Tenet*, a similar issue arose, but in this case the plaintiff alleged racial discrimination.[80] Sterling, an African American, was sent to language school for a year by the CIA to learn Farsi, but after completing the course a supervisor said that he would not be assigned to the fieldwork that leads to advancement in clandestine services at the Agency. He was told a "big black man speaking Farsi" in foreign venues would simply be too noticeable to be effective. When Sterling objected, retaliation followed, and he was eventually fired. During Sterling's case a CIA agent approached Mark Zaid, Sterling's attorney, and demanded the return of some documents released in discovery. The agent claimed that the documents would cause grave damage to national security if disclosed and that failure to return them might result in Zaid going to prison. The attorney reluctantly returned the documents, but both he and Sterling say the real reason for the demand was that the documents lent support to Sterling's claims.[81] George Tenet successfully argued that the suit could not go forward without exposing information that, while perhaps not all classified, would nonetheless provide a classified picture of intelligence-gathering sources and methods.

The disturbing possibility exemplified by *Tilden* and *Sterling* and other discrimination cases is that intelligence agencies may simply opt out of compliance with federal statutes. Especially after 9/11, it may be highly embarrassing and cause severe congressional scrutiny for agencies to admit to cases disclosing illegal employment practices, since such allegations go right to the heart of agency effectiveness to combat the war on terror. If agencies are engaging in prohibited practices, it means that the full resources and talents of national security employees are not being exploited and that the very people on whom we depend upon for intelligence of a forthcoming attack, people of color and of various cultural backgrounds, are being discouraged in their employment.

Similarly, *Halkin,* discussed briefly at the beginning of this chapter, demonstrates that wholesale constitutional violations can also go unremedied. Although the revelation of the interception of thousands of phone and electronic communications of United States citizens created tremendous controversy, those who initiated the policies and procedures of methodical violation of the constitutional rights of citizens were never held to account for their actions. The *Halkin* court shrank from its constitutional duty to constrain the executive from violating the constitutional rights of citizens because the wrongdoing of government administrators was closely entangled with classified operations.

Most recently, of course, leaked information published in December 2005 disclosed President Bush's authorization of warrantless electronic surveillance, which resulted in the interception of many communications by United States citizens. The Bush administration asserted the state secrets privilege in all of the cases filed to challenge the surveillance program.

In numerous instances, courts terminate actions not because the plaintiffs' cases are without merit, but because the courts do not see how they may proceed without exposure of classified information during the proceedings. Sometimes the concerns descend to the mundane, as in the reported case of a court's refusal to have a CIA employee produce personal financial records in a divorce case because the records might reveal sensitive information.

Other cases are far more dramatic. In the case of *Arar v. Ashcroft,* the U.S. government kidnapped Maher Arar, a Canadian citizen, from United States soil and flew him via CIA jet to Jordan. From Jordan, Arar was transported to Syria to be tortured and interrogated for a period of several months.[82] The kidnapping was in error; Mr. Arar had no connection with terrorists and had committed no crimes. He filed suit against the United States, and the Department of Justice asserted the state secrets privilege. The government denied requests for discovery, asserting that "the information forming the basis for each of these decisions [to kidnap and give Mr. Arar to the Syrians] is properly classified" and that "its disclosure would interfere with foreign relations, reveal intelligence-gathering sources or methods, and be detrimental to national security."[83] Presumably, some of the intelligence-gathering methods and sources that may be compromised are also the embarrassing ones that concern agreements with foreign countries to engage in torture on our behalf. The government concluded that "disclosure of the information necessary to litigate plaintiff's claims" could reasonably be expected to cause grave damage to the national security.

In the state secrets privilege, the government gets a free pass in the area of national security, with all of its abuses, illegalities, and embarrassments protected from disclosure. This result is at odds with the basis of our democracy and is a warrant for unaccountable presidential authority.

THE MOSAIC THEORY

The mosaic theory is perhaps the most astounding and perplexing mechanism of avoidance used by judges in cases potentially involving national security information. Simple in formulation, it is far-reaching in its consequences. This theory holds that privileges against disclosure will be upheld against requests for even unclassified information, if that information may be assembled into a classified "mosaic" of national security activity. In other words, unclassified, banal information may be withheld whenever the government may make an argument that it will combine with other unclassified information to yield a classified picture of government activity.

The logic of this argument, which not only is accepted by courts but was originally conceived by the D.C. Circuit Court of Appeals in *Halkin,* is stunning in that it provides a limitless means to protect unclassified information from disclosure. To be sure, government attorneys are careful not to overuse the privilege so as not to tempt judges to dilute its potency, but the mosaic formulation means that in any case where bureaucrats need to hide embarrassing facts or criminal activity they may even protect unclassified material from disclosure. And since the state secrets privilege may be invoked against private parties, over documents not under government control, in actions to which the government is not a litigant, it is the perfect tool for preventing disclosure of information in especially sensitive matters no matter by whom and where they are raised.

Judges often accept invocations of the privilege because they do not feel competent to make a determination of what information is or is not dangerous to national security if revealed. They are extremely reluctant—understandably so—to replace administrative judgment on matters of national security with their own. There are some cases where the injustice caused by this reluctance is of a sharp and disturbing nature. *Frost v. Perry* and *Kasza v. Browner,* the Area 51 case discussed at the opening of this chapter, are good examples of perverse and harmful uses of the privilege.[84] In the Area 51 case, the government had violated numerous criminal and civil environmental statutes but prevailed after asserting the state secrets privilege. The workers never did discover what chemical wastes they were exposed to.

The *Kasza* court noted that "if seemingly innocuous information is part of a classified mosaic, the state secrets privilege may be invoked to bar its disclosure."[85] And in the same line, although never considering the mosaic theory specifically, the Supreme Court noted that, "superficially innocuous information" may divulge valuable intelligence.[86] This leads to the obvious conclusion that the state secrets privilege may now prevent disclosure of unclassified information that cannot in any sense be reasonably characterized as a state secret. This is a rather stunning reach for a privilege that started out as a device to protect only the most sensitive information. Under the mosaic theory, literally any piece of information may be argued to be a potential tile in a mosaic leading to a classified picture of United States operations. President Clinton provided protection against future suits by issuing a Presidential Determination specifically exempting Area 51 from compliance with environmental regulations and prohibiting release of any information about Area 51.[87]

The privilege also sometimes shields malicious actions of administrators in the business world as well as those of government administrators. *Maxwell v. First National Bank of Maryland* is a disturbing case involving illegal arms shipments and money laundering by the CIA. At the request of his supervisor, Robert Maxwell, a bank officer, handled a number of transactions that were suspicious and lacked proper documentation. Maxwell subsequently learned the transactions were in support of CIA operations and that his name was attached to additional transactions of which he knew nothing. Sternly warned not to keep any personal copies of these transactions and monitored closely at his office and home, Maxwell nonetheless surreptitiously made copies of numerous money transfers. When Maxwell finally expressed concern about the legality of the transactions, he and his family were threatened with harm.

Federal agents allegedly harassed and surveilled Maxwell for years after he left the job with the bank and interfered with his efforts to procure positions at other banks. When Maxwell sued the bank, the government successfully intervened, asserting the privilege to prevent the release of any documents relevant to the case. Most of these documents were held by the bank and were not state secrets in any common understanding of the term; they were ordinary financial documents that numerous uncleared personnel had seen and handled.

Moreover, the court precluded the use of information at trial that would establish the existence of a relationship between the CIA and the bank and even held information to be inadmissible that had already been publicly disclosed. The court cited the mosaic theory as the basis for these determinations; overruling First Amendment claims to the right to testify, the court prevented Maxwell "from offering in evidence bank documents already in his possession or his own testimony about alleged admissions by bank officials concerning the relationship of [the bank] and the CIA."[88] This is an astonishing result: a plaintiff was victimized by the government in collusion with private business; was prohibited from testifying in a case concerning unclassified matters in his own knowledge when he owed no duty of secrecy to the government; was not allowed to admit into evidence documents that had already been published and were in the hands of reporters.

The mosaic theory turns many of the assumptions of liberal democracy inside out and allows the government to make information secret and put it beyond the reach of judicial requests when that information could not properly be classified either under executive order or statute.

THE SEPARATION OF POWERS

Misplaced judicial deference to the assertions of privilege means more than citizens left without legal remedies; sometimes it creates instability in constitutional arrangements of power. The danger such deference presents to our constitutional framework is highlighted by the Clinton administration case of *Barlow v. United States*. Barlow, a former CIA employee, was fired from his job at the Department of Defense Office of Non-Proliferation Policy. He believed that the CIA and the Department of Defense were giving false information and testimony to Congress in an effort to manipulate it into passing legislation and funding specified programs. Specifically, Barlow knew that executive branch officials were concealing information about Pakistan's nuclear weapons program and that this concealed information presented a grave risk to the United States. Barlow also discovered information concerning the A. Q. Khan network, which most recently has been found to have been the chief source of illegal dissemination of nuclear weapons technology. Questions remain as to whether or not the Khan network passed material and crucial information to Al Qaeda.[89] But at the time of Barlow's intelligence discoveries, the Soviet Union was mired in the bloody fight in Afghanistan, and we needed Pakistani cooperation to supply the Afghani resistance with weapons and intelligence.

Barlow alleged that executive branch officials had lied to Congress in order to prevent triggering the Pressler-Solarz Amendment to the Foreign Assistance Act, which would have blocked a $1.4 billion sale of fighters to the Pakistani government.[90] Executive branch officials worried that if the sale of the fighters to Pakistan were blocked, it could jeopardize Pakistan's willingness to assist the United States in supplying the Afghani resistance. Barlow brought his complaints to his supervisor and stated that he would try to establish contact with members of Congress to inform them of his allegations. He was ordered not to contact members of Congress, even though the members he wished to talk to held security clearances and were already receiving the allegedly false information from the CIA and other intelligence agencies. Barlow argued that he was fired out of suspicion that he could not be trusted to keep the efforts to deceive Congress secret.

The U.S. Senate passed a resolution referring Barlow's case to the U.S. Court of Claims, where Barlow sued the United States under the Whistleblower Protection Act.[91] His counsel made very focused discovery requests, and Director of Central Intelligence George Tenet successfully asserted the state secrets privilege. In attempting to counter the claims of Tenet that the materials requested could not be turned over for evidence in the case for reasons of national security, Barlow submitted an affidavit from Charles Burke, once a "high-ranking" CIA employee. Burke stated that disclosure of the requested information would not jeopardize national security; like Barlow, he believed that Congress had been lied to. Burke also implied that Director Tenet asserted the state secrets privilege to prevent the disclosure of material that would substantiate Barlow's claims that intelligence agencies had intentionally deceived Congress.[92] Despite the importance of the issues involved and in the face of rather clear evidence of the likely misuse of the state secrets privilege, the court declined to look past the bare assertions of the government. According to Barlow, government counsel would stand up every time the state secrets privilege was asserted with respect to some question being asked; by the end of the testimony the attorney was so tired he could barely walk. Few sentences were allowed to escape Barlow's mouth without government counsel asserting the privilege, and Barlow lost his case.

If Congress must rely solely on executive branch intelligence agencies for information in making decisions without any means of verifying that information, it is completely at the mercy of the president and the executive bureaucracy. Judicial deference to the privilege in cases such as *Barlow* amounts to complicity with the executive branch in undermining congressional power and responsibility. And on occasion judicial functioning seems coopted by the perspective of secrecy that pervades executive agencies, making it unable to do its part in maintaining the separation of powers. In *In re United States,* judge Douglas Ginsburg withheld two-thirds of his dissenting opinion, stating, "unfortunately, I am unable fully to explain my disagreement with the court . . . without discussing [classified information] and thus the bulk of this opinion will be available only to a limited readership."[93] That limited readership included government attorneys but not plaintiff's counsel. In appealing such a ruling, it is unclear how a litigant would be able to go about addressing arguments it may not see, drawn from evidence it may not review. The perversity of a hidden system of law is richly discussed in literature; it may be a cliché to invoke Kafka in discussing legal matters, and often hyperbole at that, but when it comes to state secrets cases, *Kafkaesque* accurately captures the judicial ambience.

The Present Use of the Privilege

Recent use of the state secrets privilege shows a tendency on the part of the executive branch to expand the privilege to cover a wide variety of contexts. Conflict of interest is a fundamental problem afflicting the current arrangement for assertion of the privilege and the deference with which courts feel obliged to treat such assertions. Lord Coke famously remarked, "The King cannot be judge of his own cause, therefore the case must be judged by the Lords."[94] In this spirit, Executive Order 12958, issued by President Clinton, commands that "in no case shall information be classified in order to . . . conceal violations of law, inefficiency, or administrative error [or to] prevent embarrassment to a person, organization, or agency."[95]

In 1998, on the issue of disclosure raised by E.O. 12958, Congress debated statutory language that would allow executive branch employees to inform members of Congress or their staff representatives of violations of law, waste, or fraud by administrators. The Office of Legal Counsel at the Department of Justice opposed the language, arguing that it violated the separation of powers, and the threatened legislation failed. In the course of the debate, Senator Charles Robb asked Deputy Attorney General Randolph Moss the following hypothetical: if an executive branch official signed a specific, illegal finding authorizing the assassination of a foreign head of state, would an executive branch employee be authorized to report the act to Congress? In an astonishing reply, Moss essentially said no, only weakly noting that "the National Security Act require[s] reporting to Congress by the President" of violations of law.[96] But it is unreasonable and constitutionally unsound to rely on presidents and administrators to report their own misconduct, and it is an insult to Congress that the Department of Justice had no better justification in law or the Constitution to support its position. It is tantamount to saying that the president will do what he wishes and can prevent reporting of even illegal activity to Congress. This is a position that allows no room for recognition of Congress's constitutional duties of oversight of executive branch activity.

The Bush administration is even more committed to secrecy and maintenance of executive power than previous administrations, and a number of key personnel have histories of involvement in withholding records under unusual circumstances. For example, former Secretary of Defense Donald Rumsfeld, as both counselor to President Nixon and executive director of the Cost of Living Council, withheld documents requested by Congress in 1970 on two occasions. In both instances, Rumsfeld and Nixon claimed that a "confidential relationship" between them precluded compliance with congressional requests for information.[97]

And former attorney general John Ashcroft imposed stringent guidelines concerning Freedom of Information Act requests. The previous policy, by Attorney General Janet Reno, authorized withholding information only when an agency "reasonably foresees that disclosure would be harmful" to national security.[98] Ashcroft's memorandum, which superseded Reno's, directed agencies to withhold information where there is a "sound legal basis" to do so.[99] Given the reach and effectiveness of the state secrets privilege, such a directive is tantamount to making disclosure of any particular piece of information subject to the idiosyncratic discretion of administrators. A "sound legal basis" for withholding information under the state secrets privilege may be manufactured for virtually any document an administrator does not want the public to see.

The recent case of Sibel Edmonds presents a textbook example of questionable use of the state secrets privilege. Edmonds, a contract linguist for the FBI, made serious security allegations against a co-worker, that "amounted to an accusation against the co-worker of possible espionage." The Department of Justice Inspector General found that "the FBI did not, and still has not, adequately investigated these allegations." What the FBI did instead of investigating possible espionage was "to have discounted Edmonds' allegations, believing she was a disruptive influence and not credible, and eventually terminated her services." The inspector general "found that many of Edmonds' core allegations relating to the co-worker were supported by either documentary evidence or witnesses other than Edmonds . . . [and] concluded that, had the FBI performed a more careful investigation of Edmonds' allegations, it would have discovered evidence of significant omissions and inaccuracies by the co-worker related to these allegations." Finally, the inspector general concluded that Edmonds's allegations against her co-worker were "in fact, the most significant factor in the FBI's decision to terminate her services."[100]

Edmonds filed suit against the FBI under the Privacy Act and the First and Fifth Amendments to the Constitution. In response, Attorney General Ashcroft, allegedly at the behest of FBI Director Robert Mueller, formally filed an assertion of the state secrets privilege with the federal district court hearing Edmonds's case and "filed a motion to dismiss the case, because the litigation creates substantial risks of disclosing classified and sensitive national security information that could cause serious damage to our country's security."[101] Judge Reggie Walton found that because the "documents related to the plaintiff's employment, termination and security review that comprise the system of records are privileged, and because the plaintiff would be unable to depose witnesses whose identities are privileged or to otherwise identify through discovery the individual or individuals who purportedly released the privileged information, the plaintiff is . . . unable to proceed with" her claims.[102]

When Edmonds claimed in the media that the FBI's Language Services Section was egregiously backlogged, negligently managed intelligence bearing on the 9/11 attacks before they took place, and was in managerial disarray, she was subpoenaed to testify in a civil suit. Attorneys representing some 500 family members pursuing combined actions against various organizations for the wrongful death and injury of their relatives on 9/11 sought to depose Edmonds. Again, Attorney General Ashcroft asserted the state secrets privilege, and again the court held that the privilege applied.[103] A civil suit filed under FOIA by Edmonds met the same fate, so now Edmonds was prevented from suing for her termination and the public release of confidential employment information about her and was blocked from giving a deposition in another trial. Finally, Ashcroft retroactively classified previously unclassified information concerning Edmonds in order to intimidate members of Congress into not using the information in public hearings or in communications. Republican Senator Chuck Grassley found it "ludicrous to classify information that's been in the public domain for two years" and had "questions about whether this has anything to do with genuine national security."[104] Ashcroft even held that Edmonds's date of birth, the college she attended, and the languages she speaks were classified information, even though all of this information had been reported in the news. Judge Walton dutifully went along with these claims, finding that the state secrets privilege applied in each case.[105]

As cases against the Bush administration wend their way through the courts, judges are beginning to see broad assertions of executive power from administrators to withhold information from the public, the courts, and Congress. In a case against Vice President Richard Cheney to force the release of documents concerning meetings of the National Energy Development Group, now famous as the "energy task force," Judge Emmet G. Sullivan found Bush administration claims of privilege to "reflect what appears to be a problematic and unprecedented assertion, even in the face of contrary precedent, of Executive power." Sullivan then took note of a pattern of behavior on the part of Bush administration attorneys: "The fact that the government has stubbornly refused to acknowledge the existing controlling law in at least two cases, does not strike this Court as a coincidence. One or two isolated mis-citations or misleading interpretations of precedent are forgivable mistakes of busy counsel, but a consistent pattern of misconstruing precedent presents a much more serious concern."[106]

Bush has asserted the state secrets privilege more times than any president in history, and though he has prevailed in virtually all of these assertions, some district courts show a developing wariness concerning use of the privilege. But this has not chastened the Bush administration.[107] Indeed, recent cases indicate that Bush administration lawyers are using the privilege with offhanded abandon. In one case, Department of Justice attorneys raised the privilege on 245 separate occasions yet failed to follow through and meet the formal criteria prescribed in *Reynolds* for invocation of the privilege.[108] This conduct indicates that agencies may be asserting the privilege to prevent discovery or disclosure of information even in cases where the privilege is not warranted.

Undaunted by mounting criticism, Bush issued an executive order in November 2001 modifying procedures under the Presidential Records Act. The order has far-reaching implications. E.O. 13233 extends the power of asserting the state secrets privilege to former presidents to prevent disclosure of information generated during their presidencies. There, Bush stated, the "President's constitutionally based privileges subsume privileges for records that reflect: Military, diplomatic, or national security secrets (the state secrets privilege). . . .The former President independently retains the right to assert [these] constitutionally based privileges."[109] As discussed earlier, the state secrets privilege is not a component of executive privilege, and Bush's language stretches executive power beyond anything previously claimed. He simply asserts that the state secrets privilege is a *constitutionally* based privilege, not merely a common law evidentiary privilege—a direct claim that recent presidents had been careful to avoid.

Presidents from Jimmy Carter onward have claimed that certain statutes or requests by Congress are void to the extent that they impair the president's power to raise the state secrets privilege, but they have not claimed that the privilege inheres as a prerogative power in the presidency. This is an important distinction: it is one thing to say that Congress may not impair the power of the president to protect United States interests; it is quite another thing to say that the privilege is a prerogative power that Congress is constitutionally forbidden from tinkering with. The privilege is available to presidents to protect United States interests upon an appropriate showing of potential grave damage, but it does not arise from Article II powers. Indeed, as we have mentioned, it is easy to imagine instances where Congress or federal judges could raise the privilege independent of the executive branch. It is true that the procedure for asserting the privilege is tailored for the executive bureaucracy, but it is evident that this procedure would bend around novel situations arising outside of the executive branch to protect United States interests. At any event, Bush is attempting, with all indication of success so far, to reformulate the privilege as a prerogative right of the presidency.

This is a power heretofore unrecognized either in courts or general political life. In *Nixon v. Administrator of General Services,* the Supreme Court was ambivalent on the point of whether or not a former president could assert the so-called presidential communication privilege. Justice Brennan, writing for the Court, found that despite strong arguments weighing against it, there is at least a weak power in former executives to assert the communication privilege. But the Court found it clear and uncontested that the "very specific privilege protecting against disclosure of state secrets . . . may be asserted only by an incumbent President."[110] When questioned about the order, President Bush appeared to confirm the unprecedented reach of the privilege: The order "lays out a procedure that . . . is fair for past Presidents. . . . [A] process that I think will enable historians to do their job and at the same time protect state secrets."[111] The clear implication of this statement is that even former presidents may assert the state secrets privilege to protect against disclosure of documents from their administrations, regardless of Supreme Court precedent to the contrary.

Richard Nixon fought to the end of his life, and his heirs have continued the fight on his behalf, to control the process by which his tapes and other records would be preserved and stored.[112] Unsuccessful in asserting the state secrets privilege to prevent disclosure of embarrassing and damaging information, Nixon shifted his attack, attempting to limit the material released and to control the form in which it was released. The protracted litigation, combined with lack of full cooperation from the National Archive, had the effects of limiting access and continuing secrecy with regard to the Nixon tapes. If President Bush is successful in extending the state secrets privilege to past presidents to cover presidential records, however, the access problems will become insurmountable, and the ongoing disputes over when and how the archival records of past presidents can be researched will be eclipsed by the threshold question of whether anyone may see them at all without a former president's consent.

Just as the Bush administration's stance threatened to unsettle the presidential records secrecy question, so too did it complicate the oft-raised matter of the continued publication of the *Foreign Relations of the United States,* a documentary history of U.S. foreign relations. President Reagan sought to limit publication of the volumes in this series, much to the dismay of historians and archivists who rely on it as a critical research source for understanding the history of American foreign policy. Although the *FRUS* was already subject to a thirty-year publication delay, ostensibly for reasons of state secrecy, Reagan issued E.O. 12356 in 1982 requiring "protection of information that 'alone, or in the context of other information' could cause damage to national security." The wording here seems calculated to import the mosaic theory into decisions concerning *FRUS* publication. When the Advisory Committee complained about "overclassification" with regard to *FRUS,* the State Department changed the composition of the Committee "to dilute the voice of its historian members."[113]

The Bush administration also relied on the state secrets doctrine to buttress its decision to allow secret military tribunals to prosecute foreign terrorists. Anticipating that information brought into evidence in order to convict terrorists will often be classified, the military order establishing the tribunals mandates that trials are to be closed to outside observers and that all issues of fact and law are to be determined by the tribunal rather than by a jury. Bush's order on the subject directs that consideration against disclosure of state secrets will regulate "the conduct, closure of, and access to proceedings" and that this secrecy extends to "pretrial, trial, and post-trial procedures, modes of proof, issuance of process, and qualifications of attorneys."[114]

Considering the power of the privilege, we imagined that there would be policy documents concerning its use and invocation, but we were wrong. Our attempts to obtain policies for assertion of the state secrets privilege were met with failure; there appear to be no policy guidelines on the use of the privilege in any major department or agency of the executive branch. Freedom of Information Act requests to some three dozen agencies and their various subcomponents yielded nothing in the way of documentation of guidance for use of the privilege. Any limitations on assertion of the privilege appear to be self-imposed by the individual agencies, and use of the privilege seems to be carried out *ad hoc* at the discretion of department heads. The general feeling of administrators concerning the privilege was perhaps best summed up in a Department of the Navy memorandum, which crowed that "there is nothing but good news about the state secrets privilege" as a tool to prevent disclosure of information.[115]

The current structure of the state secrets privilege virtually guarantees that its assertion in any particular case will be successful and that the costs for abuse of the privilege will be minimal or nonexistent. The existence of such an effective tool of executive power provides a ready context for understanding the impulse of presidents to expand the use of the privilege to prevent scrutiny and information gathering by Congress, the judiciary, and the public. The state secrets privilege is more secure now than it ever has been, and it is expanding concomitant with presidential decisions to extend classification authority among the various agencies and to secure the country against terrorist attacks. While this expanded secrecy may or may not yield a more secure nation, it certainly ensures, as we have discussed, a great deal of public ignorance and injustice. Because the privilege is of judicial origin, it is the task of the courts to take the first concrete and measured steps to check the reach of the privilege, especially where that reach threatens to undermine the constitutional balance of power and to invade public interests.

But the chances for such reform are slim, since the Supreme Court has indicated that the executive branch does not have *enough* protection for national security material and its intelligence-gathering functions. The Court has clearly indicated that it will continue to give ground to presidential secrecy in matters claimed to affect national security.

CHAPTER FOUR

The Shadow President: The Attorney General, Executive Power, and the New Anti-Terror Laws

Absolute discretion, like corruption, marks the beginning of the end of liberty.

—*William O. Douglas*

A spate of legislation followed the terror attacks of September 11, 2001. The USA PATRIOT Act (hereafter the Patriot Act) passed Congress in October 2001 while the nation was still recovering from the attacks, and the massive administrative restructuring program contained in the Homeland Security Act became law thirteen months later.[1] In between those two major statutory reforms, other laws and regulations were enacted that aimed at fighting terror, including the Enhanced Visa and Border Security Act of 2002.[2] Often viewed of a piece, these laws did not spring full-blown from the besieged and defensive mindset that pervaded the United States after 9/11; they must also be seen as a continuation of the trend of increasing executive secrecy and power that began decades ago, in the post-Watergate period.

Indeed, some security-related initiatives revisited after 9/11, such as the Foreign Student Monitoring Program, were already fixed in law before 9/11.[3] This is not to deny or understate, of course, the impact of 9/11 on the lawmaking process: the harm to Americans from all walks of life brought national security problems to the forefront of public debate and generated urgent necessity for changes in law enforcement and intelligence-gathering methods. There is no question that the terror attacks produced an urgent sense on the part of the public that extensive changes in our approach to national security were needed or that this public sentiment generated great political momentum for new efforts to prevent and punish terrorist acts. Nonetheless, we contend that despite the exigency of the circumstances under which they arose, the new anti-terror laws must be viewed as the extension of a trend of increased executive secrecy and consolidation of executive power that long predates 9/11. These recent efforts represent the latest—and the most rapid and extensive—institutionalization of presidential powers, which threaten both to destabilize constitutional divisions of responsibility between the various branches of government and to diminish civil liberties.

Most significantly, the anti-terror laws create a concentration of executive power within the executive branch in the office of the attorney general. We call this newly strengthened office the *shadow president*: an unelected executive official who can act without possibility of review to execute direct actions on individuals, change established law and policy, and reengineer the accepted understanding of constitutional limits of governmental action. Much of the waging of the "war on terror" is done by the attorney general's office (and to a lesser extent, the secretary of homeland security), as detailed below: in practice, the president's symbolic pronouncements have been translated on the ground by Attorneys General John Ashcroft and Alberto Gonzales.

The office of the attorney general arose from the clause in Article II, section 2 of the Constitution, which directs that the president "take care that the laws be faithfully executed." Section 16 of the Judiciary Act of 1789 explicitly created the office for the following functions: "To prosecute and conduct all suits in the Supreme Court in which the United States shall be concerned, and to give his advice and opinion upon questions of law when required by the President of the United States or when requested by the heads of any of the departments, touching any matter that may concern their departments."[4] The attorney general's office has since grown to become "the head of a great executive department; the great majority of her time necessarily is devoted to directing the policy and administration of the activities of the Department of Justice."[5]

In the configuration just described, the attorney general is an agency head wielding great power and enjoying wide discretionary latitude. Given the post-9/11 climate of massive anti-terror law enforcement initiatives, it is especially important to consider the potential dangers of wide-ranging and sometimes absolute discretion vested in a single agency head. The respected administrative law scholar Kenneth Culp Davis saw the dangers in such discretion, even as he argued that it is a practical necessity in some cases. Thus, Davis not only argued for "discretionary justice" as necessary and unavoidable but also offered means by which abuse of discretion could be prevented. Davis suggested that administrative rulemaking, "one of the greatest inventions of modern government," could help to confine administrative discretion—even better than the use of adjudicative opinions could.[6]

While rulemaking does not remove discretion, it certainly creates openings for dissent and opposition along the way to the final rule adoption, as the notice and comment requirements of the Administrative Procedure Act stipulate.[7] Moreover, it commits the agency head to a position in future cases and confers publicity on administrative actions; arbitrariness and overreaching can be seen more clearly against the backdrop of a formally adopted rule. While rulemaking has been undertaken in some sub-areas of anti-terror policy (for example, in response to the Supreme Court decision in *Zadvydas,* discussed below), rulemaking has not been done in other crucial instances, such as the expansion of the material witness statute, also discussed below. One might suspect that the absence of rulemaking in the material witness area is a result of the executive's fear of exceeding statutory limits—as such, material witness policy appears to provide a good example of the abuse of discretion that worries Davis.

Davis also mentions legislative checks on administrative discretion.[8] While legislative supervision, oversight, and appropriations control are complex political mechanisms susceptible to varied and conflicting results, they too offer means to controlling the attorney general's discretion. However, Attorney General Ashcroft quickly made it clear that he would impose limits on the oversight process. Testifying before the Senate in the aftermath of 9/11, he had this to say: "Congress' power of oversight is not without limits. . . . In some areas, I cannot and will not consult you. . . . I cannot and will not divulge the content, the context, or even the existence of such advice to anyone—including Congress—unless the President directs me to do so."[9]

The attorney general compromised another avenue of confining discretion as well: the use of administrative adjudicatory and appellate tribunals, particularly in the immigration area. As we explain below, Ashcroft instituted measures that undercut the administrative appeal process by selecting cases that would be treated differently and would be subject to strict secrecy. Thus, he interfered in the administrative adjudication of cases with the likely result that thorough procedural protections at the trial and appellate levels will not be available. The availability of openness—of publicity—in controversial cases involving unpopular defendants is an important safeguard of fair procedures. Taken together, the means for limiting administrative discretion advocated by Davis will not be of much use in the anti-terror context. That these suggestions come from a respected commentator who advocates administrative discretion (even absolute discretion in some cases) makes their unavailability here even more striking.

Events during 2003 gave reason to suggest that the discretion vested in the attorney general had been abused. First, with regard to the anti-terror laws themselves, even Republican congressional leaders lamented the difficulty of getting information about the Patriot Act, complaining that "it's like pulling teeth" and comparing the administration to "a big black hole."[10] Withholding information goes beyond substantive discretionary decision-making. When the attorney general is asked for information and refuses to provide it, he is not executing a policy or rendering of a discretionary decision but simply refusing to act. Nonetheless, the inability of the legislature to obtain information about controversial executive actions makes oversight impossible.

After a senior administration official leaked the identity of a CIA operative to the press, apparently in retaliation for criticism voiced by the agent's spouse, investigation of the leak ensued, as it could constitute a federal crime.[11] Although some people questioned the attorney general's ability to be impartial in the investigation since he had worked with many of the administration staff under suspicion, he refused to appoint a special prosecutor, insisting that "the prosecutors and agents who are and will be handling this investigation are career professionals with extensive experience in handling matters involving sensitive national security information and with experience relating to investigations of unauthorized disclosures of such information."[12] His avoidance of the question of impartiality merely underscored the dangers of such a closed and secretive approach to running the Department of Justice. Here again, a chance for oversight was fended off, at least initially, by Ashcroft himself.

The substantive content of the anti-terror laws of 2001 and 2002 demonstrates the nexus between secrecy and efficiency: the executive branch operates most efficiently when it works in secret. The efficiency/secrecy nexus is a recurring theme in the Bush administration's anti-terror policy since 9/11, and in what follows we offer an exposition of the efficiency/secrecy relationship as a framework for understanding the global war on terror. The public understandably called for a prompt and effective governmental response after 9/11, and the executive branch responded by proposing initiatives to increase the efficiency and scope of existing powers, including expansion of investigative powers and a streamlining of agency organization and the decision-making hierarchy. The tradeoff, however—sometimes explicit, sometimes tacit—is a public acceptance of greater government secrecy (to the extent the public knows that secrecy is being employed) in exchange for the efficient operation of anti-terror programs. Thus, this chapter will start by outlining the various laws that comprise the Bush administration's anti-terror campaign. We will also analyze the various component programs, the webs of secrecy they generate, and the danger that secrecy poses to citizens and to democracy itself.

In the wake of 9/11, Attorney General Ashcroft bluntly announced his position: "Aggressive detention of lawbreakers and material witnesses," he warned, "is vital to preventing, disrupting, or delaying new attacks."[13] This statement revealed two key elements of the administration's anti-terror strategy: that it would be a focus on terror prevention rather than terror response, and that prevention-centered policy would involve detention of witnesses as well as defendants even in advance of criminal prosecutions. While concentrating resources on prevention of terrorist activity is no doubt crucial, it also provides a fertile environment for law enforcement and intelligence agents to engage in abusive and biased behavior by undertaking activity against people and groups without sufficient cause. Such actions may in many cases violate constitutional and statutory rights, but the secrecy surrounding governmental activity in the execution of post-9/11 statutory authority may prevent such abuses from being remedied or even coming to light. The chief legislative initiatives to be discussed here in the context of executive secrecy and possible abuse of authority are the Patriot Act (October 2001; this includes its proposed successor), the Homeland Security Act (November 2002), the enhanced use of the existing material witness statute, the various alien detention policies, and the military order authorizing military tribunals.

The Patriot Act

As the full name of the Patriot Act tells us, the measure is designed to bring about the "Uniting and Strengthening [of] America by Providing Appropriate Tools Required to Intercept and Obstruct Terrorism." Indeed, Attorney General Ashcroft said repeatedly that the goal of the government's anti-terror efforts is prevention rather than prosecution. While it is difficult to fault prevention of terror as a policy goal, the vast expansions of executive secrecy facilitated by this new law are cause for concern and, at the very least, require close examination. The Patriot Act is over 100 pages long, and it grants new powers to the executive branch while strengthening other executive powers already in existence. For our purposes here, however, rather than reviewing every portion of the act, we will concentrate on the provisions that relate to government secrecy.

Electronic Surveillance

Title II of the Patriot Act enhances the government's electronic surveillance capabilities and facilitates the inter- and intra-agency sharing of information obtained through surveillance. To accomplish these ends, the act blurs what had been a rather clear line between intelligence and law enforcement activities. Prior to the act's passage, federal surveillance activities were governed by a specific statutory scheme when they were directed at counterespionage rather than at criminal investigation. In other words, intelligence-related and law enforcement–related surveillance were subject to separate and distinct legal standards, reflecting their differing purposes. Law enforcement, as part of criminal law, followed a time-honored "probable cause" standard: to obtain court approval for surveillance of a crime suspect, federal authorities had to show, among other things, probable cause that a crime was being committed. Upon that showing and other requirements contained in Title III of the Omnibus Crime Control Act, which governs the issuance of warrants for electronic surveillance, a surveillance warrant or search warrant would be granted.[14] By contrast, surveillance of suspected foreign agents was carried out by intelligence personnel who needed to show probable cause only that the subject to be surveilled was an agent of a foreign power.

This second probable cause standard is plainly easier to meet than the first, and there is a reason for the difference: in the first case, the primary aim is prosecution of a criminal defendant, while in the second case the aim is the gathering of information. A suspected criminal faces greater harm from surveillance (in the form of criminal prosecution and sentence) than a suspected foreign agent does. The Foreign Intelligence Surveillance Act is the statutory authority governing intelligence-related surveillance, and it provides for a detailed procedure as well as a special statutory court to hear warrant applications.[15] Since we discuss FISA at length in the next chapter, it is not the primary focus here. But for the purposes of this discussion it is important to appreciate the greater ease with which the "agent of a foreign power" standard can be met. Any person an intelligence agency suspects of spying is likely to meet the standard. Rather than showing criminal activity, intelligence personnel must show only the possibility that an individual is working to further the interests of a foreign regime. As we note below, even a political dissident can be designated the agent of a foreign power, because neither certainty (a probable cause requirement, not a certainty requirement) nor affirmative acts need be shown.[16]

In modifying FISA and federal criminal law to enhance information-gathering, however, Title II of the Patriot Act blurs the line between intelligence and law enforcement by permitting agents conducting FISA-governed espionage investigations to furnish information to law enforcement personnel. The Patriot Act's "significant purpose" clause is the specific language change to the FISA that legalizes joint-purpose surveillance.[17] Before 9/11, a FISA warrant could only be granted if the purpose of the surveillance was to gather foreign intelligence. Now, under the Patriot Act, foreign intelligence need only be a "significant purpose" rather than the primary purpose of an investigation (it can be primarily a law enforcement investigation), a new standard that is obviously much easier to meet.

The implications of this change are disturbing. Under a legal regime in which intelligence and law enforcement agents are working together and sharing information, it becomes possible for the government to obtain court permission to wiretap subjects who could never be reached under normal law enforcement procedures and standards. When law enforcement and intelligence gathering become indistinguishable in practice, surveillance warrants can be obtained under the simpler "agent of a foreign power" standard. Once it is unnecessary to show probable cause of criminal activity before obtaining a surveillance warrant, the government will be able to obtain surveillance warrants much more easily, and it can obtain them against individuals who are not even arguably engaged in criminal activity. If an agent need show only that it is plausible that a surveillance target is the agent of a foreign power, then government agents can legally wiretap individuals who have done nothing more than criticize U.S. foreign policy, for example. Potentially, this law change could enable the government to legally surveil virtually anyone it distrusts or anyone who disagrees with administration policy. The mere potential for this kind of misuse of the anti-terror laws alone should give us pause before we endorse the heightened executive power that the Bush administration has engineered to fight terror.

In addition to being easier to obtain, wiretaps are now more far-reaching and more productive of detailed, individualized information under Title II of the Patriot Act. There are no geographical limits to surveillance warrants; virtually any means of communication may be intercepted, and virtually any means of video surveillance may be installed in implicated facilities and dwellings, including private homes. Phone surveillance can be authorized to cover an individual, regardless of the telephone sites he or she uses. And warrants are essentially granted in blank form when addressed to Internet sources, leaving the government to search as it will—a procedure that surely vitiates the purpose of a warrant requirement itself. Finally, under FISA, a target will most likely never be aware that she or he was the subject of surveillance, as the statute contains no notification requirements, and indeed contemplates that targets, unless FISA intercepts are introduced at trial, will not be informed of surveillance.[18]

Grand Jury Proceedings

Information-sharing is enhanced by other Patriot Act provisions as well, including the publication of grand jury records. Under U.S. law, federal grand juries are charged with the responsibility of hearing evidence and determining whether there is enough evidence against a potential defendant to go forward with a criminal prosecution. Grand jury records, historically secret under the Federal Rules of Criminal Procedure, are now available to myriad intelligence agencies under Title II. Now grand jury proceedings may be divulged "when the matters involve foreign intelligence or counterintelligence . . . or foreign intelligence information . . . to any Federal law enforcement, intelligence, protective, immigration, national defense, or national security official."[19] There is very little that cannot be squeezed into the frame of "foreign intelligence information" when the government so desires, since this condition is met by any information that "relates to . . . national security" or "foreign affairs."[20] It is hard to imagine what could not be brought under the ambit of these elastic terms. Indeed, in various proceedings, government attorneys have claimed that virtually any piece of information, in an appropriate context, actually could legitimately be either foreign intelligence information or implicate foreign intelligence information. While this may be true, it does leave available an uncontrollable means for government agents to troll through grand jury proceedings.

Thus, the Patriot Act entails two secrecy-related consequences in this regard: involving the intelligence community in domestic law enforcement, and removing the protective functions of grand jury secrecy. Here, it seems, the executive branch can increase its capacity to obtain and conceal information while depriving individuals of the protections of legally mandated grand jury secrecy. As a result of the lifting of grand jury confidentiality, the balance between government efficacy and individual privacy shifts decisively in favor of the government. When a grand jury decided not to indict a suspect prior to the Patriot Act, the proceedings ended there. Innocent grand jury defendants were thereby protected from the public stigma of criminal proceedings. But with grand jury information open to the government, that protection no longer exists.

Moreover, witness cooperation in grand jury proceedings will likely be harder to secure if the potential for publicity becomes known among participants, for grand jury secrecy is "as important for the protection of the innocent as for the pursuit of the guilty."[21] Witnesses will have more to fear after participating when they know their testimony is no longer to be kept secret. It should be noted that grand jury testimony is often far-ranging, involves hearsay and other questionable sources of information, and frequently requires witnesses to reveal highly personal facts about themselves, their families, and others. As the Supreme Court noted, the grand jury is "a grand inquest, a body with powers of investigation and inquisition, the scope of whose inquiries is not to be limited narrowly by questions of propriety or forecasts of the probable result of the investigation, or by doubts whether any particular individual will be found properly subject to an accusation of crime."[22] The confidential nature of grand jury proceedings is "older than our Nation itself" and is meant to ensure that grand jurors act efficiently and in good faith and that witnesses are forthcoming in their testimony.[23]

Even though the confidentiality of grand jury proceedings is controlled by the Federal Rules of Criminal Procedure (FRCP; now amended by Title II of the Patriot Act), historically the judiciary exercised broad control over disclosure of grand jury testimony in any particular case or request. Heretofore the government could only achieve disclosure of grand jury proceedings upon a showing of specific need falling within the scope of one of the exceptions to secrecy contained in the FRCP. And the Supreme Court has held that DOJ prosecutors may not grant "automatic" access to grand jury materials to Civil Division attorneys.[24] Normally, even government attorneys must procure a court order or notify the trial court judge before divulging grand jury information to colleagues.

The new rule concerning disclosure of foreign intelligence information is extraordinary. It is contrary to four centuries of legal practice in that it allows a government attorney to divulge grand jury material with impunity to almost any agency for any reason that is even tangentially connected to national security. The Patriot Act only requires that "within a reasonable time after disclosure is made, . . . an attorney for the government must file, under seal, a notice with the court in the district where the grand jury convened stating that such information was disclosed and the departments, agencies, or entities to which the disclosure was made."[25] In other words, judges have no control over the disclosure of grand jury material, over the ability to evaluate the reasons proffered in support of disclosure, or over the ends to which the information is used. Further, since the court is notified under seal, the public or participants in the grand jury hearing will never know that grand jury materials were disclosed. As we discuss at numerous points throughout this book, the growth of executive secrecy gravely encroaches upon traditional common law and Article III powers of the judiciary. Removal of judicial discretion to keep grand jury proceedings secret is an example of such an encroachment, as Congress, in its haste to respond to the events of 9/11, altered the FRCP to increase executive authority while at the same time denuding traditional judicial powers squarely at the heart of the legal process.[26]

Access to Records

Title III of the Patriot Act authorizes ex parte applications for student records kept by educational institutions.[27] Thus, colleges and universities can be judicially compelled to provide confidential information about individual students to the federal government, even though the schools had no opportunity to contest in advance the government's claims of appropriateness and need regarding the information. Because the requests can be made ex parte, the school's first notice of legal proceedings to obtain a court order for educational records is likely to be the court order itself requiring disclosure of the records. Schools are unlikely to challenge such orders because of the expense involved and fears of reprisal, perhaps in the form of denial of government research grants.

Though not a student records action, the case of Steven Hatfill is instructive on this point. Attorney General John Ashcroft declared Hatfill to be a "person of interest" in the mailing of letters containing anthrax spores to several politicians and members of the news media. Even though no evidence ever came to public light to implicate Hatfill—indeed, exculpatory evidence supports his innocence—Louisiana State University fired him from his job as an associate professor at the National Center for Biomedical Research and Training only a few days after he was hired.[28] The Department of Justice Office of Justice Programs explained that "it directed LSU to cease use of the services of Mr. Hatfill" at the National Center.[29] The National Center receives the bulk of its funding from the Department of Justice, so it is not hard to understand why Louisiana State University acquiesced in firing Hatfill without argument. The threat to deny funding to universities is a powerful tool that the Department of Justice has at its disposal to ensure cooperation over matters such as compliance with requests for student records and other information.

And of course, the individual students may never learn that their confidential records were furnished to the government as part of a terror investigation. This provision, like many others contained in the Patriot Act, essentially gives the government a fishing license to sift through the private material of residents without having to justify such actions in an adversarial setting and without the requirement that people subjected to such surveillance be notified. It would be naive to believe that people wholly innocent of any wrongdoing subjected to such searches would not suffer adverse consequences. Such searches would no doubt leave information trails that would be difficult, if not impossible, to eradicate. Information is passed between law enforcement and intelligence agencies; even if it is removed from one or more databases, it may still be freely available on others or reside on individual computers. It is not hard to imagine that people subjected to student record requests or other surveillance actions will encounter difficulties when applying for federal jobs, private employment requiring security clearances, or private employment involving the handling of material that could be used for purposes of terrorism.

Title II similarly amends the FISA to allow for search and seizure of business records.[30] These changes to existing law underscore the two-sided problem of blurring the line between law enforcement and intelligence gathering that is central to the anti-terror laws. First, the changes make it easier for the executive to obtain information about individuals and share it among the various divisions of the Department of Justice as well as with state and local law enforcement. More information can now be obtained more quickly, and it can be disseminated effectively as well, allowing the government more opportunities to act on it. Second, the secrecy with which the information is gathered disadvantages the individual subjects of investigation by leaving them unaware that the Department of Justice has seized and studied their records. The procedure can continue more efficiently, of course, if it is unknown and therefore unchallenged.

"Sneak-and-peek" searches, in which the target of the search may never be notified that a search occurred, are authorized by Section 213 of the Patriot Act.[31] As an obvious departure from settled understandings of the constitutional law of search and seizure, these searches have been controversial since the Patriot Act authorized them, but an attempt to remove that part of the law failed after only the House voted for amendment.[32]

Immigration Policy

In the area of immigration policy, the Patriot Act changes prior law by making noncitizens deportable for a wider range of conduct. Prior to the act, an alien became, according to legal scholar David Cole, "deportable for engaging in or supporting terrorist activity, but not for mere association."[33] Title IV of the Act, however, now renders aliens deportable for wholly innocent associational activity with a "terrorist organization," whether or not there is any connection between the alien's associational conduct and any act of violence, much less terrorism. Because the new law defines "terrorist activity" to include virtually any use or threat to use a weapon, and defines "terrorist organization" as any group of two or more persons that has used or threatened to use a weapon, the Act's proscription on associational activity potentially encompasses every organization that has ever been involved in a civil war or a crime of violence, from a pro-life group that once threatened workers at an abortion clinic, to the African National Congress, the Irish Republican Army, or the Northern Alliance in Afghanistan.[34]

Cole points out, further, that the State Department itself opposed a 1994 proposal to "make membership in [the terrorist group] Hamas a ground for denying visas" because of the associational problem described above: groups designated "terrorist" often engage in legal as well as illegal activities, social welfare as well as violence, so it is problematic to assume that every contribution and every association with the "terrorist" group is intended to further terrorism.[35] Nonetheless, the Patriot Act changed previous law to permit deportation of noncitizens for purely associational activities, regardless of the connection between association and terrorist acts. This change facilitates greater exercise of executive discretion upon a far lesser legal showing than what was previously required, and the broader standard and lesser proof requirement serve to enlarge the space in which the executive can operate free from judicial oversight. Since the president also determines which groups shall be designated terrorist organizations, the executive branch has nearly unfettered ability to manipulate matters to achieve whatever outcomes are desired.

The Intelligence Reform and Terrorism Prevention Act of 2004 brought some modifications to the standards for declaring a person a terrorist or terrorist supporter.[36] In response to proceedings in the Ninth Circuit Court of Appeals, Congress imposed a knowledge requirement on the Patriot Act standards. Thus, the prosecution must now show that a person who contributes money, for example, to an organization must have some knowledge of its terror-related activities before that person can be convicted of supporting a terrorist organization.[37] The act also expands executive capacity for FISA surveillance by authorizing surveillance of "lone wolves" who are not clearly working for a foreign power. Prior to the act's passage, officials needed to establish (to a probable cause standard) that an individual was an "agent of a foreign power."[38] The act also provides for a Privacy and Civil Liberties Oversight Board, whose members are housed within the executive office of the president and appointed by the president.[39] Here again, the institutional structure of the anti-terror bureaucracy confers almost total control to the executive in general and to the president in particular: protection of civil liberties and privacy is entrusted to the executive, who enjoys vastly increased powers of enforcement and investigation. It is worth noting, too, that the act passed at the end of a year (2004) during which the executive branch came under heavy criticism following the revelation of shocking prisoner abuses in Iraqi detention centers.[40] Congress nonetheless passed legislation entrusting civil rights protection directly to the White House.

The Bush administration's policy in the immigration area is its boldest use of both secrecy and unchecked discretion. The administration asserts that the attorney general, by fiat, may hold immigration hearings in secret. After 9/11, Attorney General Ashcroft ordered Chief Immigration Judge Michael Creppy to issue a memorandum to all immigration judges and court staff outlining procedures for the handling of "special interest" cases. Creppy ordered that "the courtroom must be closed for these cases—no visitors, no family, no press." Even the docketing information, including names of the parties to actions, is to be kept secret, and all courtroom personnel must be instructed not to discuss these cases. Further, these secrecy procedures "apply to all cases selected by the Attorney General," and immigration judges are without authority to inquire into the reasons for the "special interest" classification in any particular case.[41]

Under these circumstances, judges are powerless to open hearings in a case designated as "special interest," even when it is obvious to the judge that the classification power is being abused by the attorney general. Plaintiffs in cases seeking to overturn the Creppy rules alleged that hundreds of hearings were ordered closed by the attorney general, and it appears that an entirely secret system of adjudication with respect to aliens was being created. A New Jersey federal district court found the rules to violate the First Amendment right of public access to trial and enjoined the attorney general from using the "special interest" case procedures.[42] In overturning this decision, the Third Circuit Court of Appeals relied on an argument that has been utilized in the state secrets context.[43] The argument, at least concerning state secrets, is often referred to as the "mosaic theory" but may also be called the "ignorant judge claim."

The Third Circuit argued that while an immigration judge may see no harm in opening a hearing to the public that the attorney general has deemed a "special case," the judge does not have the skills or expertise to make the judgment that opening the hearing will not imperil national security. The court explained that "insight gleaned from open proceedings might alert vigilant terrorists to the United States' investigative tactics and could easily betray what knowledge the government does—or does not—possess" and that "even details that seem innocuous in isolation, such as the names of those detained, might be pieced together by knowledgeable persons within the terrorist network, who could in turn shift activities to a yet-undiscovered terrorist cell."[44] In other words, innocent facts that seem to present no danger to the security of the United States or the public may in fact be assembled into a mosaic of United States capabilities and activities that may assist terrorists. Based on this logic, the court reached the conclusion that since "immigration judges cannot be expected accurately to assess the harm that might result from disclosing seemingly trivial facts, . . . seeking closure on a case-by-case basis would ineffectively protect the nation's interests."[45] This decision gives the executive plenary power to dictate to the judiciary which of its immigration proceedings may or may not be open to the public. As we noted earlier and will note at numerous points in this book, the judiciary—not merely since 9/11 but also over the last several decades—has become a willing participant in the destruction of its own constitutionally granted powers where the president claims matters of secrecy or national security.

The cynical view of the attorney general's efforts to classify massive numbers of actions involving aliens as "special interest" cases would suggest that he was seeking to prevent the public from seeing how the new powers granted to the executive branch by the Patriot Act are being used in deportation hearings. One legitimate fear is that the attorney general is using powers under the act combined with the discretion to designate terrorist organizations and keep deportation hearings secret in a wholesale effort simply to deport as many Arab aliens as possible without concern for the individual merits of the cases. As in the surveillance and grand jury examples above, shifts in power relations effected by the Patriot Act amount to a zero-sum game: the loss of individual civil liberties corresponds precisely to the gain in executive power; the loss of individual privacy corresponds to the gain in executive secrecy.

In its anti-terror policy, the Bush administration offers what is in essence an implicit bargain to the United States public. In order to focus on prevention of future terror attacks, the executive must be afforded greater discretion and fewer limitations on its powers. The administration often speaks in terms of sacrificing civil liberties for security in this new context of global terror. For example, former attorney general Ashcroft has quoted Lincoln to say that "the dogmas of the quiet past are inadequate to the stormy present," and "as our case is new, so must we think anew, and act anew."[46] Lurking beneath that question, however, is a deeper one: what amount of increased secrecy, in a nation that has traditionally been hostile toward government secrecy, and executive secrecy in particular, must be ceded to the executive in order for the executive to be able to do its job of keeping the nation safe? To be sure, it is not entirely accurate to talk in terms of a "bargain" with the United States public because the public is hardly free to reject, immediately, the changed terms of the state/individual relationship. However, to the extent that it need concern itself with public opinion, the administration has sought to construct an either/or question about increased state power and public safety. Moreover, the administration has counted on the rhetoric of safety and prevention to preclude opposition to the new configuration of power.

Beyond the Patriot Act

In February 2003, a second Patriot Act proposal (entitled "The Domestic Security Enhancement Act of 2003") was "leaked" from the administration before a draft was even presented to Congress, though Speaker of the House Dennis Hastert received a copy, and it appears that the proposed legislation also went to Vice President Cheney's office.[47] Through this draft legislation, even greater investigative and administrative powers would be conferred on the executive via the office of the attorney general. For example, Freedom of Information Act (FOIA) requests related to terrorist suspects in custody or to hazardous materials threats to residential communities would be easier to deny lawfully. In the latter case, the attorney general had already explained that community contingency disaster plans, which communities use in the event of chemical spills and other toxic accidents, might also help terrorists to plan an attack; consequently, they must be kept secret.[48] The balance struck here between government secrecy and individuals' access to information they need to protect themselves, is reminiscent of the "Area 51" government secrecy cases.[49] In both cases, the asserted need for secrecy—and nothing more—trumps the need of citizens to obtain information critical to life-and-death decision-making. By suggesting that the disaster plans might be used by terrorists, the government implicitly prioritizes law enforcement over the public's need to protect itself against disaster. Ironically—and one hopes, of course, that this never occurs—the unavailability of disaster plans to the public might exacerbate casualties resulting from a terror attack on precisely those facilities covered by the plans.

The public review of items such as disaster contingency plans is also beneficial for providing accountability of government action, as review exposes such plans to expert independent review. The attorney general's argument that access to such plans by terrorists endangers public safety seems plausible in the abstract, but there are precious few categories of information that, in the abstract, would not be of aid to terrorists seeking to do us harm. The conclusion that we can draw from the behavior of President Bush and his advisors is that there is a concerted effort to pursue broad means of concealing executive branch governmental activity, irrespective of legitimate needs to keep such activity secret.

Further, the proposed legislation would invalidate consent decrees reached by state law enforcement, because those decrees allegedly could interfere with federal surveillance efforts. It would also make it possible to strip a U.S. citizen of citizenship based on an association with a group designated "terrorist." In other words, a citizen's intent to relinquish citizenship would be "inferred from conduct," whereas before a citizen had to state the intention explicitly before being expatriated.[50] When confronted about this new proposal, the administration downplayed its significance, treating it as one of numerous policy alternatives discussed only at a highly theoretical level.[51] We might well ask why a plan that was purportedly only discussed in vague and theoretical terms took up voluminous pages of detailed legislative text, obviously requiring thousands of hours of attorney time in its drafting.

These semi-secret legislative proposals are clearly extensions of the initiatives of the original Patriot Act, and in several cases track specific Patriot Act provisions rather closely. The proposal calls for presumptive detention in terrorism cases, which continues the Patriot Act's trend of facilitating detention prior to conviction. In the Patriot Act, the attorney general is authorized to detain suspected terrorists indefinitely rather than deporting or releasing them.[52] And the current use of the material witness law, though not technically part of the Patriot Act, works to the same end: detaining aliens in cases where there is insufficient evidence to charge them. The administration's new legislative proposal extends these two initiatives by establishing a legal presumption of detention in cases where terrorism is suspected so that the burden is on the detainee to rebut the presumption and not on the government to justify detention.[53] Presumptive detention would likely function as an additional blanket of secrecy over the administration's investigatory activities as a result of the lesser showing required in each case. A simple showing of suspected terrorism would be sufficient to trigger the presumption of detention, and the government would not be obliged to reveal anything further, at least in the initial stages, about its investigation or its evidence.

The provision invalidating state court consent decrees in law enforcement matters tracks Patriot Act provisions regarding enhanced surveillance and information sharing. As demonstrated above, the Patriot Act allows intelligence agents to share their findings with law enforcement personnel. Consent decrees restraining state law enforcement officers from carrying out surveillance would limit their ability to obtain information, which they could then share with federal authorities; nullifying such decrees, on the other hand, removes any such limita-tion. The problem, of course, is that such decrees are negotiated and submitted to terminate civil rights lawsuits in the state courts. One might suspect that when such suits are settled by consent rather than dismissed or taken to trial, there is likely some merit to them. Thus, some social gain in terms of the scope of civil rights protection or improved community relations results from settlement by consent decree. If civil rights consent decrees are invalidated by the federal gov-ernment, however, all such gains will be lost.

The desires of the Bush administration on this score also seem to track a recent trend in judicial action. In the aftermath of 9/11, courts began to revisit consent decrees designed to prevent longstanding law enforcement abuse of civil liberties in certain communities. In New York City, for example, a succession of abusive New York City Police Department organizations with lineage back to 1904 were brought to heel by consent decree in 1984, in the *Handschu* litigation.[54] That de-cree was recently gutted of many of its protections in response to the city's claims that the decree prevented it from effectively investigating terrorist threats.[55] Here again, the balance between civil rights and government access to information tips further in favor of the government, even in cases where the civil rights gains and the government investigatory needs arise in separate cases. The *Handschu* case originated long before the "war on terror."

There are other concerns resulting from the proposed nullification language. First, in terms of federalism, the proposed nullification process represents a new avenue of federal incursion on state sovereignty. The system of government in the United States is based on federalism: the sharing of political power between federal and state government. We live under a governmental system of dual sovereignty, in which federal and state powers are absolute in their own spheres. Under the new proposals, however, the attorney general himself would act as a reviewing court over matters clearly subject to state court jurisdiction. Not only does the state lose the right to make rulings on properly filed cases in a regime allowing federal nullification, but the attorney general also takes the role of some-thing like an appellate court—a role normally performed, in state systems, by state appellate judges installed on the appellate bench, whether by election or appointment, pursuant to state law.

Additionally, under this federal nullification process, the finality of judicial orders would be compromised. To all parties involved in settlement negotiations, court-approved settlements would stand ever in limbo, with the specter of federal intervention and nullification looming throughout the settlement process and beyond. Agreements between parties in state court would be subject to dissolution and would therefore be of questionable value to the litigants, thus diminishing the incentive to settle.

A final thread of continuity between the Patriot Act and the proposed legislation can be found in the provisions restricting FOIA access. Since 9/11, the administration has been reluctant to provide information about detainees in general, whether held as material witnesses, criminal suspects, or immigrants out of status. In January 2003, nearly 1200 Arabs and Muslims were being held under the Immigration and Naturalization Services' special "registry" program, which we discuss below. By June 2003, more than 13,000 Arabs and Muslims faced deportation as a result of terror-related anti-immigrant initiatives undertaken by the federal government.[56] Moreover, much of the information on detainees has remained secret, so that it is impossible for the public to know the total number of detainees, past or present. The inspector general of the Justice Department, Glenn Fine, released a report that summer indicating "significant problems" of mistreatment of immigrant detainees: holding them after the FBI had cleared them of suspicion and subjecting them to harsh prison conditions.[57] Nonetheless, Attorney General Ashcroft insisted, in the face of these findings, that more secrecy was needed via strengthened legislation to authorize ongoing and future investigations.[58]

The proposed legislation codifies these detention practices, shielding the administration from criticism at least pending a legal challenge. The attorney general or the CIA director must authorize release of identifying information before it can be provided to the public. The analysis of the proposed legislation indicates that such information could cause co-conspirators to flee or to attempt rescue. These risks are not unique to terror cases, and the question therefore arises why a new, pro-government balance between law enforcement and publicity was necessary. The analysis also indicates that this FOIA exemption strengthens one that already exists and that strengthening it will eliminate the need to defend "this [existing] interpretation through litigation," which "requires extensive Department of Justice resources, which would be better spent detecting and incapacitate [sic] terrorists."[59] Increasing the number of exception categories within FOIA is an effective avenue to protecting information because it avoids negative publicity: it limits the actual categories of information available to the public while appearing to reaffirm the Freedom of Information Act in principle. Public access to information is an important principle, the text seems to say, but there are some cases where it is inapplicable. And the areas carved out as additional exceptions are two such cases. It is a repeated theme of administration anti-terror efforts that the mention of national security threats in the form of possible terror attacks trumps any other concern that anyone might assert—including the competing interests in these two examples: public safety and the preservation of due process.

The political climate changed in the wake of the 9/11 Commission Investigation and Report in 2004.[60] The commission's recommendations addressed multiple intelligence failures in the months leading up to 9/11, and its report redirected the current of reform somewhat. When the Intelligence Reform Act (cited above) passed Congress late in 2004, it contained some strengthened powers but also addressed coordination of intelligence functions for greater effectiveness. Thus, the "PATRIOT Act II" was not adopted wholesale into law, but it remains, in its constituent parts, as potential future reforms. When Congress voted on March 8, 2006, to extend key provisions of the Patriot Act, the possibility of such future changes was resurrected.[61]

Bureaucratic Restructuring, Greater Secrecy: The Homeland Security Act of 2002

In response to the terrorist acts of 9/11, the federal government designed and submitted for congressional approval a massive overhaul of many administrative agencies whose functions include security. Congress signed it into law in November 2002; according to a timetable contained in the final bill itself, the restructuring took effect during the year 2003. At the time of the law's passage, President Bush promised that under the new homeland security regime, "the continuing threat of terrorism, the threat of mass murder on our own soil, will be met with a uniform, effective response."[62] The law creates a 170,000-employee department in which multiple agency functions will be directed and supervised by one person: the secretary of homeland security, initially Tom Ridge.[63]

The agencies subsumed under the Department of Homeland Security (DHS) are reassigned to four divisions: Information and Infrastructure Protection, Science and Technology, Border and Transportation Security, and Emergency Preparedness and Response. Each of these divisions is headed by an undersecretary who reports directly to the DHS secretary. The DHS secretary directs a large portion of the federal bureaucracy and commands access to an unprecedented amount of information. In fact, only the president can limit the DHS secretary's access to information. The DHS secretary is also empowered to assert a privilege over national security–related information—much like the state secrets privilege but applicable more routinely outside of litigation.[64] The construction of this powerful administrative position clearly moves the line between secret information and available information decisively in favor of the government—particularly, in favor of one executive official. At the same time that the DHS secretary enjoys almost unlimited access to information, he or she can also unilaterally deny access to others without possibility of review.

The asymmetrical information access allowed by the act works to undercut the oft-stated benefit of the act's statutory structure. Comptroller General David Walker suggested that "a statutory basis for major homeland security functions allows for more effective congressional oversight and input."[65] However, this benefit will be difficult to realize because the act itself blocks oversight by concentrating and limiting access to information in the DHS secretary's office.

The Bureau of Citizenship and Immigration Services (BCIS), which assumes the functions of the INS under the new administrative regime, is part of the larger Border and Transportation Security section of the HSA. It is responsible for strengthening previous immigration initiatives of the 1996 immigration reform law and for implementing the Enhanced Border Security and Visa Entry Reform Act of January 2002. Foreign student monitoring is a key part of these immigration laws. Foreign student monitoring was already required under the 1996 law, but the discovery that several of the 9/11 hijackers were foreign students led to renewed, intensified monitoring efforts.[66]

The BCIS estimates that there are about one million non-immigrant (that is, temporarily residing) foreign students in the United States each year. One of the most important means to tracking those students is the requirement that schools alert the government each time a foreign student is admitted to the United States for study but fails to enroll. This measure would detect "individuals who never intended to attend school in the United States [but who] . . . obtain a student visa, enter the country, and then disappear." Moreover, schools must report foreign student information to the BCIS, including address information. Student records would normally be confidential and protected from disclosure, but the 1996 immigration reform law allows a waiver of the confidentiality that would otherwise apply.[67] With these improved capabilities, the BCIS is far better able to track the activities of foreign students in the United States. In addition, stricter rules about timetables and course of study make it more difficult for students to remain in the United States during breaks in study or to arrive in advance of the program start date. While these rules appear to be reasonable and will undoubtedly improve foreign student monitoring, they also increase the attorney general's discretion to detain, interrogate, and deport students. Given the increased detention powers vested in the attorney general, as discussed earlier in this chapter, the rules will probably lead to more students falling out of legal status and therefore becoming subject to surveillance and confinement, providing law enforcement with pretexts to arrest parties of "interest." With so many ways for foreign students to run afoul of status requirements, the Department of Justice is given another means to circumvent normal investigative techniques and evidentiary requirements to engage in wholesale or random shakedowns of foreigners in the United States.

Significantly, the CIA and the FBI remain outside the jurisdiction of the DHS. Some intelligence experts find this problematic, given the historical tendency of the CIA to control intelligence information and the longstanding information-sharing disputes among the CIA, the FBI, and the NSA. In fact, Senator Richard Shelby of Alabama charges that "sadly, the CIA seems to have concluded that the maintenance of its information monopoly was more important than stopping terrorists from entering or operating within the United States."[68] Paradoxically, the impetus for the government restructuring represented by the Homeland Security Act came from the information gaps and miscommunication reported widely and frequently in the news media after 9/11. Yet the two agencies often mentioned in connection with the miscommunication were left outside the administrative restructuring effort. Whether it is the agencies' clashing institutional cultures, a strategic decision by the administration, or some other factor that is responsible for the continued independence of the intelligence agencies from Homeland Security, it remains clear to the commonsense observer that this omission makes little sense in view of the stated goals of the DHS.

The new Office of Homeland Security (OHS) drew battle lines early, indicating in statements that it will avidly practice secrecy and resist public demands for information about its operation. In response to a lawsuit filed by the Electronic Privacy Information Center, the OHS claimed that it is not an "agency" and is therefore not obligated to release records of its operation. Early in 2003, a U.S. district judge ruled against the OHS in its attempt to have the lawsuit dismissed summarily.[69]

A similar claim was made years earlier by the National Security Council in response to efforts by a group of journalists to halt destruction of NSC e-mail records from the Reagan administration. After years of litigation, government lawyers raised the claim that the NSC was not an agency and was therefore not subject to the records disclosure requirements governing federal agencies. The U.S. Circuit Court of Appeals for the District of Columbia accepted the government's argument in 1996, terminating that litigation.[70] Thus, there is precedent for excluding executive officials from the channels of oversight normally used to supervise administrative agencies. In the case of the DHS, however, it strains credulity to assert that claim. An agency made up of various previously existing agencies which, taken separately, were unquestionably administrative agencies cannot easily disclaim its own status as an agency. To deny its agency status would be to say that DHS is somehow less than the sum of its parts. The argument put forward by DHS is understandable in view of the central role of secrecy in the administration's anti-terror program, but it is a difficult claim to defend.

It has been pointed out more than once that the administration's anti-terror policies are structured like wartime policies; indeed, the "war on terrorism" is now an established part of our lexicon. Tactics such as the fight to preserve agency secrecy discussed in the preceding paragraph reinforce the point that the administration is fighting a war, and that its policies are, more often than not, a product of that fact. In administrative theory, however, a line is frequently drawn between civil-associational organizations on the one hand and purposive organizations on the other. The typical political institution is a civil association, and this is true in both a descriptive and a normative sense: it is the more frequently observed type of organization as well as the more preferred one. Agreed-upon rules for member interaction and limitation of state power are central features of the civil association. In times of war, according to Michael Spicer, political organizations often move into a purposive style rather than the "normal" civil-associational style. Purposive administration is marked by more efficient, more coercive institutional behavior, as governmental resources are focused on winning the war and vanquishing the external threat—so that normal life may resume. As Spicer puts it, "Concentration of political power will be seen here as facilitating the efficient and effective accomplishment of state purposes, and therefore will be seen as desirable. Consequently, there will be little patience with the type of constitutionalism that is understood, in the English and American sense, as a means or a set of devices for dispersing power or checking the abuse of power. Rather, such constitutional devices as separation of powers, judicial review, or federalism will be seen as little more than impediments or obstacles to the pursuit of a state's ends."[71]

But while purposive organizations are more efficient, that form brings costs—in terms of morale and institutional culture. These costs intensify over the long term. For that reason, governmental entities ought to resume the civil-associational style as soon as practicable. As an example, Spicer mentions the "cold war, a war that lasted some four decades or so [and] contributed significantly to the strengthening of executive power within our constitutional system."[72] And while rhetoric of protracted, "new" war against a vague and nameless enemy has been politically expedient for the Bush administration, the war on terrorism incurs unique costs resulting from its character as a long-term struggle without a clearly defined endpoint. In short, the civil/purposive association problematic helps to show some of the costs perhaps temporarily deferred but looming in the future as a result of the way the "war on terrorism" is conducted. In placing efficiency above democratic values and in ignoring the long-term effects of a purposive administrative style, the president risks permanent changes in governmental culture and attitudes toward government.

Moreover, the vast scale on which resources are now arrayed and redirected with the purpose of eliminating terrorism suggests an even more pronounced effect. The administration's response to 9/11 (and Congress's approval of it) did not involve probing and pinpointing specific areas needing reform but rather focused on rearranging all relevant agencies (except the CIA, the FBI, and the NSA) and making them accountable to one agency head with almost unlimited formal power but dependent nonetheless on the cooperation of multiple agencies below him.

It is important to note the ideological and rhetorical support for the new security regime. The rhetoric purports to justify not only specific intelligence and anti-terror initiatives but also the concentrated power and virtually unlimited information access enjoyed by the attorney general and the DHS secretary. At the DHS bill-signing ceremony, President Bush explained that "the continuing threat of terrorism, the threat of mass murder on our own soil, will be met with a unified and effective response."[73] Lisa Nelson points out that the rhetoric of the post-9/11 anti-terror policy pits security against individual privacy in ways that privilege the former at the expense of the latter. The architects of the homeland security legal and policy regime, which encompasses the FBI, the CIA, the NSA, and the attorney general's office as well as the DHS itself, employ two key rhetorical moves to justify its existence. First, according to Nelson, technology is presented as universal and objective in its application. It does not single out individuals but rather looks everywhere for particular information; "its observation does not signal our guilt." In a related move, Nelson argues, the subjective expectation of privacy, which is hard to articulate in the high-tech surveillance context, is made to be seen as "a possible desecration of the common good."[74]

In sum, it appears that the administrative restructuring resulting in DHS is likely to lead to increased executive power and greater executive control over information (in the hands of fewer people) and a changed government culture. Beneficial effects, on the other hand, are not apparent. To date, there has been no showing that anti-terror activities have been more effective in catching terrorists under the new regime, Ashcroft's statements to the contrary notwithstanding.[75] Indeed, there were few actual or attempted attacks. There are serious questions about the administration's overall homeland security plan as well. For one, the policy focus has been on weapons of mass destruction rather than conventional weapons, even though the 9/11 attacks were carried out with little more than box cutters. Richard Sylves and William Waugh Jr. warn that this focus might return us to "the command-and-control approach that was common two or three decades ago, when civil defense against nuclear attack was the paramount concern."[76]

Since the heyday of nuclear threat response, command-and-control defense structures have been replaced by coordinated, comprehensive disaster response systems. Sylves and Waugh cite fears among professional disaster response planners that "the response to September 11 will bring back that earlier era rather than produce a more consensually-based and elegantly interlaced emergency management system—one that does not superimpose overbearing command systems riddled with secrecy requirements that complicate the collaboration and public involvement essential to dealing with hazards and disasters." Further, the very hierarchical structure that concentrates information access in the DHS secretary's office paradoxically gives the DHS secretary "little real authority over the myriad of departments, agencies and offices that are involved in dealing with the terrorist threat." Sylves and Waugh agree with those who suggest that a network approach might be more effective.[77] These risks of the effects of misguided planning are compounded by the lack of broad-based input into the process of creating DHS. Because of the secrecy of the DHS planning phase, the concerns raised by the authors went unheeded, and now those concerns stand as even more real possibilities.

In July 2006, *Foreign Policy* magazine published a survey of 100 foreign policy experts who agreed that "recent reforms of the national security apparatus have done little to make Americans safer." Eighty-six percent of respondents said that the world is much or somewhat more dangerous, and 84 percent disagreed that the United States is winning the war on terror. These responses indicate a solid consensus among experts that the Bush administration's anti-terror policies are not working.[78]

Detention without Criminal Charges: "Material Witnesses" and Immigrants Out of Status
The Material Witness Statute

Former attorney general Ashcroft's aggressive detention policies in the war on terrorism relied crucially on executive secrecy for their effectiveness. The greatly expanded use of the material witness statute since September 11, 2001, employs a novel interpretation of that statute that allows the federal government to gather evidence, largely in secret, outside the bounds of any pending criminal case.[79] The statute itself contemplates confinement of material witnesses in ongoing criminal cases when there is risk of losing that witness's testimony if he or she remains at large. Though the material witness statute has always been controversial for its potential effect of confining innocent persons, its present use as an information-gathering device surpasses the earlier uses and the criticism of those uses. First, it allows the government to obtain information from detainees almost entirely without oversight. Second, the confinement of uncharged persons allows the government to investigate and then charge suspects held in custody post hoc, thus using "material witness" as "a temporary moniker to identify an individual who will soon bear the status of defendant."[80] Shielded from scrutiny by the material witness statute, it is much easier for the government to detain individuals first and search for evidence against them second—in other words, to proceed in a manner that is exactly the reverse of a normal criminal prosecution in our legal system.

In *United States v. Awadallah,* U.S. District Judge Shira Scheindlin exposed the flawed legal reasoning underlying the government's interpretation of the material witness statute in the terror investigation context. Pointing to the statute's repeated references to an ongoing criminal case, Scheindlin ruled that material witnesses could only be detained in connection with an identified, indicted defendant in a specific and ongoing investigation—and even then, such detention is strictly limited by the statute itself. In the absence of a pending criminal case, the government cannot justify holding a person as a potential witness. To interpret the detention provision of the material witness statute otherwise, she wrote, requires one to ignore the statute's plain meaning and clear structure.[81] The Second Circuit reversed Scheindlin's ruling, however, emphasizing that there was, in fact, a grand jury proceeding involved and ruling that a grand jury proceeding is a "proceeding" within the meaning of section 3144. Thus, while the Second Circuit overturned the lower court ruling, it did so on grounds applicable to grand jury proceedings—emphasizing, in fact, that "the District court noted (and we agree) that it would be improper for the government to use 3144 for other ends, such as the detention of persons suspected of criminal activity for which probable cause has not yet been established."[82] The court, then, did not approve the practice of material witness detention where no grand jury has been convened—it merely interpreted "proceeding" to include grand juries.

The policy arguments against material witness detention are familiar: it effectively treats witnesses as criminals; it potentially permits detention of dissidents who could not otherwise be validly confined by the government; it turns the constitutional presumption of innocence on its head. It is easy to imagine how the procedure could lead to injustice in particular cases. It is unnecessary, however, to construct a hypothetical "worst case" of misuse of the procedure, because such a case actually occurred. Abdallah Hijazy was staying in a hotel near the World Trade Center on September 10, 2001.[83] When officials evacuated and searched the hotel, a passport and a copy of the Koran were found in Hijazy's room. Unfortunately for Hijazy, a hotel security guard claimed, falsely, that he had found radio signaling equipment in Hijazy's room. Hijazy initially denied possessing the radio equipment but later confessed (falsely) to having it—only after a long interrogation and threats against his family, Hijazy claims. He says that the agents threatened to harm him and his family.[84] He was held in the highest security, moved around to different facilities, and repeatedly strip-searched. He stayed in a cell measuring ten feet by ten feet. He was then charged with making a false statement to federal authorities. Only after an airline pilot claimed the radio equipment as his own work gear, following an admission by the motel security guard that he lied in attributing ownership to Hijazy, did the authorities finally release Hijazy. He sought, unsuccessfully, to have criminal contempt sanctions imposed on the federal officials responsible for his month-long detention. When he was released, the authorities simply turned him loose on the street.[85] Although Hijazy claimed that the government knowingly submitted false affidavits to the court in his case, the court was unwilling to consider contempt sanctions.

The lessons of this case are disturbing. Here was a man who fell under suspicion initially for his alien status and his religious practice. Officials detained him without legal justification outside of any accepted criminal procedure. Even if the government sought to justify his confinement under the material witness statute, it could not successfully do so because there was no pending case in which he could be a witness and, moreover, no specific facts he could be expected to know. A witness can seek relief from material witness detention by filing a petition to the presiding judge (there was, of course, no presiding judge here because there was no case over which to preside), but the government denied Hijazy access to a lawyer, so he could not avail himself of that procedure either.[86] In addition, a deposition can be secured to preserve witness testimony, and the deposition can substitute for the confined witness. That no one suggested deposition as an option here is a further indication of the thin legal justification for detention: a deposition would have been pointless here because there was no set of facts on which the witness could have been deposed.

Thus, the material witness claim was clearly a pretext for the government's desire to round up and detain foreigners perceived to be Arabic or Middle Eastern. And so they did: 1,169 men were detained during a special registration of noncitizens between 2002 and 2003, and 170 remained in jail without further proceedings.[87] In another case, a New York police cadet of Pakistani descent was sought as a terror suspect—apparently only because he was a Pakistani who disappeared after 9/11. It was later determined that he had died trying to save people at the World Trade Center.[88] It appears that the administration places Muslim or Arabic persons under suspicion before looking for solid reasons or evidence that would justify such suspicion. The material witness law facilitates that process. The material witness statute has been an efficient, if improper, means to large-scale detention. And precisely because there is no specific criminal proceeding to reference in any of the detention cases—as there normally should be when the material witness statute is invoked—the government can proceed with detentions on a large scale and not trouble itself with the statutory analysis required in each case. The obvious misuse of that statute on such a scale is itself good reason to question the motives of the authorities.

One could ask whether the policy's architects sincerely believed that it was the best way to fight terrorism or whether they sought merely to create the appearance of vigorous prosecutorial activity in order to reassure a frightened public. In a sense, though, it does not matter how that question is answered, because the import is the same. In a time of national crisis, a policy that diminishes clearly settled constitutional rights and drastically alters the relationships among actors in criminal cases works efficiently precisely because it operates in secret. The efficiency of that practice is closely tied to its secrecy: because the government did not have to explain its actions in each of the many material witness detentions, it was far easier to carry them out. As for secret evidence–based prosecutions, few have been conducted thus far.[89]

Alien Detention and Deportation

In addition to material witness detention, the federal government now detains aliens for protracted periods under its immigration authority. The Patriot Act augments the existing executive authority in immigration matters, allowing the attorney general to detain, for successive six-month periods, any alien he or she certifies as a terrorist threat.[90] Since the "terrorist threat" status is renewable, this procedure effectively creates indefinite detainee status, and it functions independently of Title IV's deportation authority vested in the attorney general. In other words, the power of the executive to order deportation on broader grounds is one aspect of increased immigration power under the Patriot Act, but the power to detain indefinitely is something else. It may be used in cases where deportation has been ordered, and it may be used in cases where the executive action has simply been to detain a subject based on fear of future terrorist acts.

By a strange turn of circumstances, the executive branch managed, after 9/11, to recover power in the immigration context that it had lost just a few months before 9/11. The Patriot Act vitiated the limiting effect of the *Zadvydas* case, an immigration law decision handed down by the Supreme Court in June 2001. A narrow majority ruled in *Zadvydas* that indefinite detention of an alien in deportation status raised serious constitutional questions. The petitioner in that case had not found a country willing to accept him after deportation, and as a result he faced indefinite, perhaps permanent, detention. Attorney General Ashcroft contended that he was statutorily authorized to determine that an alien could be detained indefinitely. The Court disagreed, however, and concluded that the only way to save the statutory scheme from running afoul of the Constitution was to read into it a "reasonable" detention period of six months.[91]

The Court noted, however, that there were perhaps circumstances under which continued detention might be justifiable, and the Court mentioned allegations of terrorist activity as one such circumstance. The Bush administration (specifically, Attorney General Ashcroft) responded by ordering investigation of possible criminal charges against detainees: that approach would provide an alternative ground for continued detention. Moreover, after 9/11, the INS published rules expressly addressing the terrorism case and authorizing indefinite detention, as per the "special circumstances" dicta of *Zadvydas*, in cases where terrorism was an issue. The INS introduced the interim rules with the following statement: "It is the Attorney General who is best situated to assess the due process interests of any particular alien with respect to the matter at issue, to weigh those interests against the national security and public safety concerns presented in the case, to assess the nature and the quality of the information that triggered those concerns and to provide procedures that honor those competing interests."[92]

T. Alexander Aleinikoff worries that using "a balancing test to evaluate the constitutionality of preventive detention is likely to tip unduly in favor of the government." But even beyond the substantive legal standard to be employed, the INS makes it clear that the executive seeks to limit, or remove, judicial oversight in preventive detention matters: "The State Department is the appropriate agency to assess the foreign policy implications of the release of a particular alien. The judiciary is not well positioned to shoulder primary responsibility for determining the likelihood and importance of such diplomatic repercussions."[93] This statement articulates a view of the separation of powers in which the authority of the judiciary is relegated to cases without significant repercussions. Since the establishment of judicial review in *Marbury v. Madison* two centuries ago, the American political system has functioned in accordance with Chief Justice Marshall's statement that "it is the duty and province of the Court to say what the law is."[94] Clearly, it would make little sense to say that the scope of a dispute or of its potential repercussions should limit the ability of a court to resolve it. Neither our judicial history nor the rules for petitioning the Supreme Court for review supports the conception of the role of the courts in our governmental system upon which the INS statements seem to be based. At the very least, a greater showing need be made by any governmental entity seeking to restructure the balance of powers in such a fundamental and unprecedented way. Moreover, it is useful to recall the words of Kenneth Culp Davis in *Discretionary Justice,* cited above: absolute administrative discretion must be managed carefully to prevent its abuse. Davis argues for the availability of fair adjudicatory fora at the trial and appellate levels, and he advocates rulemaking to confer publicity and consistency on the agency head's discretionary decisions. The absence of both of these checks on administrative power sharply ensures its abuse.[95]

Some of the thousands of immigrant detainees taken into federal custody after 9/11 were seized pursuant to terror investigations and designated as material witnesses—thus placing them doubly in legal limbo: as noncitizens and as persons detained without charges. Immigration authorities detained others, though, after requiring them to appear for registration at government offices. In December 2002, immigration authorities required non-immigrant alien men between the ages of eighteen and forty from Iran, Iraq, Sudan, Syria, and Libya to report to INS offices for registration with immigration authorities. Many of those who complied were reportedly held for days in harsh conditions of confinement while the INS processed them through interviews. In January 2003, authorities repeated the procedure for men from thirteen other countries.[96]

Several startling facts emerged regarding the alien registration program. The detainees were handcuffed and shackled for the duration of their confinement, which in one case lasted five days. A computer technician and a biomedical researcher, both longtime U.S. residents, were held for days and were moved from facility to facility with little sleep. One of them reported that although he would have been "happy to talk to the FBI" to help their anti-terror investigation, his interview was "perfunctory," and the interviewer asked no questions that could help to determine the identity or location of terrorists in the United States. To make matters worse, the Arabic announcement on the INS website requiring registration of certain non-immigrants listed the wrong date for them to appear for registration.[97] These facts suggest an ill-planned and perhaps improperly motivated alien registration program whose own design prevented it from being effective. The country lists did not conform to terror risks, and the interviews carried out did not address terror risks. In short, it is clear that the aliens who sought to comply were treated harshly and subjected to extended deprivations of liberty to no clear purpose.

In response to criticisms of the program, Chris Kobach, counsel to the attorney general, retorted that all those detained had broken the law (by overstaying their visas) and that therefore all were legally blameworthy. This is true only in a technical sense. For example, one such "illegal" resident was a scholar recruited and hired by the Brookings Institution; he was arrested and detained until high-level government complaints secured his release.[98] His violation: he came to the United States to work at Brookings and was waiting for his residency petition to go through based on his marriage to a U.S. citizen. Similarly, officials detained a non-immigrant named Al-Maqtari for being out of status even though he was in the United States petitioning for permanent residency based on his wife's citizenship.[99] He was detained even after the government could find no evidence with which to charge him. Instead, federal authorities invoked the mosaic theory to justify Maqtari's continued detention.[100] As we have already seen in chapter 3, the mosaic theory is a troubling legal doctrine developed in state secrecy cases to justify withholding even material that is clearly non-secret. In the detention context, however, it raised the even more troubling concern that an alien might be held in long-term detention even without relevant and material evidence because under the mosaic theory, one piece of irrelevant information could lead one anywhere, thus justifying continued detention.

Moreover, the administration's comment to the effect that all those affected by its special registration program are breaking the law anyway—in effect, they deserve whatever they get—is an overly simplistic policy justification. The two cases mentioned above involve men who were in the process of adjusting status as a result of marriage. They had a clear and reasonable expectation of status adjustment. In fact, for one of the men, it was so clearly wrong for the authorities to arrest him that a few powerful individuals felt justified in pressuring the authorities for his release. In addition, people frequently try to change status while already in the country. To criminalize anyone who is out of status even temporarily is to ignore the everyday realities of immigration law and immigrant life here in the United States.

Scholars note historical precedents for the disparate treatment of aliens, as compared to U.S. citizens, in times of war.[101] Surveying that history from a different perspective, William Rehnquist notes the treatment of Japanese-Americans (two-thirds of whom were U.S. citizens) during World War II and concludes that the treatment of aliens may have been justified but that the restrictions on citizens are harder to justify.[102] Though their evaluations of the practices differ, commentators confirm that more restrictive measures have been applied to noncitizens in times of war. In the alienage-related provisions of the anti-terror laws summarized above, once again we see an ideological divide between citizens on the one hand and aliens on the other. Cole warns that implementation of restrictive and unpopular measures against aliens is often a prelude to their implementation against citizens: the way is made smooth, so to speak, by the less objectionable application of the policy against noncitizens; when it is broadened for use against citizens, it is more familiar, less drastic in appearance, and therefore less objectionable. He cites the Enemy Alien Act of 1798 (permitting executive detention or deportation of "enemy aliens"), the Japanese-American internment policy of World War II, and the "Alien Radical" techniques of J. Edgar Hoover (which were applied decades later by Joseph McCarthy against citizens as well) as examples of policies applied to noncitizens first and citizens afterwards.[103]

Perhaps the starkest example of this "first aliens, then citizens" approach to curtailing civil liberties can be seen in the Alien and Sedition Acts of 1798. In the same congressional term, these two laws were passed: the Alien Act first and then the Sedition Act. The former prohibited certain dissenting behavior by aliens and paved the way for the latter, expanding the prohibition and punishment to cover citizens as well.[104] These examples make it clear that citizens and noncitizens alike have an interest in resisting and protesting the measures targeting noncitizens, because eventually everyone may be subject to the measures being used initially only against noncitizens.

Secret Legal Proceedings: The Proposed Use of Military Tribunals

On November 13, 2001, President Bush issued an executive order (actually a military order) declaring that noncitizens with ties to Al-Qaeda would be tried by military tribunals rather than U.S. civilian courts.[105] Not only Al-Qaeda members but also any non-U.S. citizen who aids or harbors a terrorist or terrorist group would be subject to the provisions of the order. A military commission would serve as judge and jury in those proceedings, and a two-thirds vote for conviction would be sufficient to convict. The secretary of defense would render a final decision on the record, and no appeal outside the Department of Defense would be available.

David Cole's warning regarding retrograde civil liberties policies that begin with aliens and expand to citizens is relevant here. Basic due process rights are to be stripped from suspects who lack U.S. citizenship, but there is no reason in principle to suppose that greater security against terror attacks is to be gained by prosecuting only noncitizens in this manner. In fact, as Cole notes, we have used military tribunals to try U.S. citizens before.[106] If, as the president suggests in his November 13 order, national security requires the use of military detention and military trials for suspected terrorists, why would those procedures not be equally necessary for U.S. citizen terrorists? The citizenship distinction is a political, rather than a logical, one. Thus, one of two conclusions is possible: (1) the administration adopted this rule with motives other than effective anti-terror policy in mind; or (2) the administration is indeed guided only by effectiveness in crafting its anti-terror policy, so it must expand the rule at some future point to cover citizens as well as aliens.

Two cases involving administration detention and trial practices worked their way up to the Supreme Court. *Hamdi v. Rumsfeld* concerned detention without trial, and *Hamdan v. Rumsfeld* addressed the legality of military tribunals. Both are important tests of executive power.

The U.S. Circuit Court of Appeals for the District of Columbia ruled in favor of the administration's scaled-down civil liberties policies vis-à-vis suspected terrorist detainees. Reviewing claims by families of detainees at Guantanamo Bay that the detainment is illegal, the court ruled that because of the detainees' alien status and because they are not within the United States, they are not entitled to the constitutional protections of due process of law, defense counsel, or a speedy trial. Those constitutional provisions would normally preclude the government from holding prisoners without charges and without access to counsel, but there is precedent for treating enemy aliens differently, dating back to World War II.[107]

In *Hamdi*, the Supreme Court modified the D.C. Circuit's ruling with a 5–4 decision that essentially split the difference: the Court upheld the president's power to detain "enemy combatants" without criminal charges (over an unusual pro–civil liberties dissent by Justice Scalia), but the Court required a hearing, with counsel, in which a detainee could challenge his or her "enemy combatant" status. Thus, the power of the executive to circumvent normal criminal processes and safeguards in "enemy combatant" cases was upheld, but some measure of due process was required to validate the "enemy combatant" status. Of course, it is crucial to remember that Yaser Esam Hamdi is a U.S. citizen and that his citizen status was significant to the ruling. Justice O'Connor's opinion emphasized that the "state of war is not a blank check for the President when it comes to

the rights of the Nation's citizens." Further, the opinion drew on earlier jurisprudence to reject "a heavily circumscribed role for the courts" in cases involving civil
liberties during wartime.[108] So far, however, the government has generally managed to keep the plight of the detainees largely out of public awareness; the
deployment of secrecy has worked well to minimize public complaint.

In the fall of 2004, the Bush administration received another apparent judicial
setback. The D.C. District Court ruled that a detainee seized by the United States
in Afghanistan could not be tried by a military tribunal as envisioned in Bush's
executive order because he had not been judicially determined ineligible for
protections under the Geneva Conventions. The court rejected the administration's claim that Article II powers—that is, powers belonging to the commander-
in-chief—relieved the executive from the requirement of obtaining a judicial determination of the prisoner's status.[109] However, in July 2005 the D.C. Circuit
reversed, holding that a military tribunal was, in fact, competent not only to try
Hamdan but also to determine his pre-trial status. Thus, the military tribunal,
with its compressed set of procedural rights, was the entity permitted to determine whether it would (and should) try him later.[110]

Remarkably, the administration also argued that Hamdan could not assert his
rights under the Geneva Conventions because that treaty does not provide a
private right of action; even more remarkably, the D.C. Circuit agreed with the
administration.[111] Here, once again, a federal appeals court struck down a district
court decision and invalidated that decision's pronouncements regarding individual rights and limits to executive power. In *Hamdan* there was an additional
ruling that would bear heavily on future cases: the inapplicability of the Geneva
Conventions to military commission proceedings—and, by extension, to all other
individual judicial proceedings. Since the court makes it plain that the president
is, in its view, entitled to "great weight" for his "construction and application" of
treaty provisions, it is difficult to see how any defendant or habeas petitioner
could make out an argument claiming protection of the Geneva Conventions: the
president's contrary interpretation would be controlling.[112]

Louis Fisher has pointed out that "by 2001, the issue of military tribunals
seemed quaint if not antiquated."[113] Since the *Quirin* case in 1942, there had been
some limiting decisions but little public attention to the issue. Thus, when *Hamdan* reached the Supreme Court in 2006, the Court was poised to write a decisive
chapter in the history of American military tribunals. In a carefully reasoned five
to three decision authored by Justice John Paul Stevens (newly installed Chief
Justice John Roberts did not participate, having signed the decision below prior to
joining the Court), the Court ruled as follows:

— They had jurisdiction over Hamdan's habeas corpus action, even though the 2005 Detainee Treatment Act (DTA) limits federal jurisdiction in certain detainee cases;

— Hamdan was charged only with conspiracy, which could not properly be tried by a military commission, for it is not an offense under the law of war (four-justice plurality only);

— The Geneva Conventions applied (via the Uniform Code of Military Justice and the law of war) and were violated in Hamdan's case; and

— The specific structure and procedure of the military commission to be used to try Hamdan was illegal under the UCMJ.[114]

Here, the Supreme Court decisively limited the executive's war powers. The proposed military commission was compared with statutory standards prescribed by the UCMJ, and it was found wanting. Thus, the limits set earlier by Congress were affirmed by the Court, even while Congress itself had sought to facilitate executive discretion in the "war on terror" by passing the DTA. Moreover, the protections of the Geneva Conventions were restored, albeit in a circuitous way: the UCMJ incorporates the law of war, and the law of war incorporates the Geneva Conventions.

On the one hand, the scope of the *Hamdan* ruling is limited: it concerns one category of detainee, that is, those whose cases were pending when the DTA was passed—the DTA itself remains intact. On the other hand, though, this case is the most important decision on military tribunals since 1942, and it establishes important limitations on the executive's treatment of unpopular individuals. Further, the status of military tribunals is related to secrecy. It almost goes without saying that military tribunals preserve greater secrecy than Article 3 courts: they can even keep evidence secret, as Hamdan himself complained.[115] Secrecy can be misused, as Fisher notes regarding the *Quirin* case. In *Quirin*, "the need for secrecy was driven by two reasons: to conceal the fact that Dasch had turned himself (and the others) in, and to mete out the death penalty."[116] In short, the *Hamdan* decision stands as an important rebuke to executive secrecy.

The preceding discussion reviews the main points of the anti-terror legislation related to secrecy. They share a common, secrecy-related theme: the executive gets more ability to obtain information from a wide range of sources, and the public is denied access to the same information. As the executive gains power, the people lose power. Moreover, the executive can execute more effectively when it need not justify and report on its every act. We have pointed out the harms of the government's secrecy policy: lack of accountability, long-term effects on the morale of government and citizens, violation of constitutional rights.

However, the main point here has been to show the ways secrecy and efficiency combine and work together, producing outcomes that serve the executive's purposes while creating constitutional violations that amount to dangerous future precedents. Much of the increased executive power generated by the post-9/11 anti-terror laws accrues to the attorney general. The attorney general controls deportation and exclusion, according to his estimation of an individual's connection to terror groups. The attorney general confines people, in both the short and the long term, as material witnesses, terrorist threats, and aliens out of status. The attorney general gathers information from law enforcement and intelligence sources under a statutory mandate of information sharing. And the attorney general continues to seek expanded executive powers that are allegedly necessary to combat terrorism effectively.

While the anti-terror effort led to consolidation of many federal agencies under DHS, that process led to no reduction of the attorney general's power—quite on the contrary. Taken together, these statutory changes have effectively created within the executive a shadow president: an extraordinary investiture of executive power in the person of the attorney general. He continues to answer to the president and to comport himself in a manner consistent with the administration's broadly stated anti-terror agenda, but as this chapter shows, he enjoys a secrecy that allows him to exert his will in the shadows of presidential power and responsibility.

CHAPTER FIVE

The President and National Security Surveillance

There are citizens of the United States, I blush to admit, born under other flags but welcomed under our generous naturalization laws to the full freedom and opportunity of America, who have poured the poison of disloyalty into the very arteries of our national life . . . Such creatures of passion, disloyalty, and anarchy must be crushed out.

—*Woodrow Wilson, State of the Union Address, 1915*

Writs of assistance and general warrants are but puny instruments of tyranny and oppression compared with wire tapping.

—*Louis D. Brandeis*

Since 1940, presidents have explicitly asserted an inherent presidential power to conduct warrantless searches of foreigners and U.S. citizens where "national security" matters are implicated. Each president, for various reasons, pressed this power to the limit of constitutional credulity until, finally, the excesses of the Nixon administration brought political, legislative, and judicial opprobrium onto the office of the president. Some commentators, in gleeful terms, considered the events that befell President Nixon as good for the "institution" of the presidency. Arthur Schlesinger crowed that Watergate was "the best thing" to happen to diminish presidential power; as Theodore Lowi portrayed Schlesinger's view, it "may have shut the evil genie up in the bottle again for as much as fifty years."[1]

The genie of presidential temptation, though, was not so easily contained, and barely ten years after Nixon's fall, Lowi could get away with writing that "the Watergate case is confirmation of and consistent with the nature of the modern presidency, not an aberrant episode," and that "in every respect other than the extent of illegal activities, there is a Watergate of some kind everyday in the life of a president."[2] The actions of Nixon and his aides brought the presidency to its knees, but statutory and administrative changes since Nixon have, paradoxically, done much to relieve presidents of personal responsibility for questionable surveillance activities. Actions that would have drawn cries of presidential excess in 1968 now are institutionalized and legitimated by congressional transfers of power to the executive branch originally designed to limit presidential authority. "Congress," according to Lowi, "delegates broadly and then tries to take it back in bits and pieces," a process Lowi calls "legiscide."[3] The "daily Watergates" have been folded into the institutionalized presidency and have been placed at arm's length from presidential discretion, but their intrusiveness and questionable constitutionality nonetheless remain. Nowhere is this more true than in national security surveillance.

Lyn Ragsdale and John Theis point out that study of the presidency is most often the "individual-president approach" and that "scholars often study the 'big' decisions of presidents: Truman drops the bomb; Kennedy confronts the Soviets in Cuba; Reagan cuts the budget." This approach highlights the drama of the presidency but "preempts" both "full consideration of systematic temporal change in the office" and "systematic similarities across presidents." Ragsdale and Theis, applying the indicators of "autonomy, adaptability, complexity, and coherence" that were first proposed by Samuel Huntington, conclude that the presidency first emerged as an *institution* sometime in the late 1970s.[4] Congress aided in this institutionalization by expanding executive authority in various areas and by creating institutional processes for the exercise of that authority.

One of these grants of authority is the Foreign Intelligence Surveillance Act; a law originally designed to reduce presidential power wound up institutionalizing the very activity it sought to prevent.[5] FISA governs the issuance of warrants to federal agents to engage in electronic surveillance and physical searches of people believed to be working on behalf of foreign governments or organizations to the detriment of United States national security. It is also an effort to institutionalize a facet of claimed presidential prerogative, thus transforming that prerogative into a power subject to a system of rules and legislative and judicial oversight. Presidents frequently claim the "inherent" authority to engage in warrantless national security surveillance. But pre-FISA presidents had no legislative support in this matter, and for several decades in the middle of the last century, both legislative authority and case law mitigated against claims of inherent presidential authority to undertake "national security" searches and surveillance. Such activities were taken by presidents outside of recognized avenues of executive action and often depended on "off the books" eavesdropping initiated by personnel at the direction of J. Edgar Hoover on the authority of various attorneys general.

Beginning in the 1970s, though, the federal judiciary began to recognize a "national security" exception to the Fourth Amendment and upheld the legality of presidentially ordered warrantless electronic surveillance in a number of cases. With important exceptions, courts facing the issue of inherent presidential power to conduct warrantless surveillance sided with the president.[6] Indeed, Antonin Scalia, at the time a D.C. Circuit Court of Appeals judge, wrote the opinion in *Smith v. Nixon* holding that what appeared to be a patently unconstitutional wiretap of a journalist's home telephone authorized by Richard Nixon was within the president's power at the time.[7] The national security exception to the Fourth Amendment was proving to be rather deep and powerful, and in the wake of Nixon's misdeeds Congress searched for a means to place limits on what appeared to be uncontrolled discretionary power by presidents to surveil citizens electronically. FISA is the result of this search, though it may be that the harness of FISA is more dangerous to the Fourth Amendment and the civil liberties of citizens than the discretionary power of presidents in pre-FISA times. The institutionalization of the surveillance process and the attendant changes made to FISA in the wake of the attacks of September 11 have resulted in levels of surveillance of U.S. citizens that eclipse past activity.

And FISA did not prevent presidents from engaging in secret, judicially unauthorized, and constitutionally suspect surveillance. President George W. Bush, as we shall discuss, authorized warrantless surveillance of U.S. citizens outside of the FISA process, surveillance that apparently sifted through millions and perhaps billions of electronic communications.[8] Even discounting such unilateral presidential action, Congress's quest to tame presidential prerogative through FISA has subjected citizens to even greater incursions into their privacy and arguably given away a powerful means for checking presidential power. The story of FISA is one of caution, for the attempt to denude the president of power established, for practical purposes, an irretrievable grant of authority to the executive bureaucracy that now threatens to engulf the Fourth Amendment. This is a story of legiscide in its most consequential form, since the result is arguably that the Fourth Amendment and privacy protections of citizens have been greatly diminished, if not profoundly undermined.

Unfortunately, this chapter is an explanation and clarification of exactly how the barn door closed after the horses left; how Congress, contrary to its intentions, managed to increase executive power, undermine the Fourth Amendment, and diminish oversight of federal electronic surveillance. The path from back-alley presidentially sanctioned surveillance to the institutionalized procedures of FISA is complicated, but it reveals an interesting odyssey of executive branch power.

From *Olmstead* to FISA

In *Olmstead v. United States,* the Supreme Court opened the door to presidentially ordered wiretapping by holding that interception of telephonic communications, absent a physical trespass on a target's property, was not a search under the Fourth Amendment. Chief Justice Taft, writing for the Court, held that "the evidence was secured by use of the sense of hearing and that only. . . . The language of the [Fourth] Amendment cannot be extended and expanded to include telephone wires reaching to the whole world." The case, though, is best remembered for the scathing and eloquent dissent of Justice Louis D. Brandeis, who noted that the Framers "recognized the significance of man's spiritual nature, of his feelings and of his intellect. . . [and] [t]hey conferred, as against the Government, the right to be let alone—the most comprehensive of rights and the right most valued by civilized men."[9]

Despite Brandeis's complaints and Justice Oliver Wendell Holmes Jr.'s dissent declaring wiretapping a "dirty business," this decision gave government agents and law enforcement a clear path to engage in widespread surveillance of citizens for both legitimate and unsavory motives alike.[10] In 1931, Attorney General William Mitchell concluded that while the "dirty business" might be unethical, it was necessary for national security, and he authorized wiretaps in a number of cases.[11] A substantial industry, along with a class of professional wiretappers, grew up in the wake of the *Olmstead* decision, a class described by a chairman of the Federal Communications Commission as "the least admirable of the groups of creatures that qualify for membership in the human race."[12]

In the wake of public upset with wiretaps, Congress, on several occasions, introduced legislation to curb these transgressions but failed to pass any of the measures.[13] Then Congress enacted the Federal Communications Act of 1934, in which section 605 states that "no person receiving . . . [or] transmitting . . . any interstate or foreign communication by wire or radio shall divulge or publish the existence, contents, substance, purport, effect, or meaning thereof, except through authorized channels of transmission or reception."[14] Section 605 prescribes civil and criminal penalties for wilful violation of its provisions, but there is no evidence in the legislative record that Congress meant for the act to criminalize wiretapping by government officials or even by private investigators and citizens. Despite this, section 605 came to be known as the "federal wiretap law," a "good example of abnormal birth," since it apparently took on its importance with no intent from Congress.[15] This abnormal birth took place in *Nardone v. United States,* where the Supreme Court interpreted section 605 as making wiretapping illegal.[16]

With only two members from the *Olmstead* court remaining, Justice Owen Roberts paid little heed to government arguments, narrowing the question to the bloodless level of whether or not the wording in section 605, that "no person" shall divulge intercepted communications to "any person," contemplated federal law enforcement agents and courts. Roberts said that the plain meaning of the language allowed no exception. The Court held that section 605 prohibited wiretaps by federal agents, and the provision against divulging or publishing intercepted material prohibited the use of wiretap evidence in court. Justice Roberts found that "Congress may have thought it less important that some offenders should go unwhipped of justice than that officers should resort to methods deemed inconsistent with ethical standards and destructive of personal liberty."[17]

The case came back to the Court two years later, when Justice Felix Frankfurter conjured his memorable "fruit of the poisonous tree" metaphor to prevent use of derivative information and evidence from illegally intercepted communications as evidence in federal criminal cases. In the intervening years between the *Nardone* cases, the government had developed a strategy that while it may not be able to use evidence intercepted in violation of section 605, it could use the intercepted information for any derivative purposes, such as investigation leading to additional evidence. Justice Frankfurter dismissed this approach, finding that such a reading "would largely stultify the policy which compelled [the] decision" in the first *Nardone* case.[18]

In bolstering a mantle of dignity for the first *Nardone* case, Justice Frankfurter declared, "That decision was not the product of a merely meticulous reading of technical language [but] the translation into practicality of broad considerations of morality and public well-being."[19] But the Court decided that "morality and public well-being" did not extend to cases of warrantless interception of conversations through microphones. In the 1942 case *Goldman v. United States,* the Court found that the use of microphones to intercept conversations, when no trespass of property is involved, is not prohibited by the Fourth Amendment.[20] The *Goldman* Court also refused to extend section 605 to cover the microphone interception of a person speaking into a telephone where there is no tap on the phone itself; it also explicitly declined an invitation to overrule *Olmstead.*

The decisions in the *Nardone* cases presented the president and federal law enforcement officials with a dilemma; on the one hand they had no intention of dispensing with wiretaps, but on the other hand they now had no legal justification for their use and faced possible legal sanctions for warrantless taps. As Alan Westin noted, police and other law enforcement agents realized that section 605 was "still law, yet believing that wire tapping is a vital part of their investigatory work [they drew] a veil of concealment over their activities."[21] Officials at the White House and at the Department of Justice (DOJ) reformulated their theory, first developed between the two *Nardone* cases, that section 605 did not criminalize the fact of interception but only the act of "divulging" the contents intercepted.

On February 21, 1941, President Franklin Roosevelt wrote to a member of Congress that "I have no compunction in saying that wire tapping should be used against those persons, not citizens of the United States, and those few citizens who are traitors to their country, who today are engaged in espionage or sabotage against the United States." The focus on the use of wiretapping in espionage matters and for intelligence purposes only meant that "a new statute was not necessary if the purpose of wiretapping was to gather intelligence that would not be used in court."[22] In a precursor of what would become known as "the wall," as we will discuss in more detail, Roosevelt justified warrantless surveillance as an intelligence function rather than a law enforcement function, claiming it to be an inherent power under the president's foreign affairs duties. But such a reading certainly skirts some troublesome issues, such as why distribution of wiretap material within government channels is not a "divulgence" under section 605.

Although there were numerous efforts throughout the years to amend the Communications Act, all of them failed, so an "understanding" of sorts settled into being. The government kept its wiretapping secret and so arguably did not run afoul of section 605, but the tradeoff was that citizens were subjected to surveillance at the whim of the FBI, the attorney general, and the president. There matters stood, at least legislatively, until 1968.

Inherent Presidential Power and the Fourth Amendment

On May 21, 1940, President Roosevelt, of course fully aware of the *Nardone* cases, sent a confidential memorandum to Attorney General Robert Jackson authorizing the use of warrantless wiretaps in "grave matters involving the defense of the nation." But he "requested" that Jackson "limit these investigations so conducted to a minimum and to limit them insofar as possible to aliens."[23] Earlier that month, the House of Representatives had passed a joint resolution to the effect that national security wiretaps were both constitutional and allowed under the Communications Act, but the resolution did not pass in the Senate, thereby precipitating Roosevelt's memorandum to Jackson.[24] Roosevelt observed that the Constitution could not reasonably be read to compel the president to wait until "after sabotage, assassinations and 'fifth column' activities are completed" to come to the defense of the nation and its citizens.[25] Jackson was ambivalent about the use of wiretaps without judicial warrant, and he recognized that much immersion in such a world could spell political disaster. In transmitting the president's desires to J. Edgar Hoover, director of the FBI, Jackson perhaps saw that distinguishing enemies of the New Deal from enemies of the state might be a difficult process.

It was inescapable that Jackson, as attorney general, would need to approve such surveillance, both in support of the inherent presidential powers theory and because J. Edgar Hoover would never leave himself so exposed as to be without authorization to engage in such activity. Though Jackson needed to authorize such taps, he did not want any evidence of authorization contained in attorney general records. Accordingly, as Athan Theoharis explains, "Jackson's decision not to maintain written records of approved wiretaps or require a written justification whenever the FBI director sought approval to wiretap effectively negated the intended restrictions of Roosevelt's directive: That such uses be exceptional and limited to aliens and that the attorney general authorize each wiretap after first assessing each request of the FBI director." Further, "Attorney General Jackson's decision not to maintain records of authorized taps emboldened FBI officials," and such arrangements served a multitude of needs for all of the parties involved. The notorious consequence of Jackson's decision was Hoover's reign of wiretaps, where thousands of Americans were surveilled at Hoover's whim.[26]

The preference of Hoover, one amenable to Jackson, was that Jackson approve classes of cases where the FBI had authority to engage in warrantless surveillance. Francis Biddle, the attorney general who succeeded Jackson, recalled that Jackson "didn't like it [wiretapping], and, not liking it, turned it over to Edgar Hoover without himself passing on each case."[27] Hoover justified circumventing attorney general approval of individual cases, unsurprisingly, by invoking a need for secrecy. On Hoover's view, as expressed in a 1941 communication with Jackson, neither U.S. attorneys nor federal judges were to be trusted with wiretap information:

> Wire-tapping, in my estimation, should only be used in cases of kidnapping, extortion, espionage and sabotage. It is, therefore, imperative that the use of it not be known outside of a very limited circle if the best results are to be obtained. We are dealing with realities in this matter, and we must recognize that many times United

States Attorneys' offices are not as close-mouthed as they should be and that matters handled therein do become known to certain favored representatives of the press, with the result that items appear in columns that are many times alarmingly correct. Likewise, we know that there are certain Federal Judges who are not as close-mouthed as they should be.[28]

With a lessened possibility of records for wiretap authorizations falling into the hands of those outside the FBI, the potential for political disaster in engaging in warrantless surveillance decreased proportionately. Hoover had his authorization but could rest assured that the paper trail was unavailable to anyone outside of the FBI. Missteps and abuse were common. Revelations of the illegal bugging of labor leader Harry Bridges caused discomfort for Attorney General Francis Biddle and Hoover in 1941, leading to an occasion for Roosevelt to exclaim to Hoover, "By God, Edgar, that's the first time you've been caught with your pants down!"[29] And an ex-FBI agent disclosed in the mid 1960s that he and his team had bugged the First Lady, Eleanor Roosevelt during World War II.[30]

President Harry Truman also had little trouble authorizing wiretaps. In a July 17, 1946, memorandum to Truman, Attorney General Tom Clark apprised Truman of the 1940 Roosevelt order and advised him to expand the use of wire-tapping beyond that authorized by Roosevelt. He quoted the Roosevelt memo but pointedly neglected to include the language by Roosevelt directing the attorney general to limit surveillance to aliens as much as possible. Clark thought it desirable to maintain national security surveillance considering the "present troubled period in international affairs" and "subversive activity here at home" but then went well beyond Roosevelt's position and simply asked the president to ignore Supreme Court jurisprudence. He argued that "the country is threatened by a very substantial increase in crime," and while one must remain reluctant to use electronic surveillance for domestic purposes, "it seems . . . imperative to use [it] in cases vitally affecting the domestic security, or where human life is in jeopardy." Truman responded with the terse statement, "I concur."[31] The moment of this memorandum seems to have escaped most commentators, but to Gordon Silverstein, Truman's "rhetoric of executive prerogative moved away from the temporary, emergency claims . . . to a new constitutional rhetoric built on the broad mandate of Article II."[32]

This expanded "rhetoric of executive prerogative" coincides with the rise of the "classified president" discussed in chapter 2, presenting a remarkable profile of ambition to power. Truman's agreement with Clark's memo is a claim to engage in warrantless surveillance of U.S. citizens for reasons of mere "domestic security" apparently encompassing ordinary crimes. This is an understanding of presidential power that would make the Fourth Amendment useless with respect to surveillance, and, as table 5.1 shows, the Truman administration rivaled Roosevelt's wartime administration for pre-FISA presidentially authorized warrantless surveillance.

Both Presidents Dwight Eisenhower and John F. Kennedy adhered to the Roosevelt and Truman practices, with Attorney General Brownell, under Eisenhower, unsuccessfully seeking congressional authorization for presidentially ordered warrantless surveillance.[33] Attorney General Robert Kennedy, in the Kennedy administration, left surveillance practices intact but reiterated to Director Hoover that attorney general authorization is required before undertaking warrantless surveillance. This reflects well-known distrust between Hoover and Attorney General Kennedy and appears to mark the end of the studied ignorance of FBI surveillance activity by successive attorneys general, starting with Jackson in the Roosevelt administration.

President Lyndon Johnson couched authorization of electronic surveillance in more careful terms than those found in the Clark memorandum, but he continued various operations. Johnson claimed that he was "strongly opposed to the interception of telephone conversations as a general investigative technique . . . except in connection with investigations related to the national security."[34] Even Ramsey Clark, attorney general during Johnson's last two years as president and a fierce opponent of government wiretapping, conceded that electronic surveillance might be necessary in national security cases, but he refused to allow such intercepts to "be available for investigative or litigative purposes."[35] This self-imposed restraint lasted only until Nixon's election.

Despite the chilly legal climate, during the period between the *Nardone* cases and *United States v. United States District Court* (also called *Keith*), which held warrantless domestic surveillance authorized by presidents to be unconstitutional, presidents and their attorneys general authorized large numbers of wiretaps and microphone surveillance.[36] Between 1940, the first year records on such activities were kept by the DOJ, and 1972, when the Supreme Court decided *Keith*, DOJ records reflect a total of 7,805 telephone wiretaps for an average of around 240 taps each year. Excluding the year 1940, when only six taps were recorded, the smallest number of taps in a year was 1941, with 67, and the high-water mark was 1945, with 519. During the same period, 2,244 instances of microphone surveillance were authorized, for an average of 68 per year. In three years—1952, 1953, and 1967—there are no recorded uses of microphones authorized by the attorney general. The most microphones operated in a single year was 198, in

TABLE 5.1
Surveillance by Presidential Administrations, from Roosevelt to Nixon

President	Total Telephone Taps	Average Telephone Taps/Year	Total Buggings	Average Buggings/Year
Roosevelt	1,630	296	603	110
Truman	2,724	363	536	71
Eisenhower	1,574	196	564	71
Kennedy	582	194	268	89
Johnson	862	172	192	38
Nixon	700	122	151	26

NOTE: Numbers are approximate because some wires overlap across administrations.

1944. Between February 1952 and May 1954, "the [Justice] Department's position was not to authorize trespassory microphone surveillance because of . . . concern over a possible violation of the Fourth Amendment." But Attorney General Herbert Brownell reversed this policy and advised J. Edgar Hoover that "considerations of internal security and the national safety are paramount and, therefore, may compel the unrestricted use of this technique in the national interest."[37]

President Richard Nixon followed the lead of Clark's memorandum to Truman and the sentiments of Brownell and purposely held national security to encompass domestic security. Even as his days in office waned, and even after the *Keith* decision, Nixon still refused to separate domestic security from foreign threats to security. A year before his resignation he proclaimed in a speech that "in internal security matters, the President has the power to authorize wiretaps without first obtaining a search warrant."[38] Although Nixon's abuses of electronic surveillance are notorious, the main reason for this is that they were exposed in the context of a pattern of additional criminal behavior.

Compared to his predecessors, Nixon's use of electronic surveillance was restrained. Nixon had the lowest yearly average of both telephone taps and buggings of any president since 1940; though he targeted people for illicit reasons, this is not much different from the behavior of previous presidents. According to the Senate Church committee investigations of the mid-1970s, presidents from Roosevelt to Nixon engaged in politically motivated surveillance: Roosevelt-authorized surveillance recorded trysts between John F. Kennedy and Inga Arvad in 1942; Truman authorized wiretaps and surveillance against a former aide to Roosevelt; the Kennedy and Johnson administrations surveilled Martin Luther King by various methods; the Kennedy administration is the only one known to have ordered warrantless bugging of a sitting member of Congress and congressional staff members.[39] Attorney General Francis Biddle even authorized wiretaps on the Los Angeles Chamber of Commerce. These examples reveal "the relative ease with which electronic bugging devices could be used against American citizens who posed no genuine 'national security' threat."[40]

In 1967, the Supreme Court reversed its holding in *Olmstead* and brought electronic surveillance under Fourth Amendment jurisprudence. In *Katz v. United States*, the Court held that Fourth Amendment warrant requirements apply to electronic surveillance of a telephone booth. But the Court explicitly declined to address the issue of a "national security exception" to the warrant clause, stating, "Whether safeguards other than prior authorization by a magistrate would satisfy the Fourth Amendment in a situation involving the national security is a question not presented by this case."[41] In response to this decision, Congress finally addressed the issue of wiretapping, passing the Omnibus Crime Control Act of 1968, which prescribed procedures for securing warrants for electronic surveillance and criminalized most warrantless eavesdropping. But Congress surprisingly included the following disclaimer in section 2511(3) of the act:

> Nothing contained in this chapter or in section 605 of the Communications Act of 1934 shall limit the constitutional power of the President to take such measures as he deems necessary to protect the Nation against actual or potential attack or other hostile acts of a foreign power, to obtain foreign intelligence information deemed essential to the security of the United States, or to protect national security information against foreign intelligence activities.[42]

This provision is a thicket of ill-advised concessions and ambiguity. It is a capitulation to the theory of presidential prerogative in the arena of national security. The most charitable reading of the provision is that it is merely a restatement of the truism that Congress cannot limit the constitutional powers of the president. But of course that is not the natural reading, and the language also tacitly assumes that constitutionally defined Article II powers are somehow self-evident, rather than delineated through conflicts with coordinate branches. It is clear that Congress can enlarge Article II powers simply by abnegating its own constitutionally plausible authority. The most unusual feature of the statute is that it seems to simply *give away* constitutional power or, at least, claims to constitutional power.

More important is how presidents interpreted the text, and, according to Gordon Silverstein, "the Nixon Administration positively saw the bill as a confirmation of what it interpreted to be a constitutional prerogative power vested in the president."[43] But it is important to see that despite the seemingly infelicitous grant of authority to the president contained in the statute, this authority is unaccompanied by institutional structures and its exercise is wholly at the risk and the discretion of the president. A president may claim to act under the inherent powers recognized by Congress in the statute, but the actions, if publicly disclosed, must be defended as a matter of *politics* by the president. As we will see, the structure created by Congress under FISA relieves presidents of this problem.

The Supreme Court would not reach the issue of warrantless domestic surveillance under color of national security until the *Keith* case. In *Keith*, the Nixon administration leveraged Congress's apparent capitulation to inherent presidential authority in section 2511(3) of Title III into a powerful argument for presidential prerogative. The defendants in the case were charged with dynamiting a CIA office in Michigan, and they moved to have the government produce electronic surveillance information and called for a hearing to determine if the evidence obtained without a warrant "tainted" the prosecution. In response, Attorney General John Mitchell submitted a sworn affidavit restating the language of section 2511(3) and asserting that he had authorized wiretaps in the case "to gather intelligence information deemed necessary to protect the nation from attempts of domestic organizations to attack and subvert the existing structure of the Government."[44]

Justice Lewis Powell, writing for the Court, presented the issue as "the delicate question of the President's power, acting through the Attorney General, to authorize electronic surveillance in internal security matters without prior judicial approval." Powell came to the rescue of Congress and the Fourth Amendment by reading section 2511(3) as "at most . . . an implicit recognition that the President does have certain powers in the specified areas" and that "so far as the use of the President's electronic surveillance power is concerned, the language [of section 2511(3)] is essentially neutral." The Court held that section 2511(3) "certainly confers no power" upon the president and that "it merely provides that the Act shall not be interpreted to limit or disturb such power as the President may have under the Constitution." This was clearly the most damaging interpretation that could be made against claims to presidential authority to engage in warrantless domestic security electronic surveillance. But the Court also found that "the instant case requires no judgment on the scope of the President's surveillance power with respect to the activities of foreign powers, within or without this country" and so refused to reach the question of a foreign national security exception to the Fourth Amendment.[45]

So in 1972, after *Keith*, the legality of electronic surveillance stood as follows: (1) warrantless electronic surveillance was unconstitutional and a crime under Title III; (2) federal judges and some state judges could authorize warrants for electronic surveillance consistent with Fourth Amendment standards through procedures prescribed in Title III; (3) the president had no inherent power to engage in warrantless electronic surveillance for reasons of domestic security;

(4) the president may or may not have inherent power to engage in electronic surveillance to gather foreign intelligence. FISA was meant to safeguard point (3) and address point (4), and there was strong congressional and public sentiment beginning in the early 1970s to place the collection of foreign intelligence under processes of law.

Attempts at Reform

After the resignation of Nixon and the national crisis over presidential prerogative created by Nixon's illegal activities and his refusal to divulge documents and tape recordings to Congress, President Ford appointed Edward H. Levi as attorney general. A lifelong academic with no government or law enforcement experience, Levi was selected to restore public confidence in the Justice Department. President Ford recognized that the times called for an outsider to run the DOJ, as there was little hope that anyone already with the department could allay the skepticism of Congress and the public.

Levi immediately adopted rules to govern domestic security investigations. Domestic security, as defined by these rules, included attempts to overthrow the federal or state governments, to interfere with foreign relations, or to "substantially" impair government policies or governmental functioning. Levi's rules described three levels of investigative authority for domestic security investigations: preliminary, limited, and full investigations. Each level of investigation established threshold requirements, with the most stringent requirements governing the opening of a full investigation. In preliminary and limited investigations, "techniques such as recruitment or placement of informants in groups, 'mail covers,' or electronic surveillance" could not be used. Only in a full investigation could government agents use electronic surveillance, and even then they were required to make application under the rigorous Title III procedure.[46] The rules generally were perceived by law enforcement as hamstringing investigators, and they contained numerous admonitions and concerns that investigators should not violate citizens' rights.

Though publicly President Ford said that "Ed Levi was one of my finest cabinet members," privately he and many high-level executive branch officials seethed over Levi's actions.[47] At the final national security meeting of Ford's administration, the animosity toward Levi was abundantly clear.[48] Secretary of State Henry Kissinger boldly asserted that "the Justice Department's role today is a threat to national security," and Secretary of Defense Donald Rumsfeld agreed with Kissinger, bemoaning DOJ's insistence on receiving intelligence information pertinent to criminal prosecutions before going forward with cases. George H. W. Bush, director of central intelligence, added that "we are being forced to give up sensitive information in order to prosecute" and wistfully recalled the days when defendants such as Julius and Ethel Rosenberg could be prosecuted without fear of disclosure of sensitive information.

Nowhere in this discussion is any concern for possible constitutional requirements or the acknowledgment that the government had only recently committed serious crimes and incursions upon civil liberties. Indeed, there is only animosity toward Attorney General Levi for his professed role of "representing the American people and taxpayers." Deputy Secretary of Defense William Clements claimed that Levi was "in effect arrogating the public prosecutor role to himself when he was supposed to be defending the [government]." National Security Adviser William Hyland and General Brent Scowcroft claimed that the Levi rules "prevented us from learning most of what the Soviets are intercepting of U.S. communications in this country."

Astonishingly, during the meeting Ford asked, "What accounts for the change in the situation at this time? Is it the law, the mood in the country?" There seems to be little recognition at the meeting of the depth of public and congressional resentment and the distrust of the executive branch caused by years of intelligence agency and presidential abuse of constitutional rights. Perhaps sensing that the Levi rules were an aberration to be swept away at the whim of an attorney general or president at some propitious time and responding to the public demand that executive branch abuses be curbed, Congress was poised to pass legislation controlling national security surveillance.[49]

Congress took the opportunity of public reaction against Nixon and the need of succeeding presidents to appear to be disposed against electronic surveillance to fashion a comprehensive statute concerning the electronic collection of foreign intelligence in the United States. Presidents Ford and Carter both "requested" legislation on the issue, but they were not quite ready to give up what they believed to be constitutionally conferred presidential power. In the political circumstances of the early 1970s there was plenty of motivation on the part of Congress to adopt legislation to limit and control national security wiretaps, but there was insufficient support to overcome what would be an almost certain presidential veto of such legislation. Efforts to enact a statute governing foreign intelligence surveillance began in 1974 and was met with a very chilly reception from President Nixon. Just four months before Nixon's resignation, at an April 1974 hearing on legislation that anticipated FISA, an assistant attorney general testified very simply: "Let me be very brief. We oppose these bills. That is it." In the remaining days of the Nixon administration and the first two years of Ford's presidency, the DOJ "consistently opposed the concept of legislation imposing judicial restraints on foreign intelligence wiretapping."[50]

But in the end there were several factors that put pressure on the presidency to compromise on the issue of national security wiretaps. First, the *Katz* and *Keith* decisions brought a sense of unease about the possibility that the Supreme Court could simply interpret the Constitution to preclude warrantless national security wiretaps. Even though the tone of *Keith* implied that warrantless foreign intelligence wiretaps might pass constitutional muster, this was far from certain. Second, the presidency was still attempting to recover from the Watergate scandal, and compromise with Congress over legislation on a claim of presidential prerogative central to Nixon's abuse of power would go far to heal wounds and restore confidence in the executive branch. But even these powerful reasons for compromise could not overcome presidential revulsion at relinquishing a perceived prerogative power. The presidency needed a nudge.

That nudge came in 1975 in the form of a decision of the U.S. Circuit Court of Appeals for the District of Columbia authored by the respected and canny judge J. Skelly Wright. In *Zweibon v. Mitchell,* the government had engaged in illegal electronic surveillance of Jewish Defense League members, and the court held that "a warrant must be obtained before a wiretap is installed on a domestic organization . . . even if the surveillance is installed under presidential directive in the name of foreign intelligence gathering for protection of the national security." And in dicta, the plurality opinion stated, "Although we believe that an analysis of the policies implicated by foreign security surveillance indicates that, absent exigent circumstances, *all warrantless electronic surveillance is unreasonable and therefore unconstitutional,* our holding need not sweep that broadly."[51] This position appeared to be at odds with rulings from other circuits finding that there is inherent presidential power to engage in warrantless foreign national security surveillance, but the importance of the D.C. Circuit presented clear problems for the executive branch.

The holding meant that in the future, at least in the D.C. Circuit, courts would probe claims of national security and foreign intelligence to make independent determinations of presidential motives in each surveillance case. This "second-guessing" of presidential motivation presented troubling issues for the presidency and no doubt would work to limit presidential discretion in ordering wiretaps. But the dictum was even more portentous, since it signaled that in the D.C. Circuit the presumption would be that *any* warrantless electronic surveillance ordered by the president is unconstitutional. The D.C. Circuit would also have jurisdiction over most, if not all, cases concerning presidentially ordered surveillance and therefore represented a real threat to presidential claims of inherent power to engage in warrantless surveillance.

This ruling lay open not only the possibility that evidence would be inadmissible at criminal trial but also that targets of electronic surveillance could maintain suit for damages against government agents and perhaps even the president. Immunities protect government officials from most money damages actions, but the embarrassment of such suits and the courts' unpredictable response to any particular action created uncertainty. Because of strong pressure and the threats represented by *Zweibon*, the Ford administration worked with Congress on a 1976 bill to place national security wiretaps under legal procedure. There was overwhelming support for the legislation in both parties, but Congress adjourned before the matter could be scheduled for a vote. Renewed efforts in the next Congress led to resurrection of the 1976 bill, and Congress enacted FISA in 1978.

The Foreign Intelligence Surveillance Act

FISA allows warrants against foreign powers, "whether or not recognized by the United States," including factions "not substantially composed of United States persons" and groups engaged in terrorism. The standard for surveillance of non-U.S. persons is lower than that for U.S. citizens, requiring only that the person's presence in the United States indicates, or that there is knowledge that the person is engaged or will engage in, "clandestine intelligence activities . . . contrary to the interests of the United States."

United States persons, those people who are either U.S. citizens or permanent resident aliens, may be subjected to FISA wiretaps if they knowingly engage in "clandestine intelligence gathering activities for or on behalf of a foreign power" that may violate "criminal statutes of the United States," engage in "sabotage or international terrorism," or enter the country "under a false or fraudulent identity for or on behalf of a foreign power." But no "United States person may be considered a foreign power or an agent of a foreign power solely upon the basis of activities protected by the first amendment to the Constitution of the United States." But applications against United States persons are reviewed at a very loose standard and may only be rejected if "the certification or certifications are . . . clearly erroneous."

FISA applications must be made by federal officers and require "approval of the Attorney General" that the application meets the statutory requirements of FISA. Applications also require certification by the president's national security advisor or by certain high-ranking intelligence officials designated by the president. These certifications, among other items, must state that the information sought is foreign intelligence information and that the information cannot be reasonably obtained through normal investigative techniques. Most important for our discussion, prior to the Patriot Act, FISA wiretaps could only be issued when the "primary purpose" of the wire is the collection of foreign intelligence.

The primary goal of FISA was to prevent presidentially authorized surveillance of political groups, organizations, journalists, and civic leaders for political reasons. As Representative Robert Kastenmeier noted, such surveillance, under the "guise of national security," is "particularly insidious because it is often conducted with regard to the subject's political activities."[52] And it is clear that FISA was meant to cover all presidentially ordered electronic surveillance: "The Bill establishes the exclusive means by which [presidentially ordered] surveillance may be conducted."[53] FISA repealed section 2511(3) of the Omnibus Crime Control Act, which appeared to recognize inherent presidential power to conduct warrantless electronic surveillance and was the subject of *Keith,* "eliminating any congressional recognition or suggestion of inherent presidential power with respect to electronic surveillance."[54] And section 1802 of FISA narrowly circumscribes presidentially authorized warrantless surveillance to those situations where "there is no substantial likelihood that the surveillance will acquire the contents of any communication to which a United States person is a party."

FISA has three explicit safeguards built into it. First, applications for warrants may only be forwarded after the attorney general or deputy attorney general personally reviews and signs each application, affirming that the statutory requirements for requesting a FISA wiretap have been met. In cases of surveillance of U.S. citizens, the attorney general attests that the motive for obtaining the warrant is not founded solely in the target's constitutionally protected rights of free speech. This safeguard has all but evaporated, however; as FISA applications now number in excess of 1,700 per year, it is inconceivable that the attorney general or deputy attorney general has sufficient time or resources to give each application personal consideration and become familiar with the underlying facts of each case. The process appears to have become *pro forma* with boilerplate paperwork taking the place of close inspection and consideration.

Second, the application may only be approved by one of eleven Article III judges appointed to the Foreign Intelligence Surveillance Court (FISC) by the chief justice of the United States. Each appointed judge serves a nonrenewable seven-year term. Additionally, an application denied by one FISC judge may not be considered by any other judge on the court. A denied application may be appealed to the Foreign Intelligence Surveillance Court of Review (FISCR), a three-member court also appointed by the chief justice. Theoretically, if the government lost in both the original application proceeding and on appeal, it could take its case to the Supreme Court. Since there are only eleven FISC judges, close working relationships no doubt develop between the judges and government attorneys and investigators, and questionable or borderline applications may be reserved for more sympathetic judges. Since the government gets to pick and choose among the eleven judges, all doubtful cases can be reserved for sympathetic judges. For this reason, the judicial safeguard against abuse may be undermined.

Third, each warrant authorization will specify "minimization" procedures to be employed. Minimized records must be destroyed. These procedures are designed to prevent electronic surveillance of U.S. persons that is not connected to foreign intelligence or criminal activity from being logged, transcribed, indexed, shared, or otherwise made into a permanent record held by government agencies. Most minimization is post-intercept, since virtually all FISA intercepts are performed by automated equipment and reviewed later for determination of intelligence or evidentiary value. Here, the process relies on trust that agents will indeed destroy all materials in accordance with minimization procedures, but, as we have seen in past behavior, trust in either intelligence or law enforcement agencies is not always well placed.

If information is useable or provides an advantage to an agent or to his or her agency, there is a strong temptation to keep such information, even if it is not foreign intelligence evidence or evidence of criminal activity. This suspicion is confirmed by an interview with a longtime FBI agent who worked extensively with FISA wiretaps and applications and prepared documents for the FISC. The agent said that there "really is no minimization" of intercepts. The problem, according to the agent, is that "the FBI does not discern a difference between information and intelligence."[55] If the information is conceivably useful in some context, it is not discarded. This fear is also borne out by discussions with another former FBI agent and electronic surveillance manager who confided to the authors that FISA wiretaps were being used to surveil members of Congress and judges. Presumably such activity, if it occurs, is done secretly without informing FISA judges. For example, in an internal communication with the Department of Justice Inspector General, an FBI agent claimed that during an investigation "a request for authority to conduct ELSUR [electronic surveillance] activity was based on unreliable source information. Due to the sensitive nature of this investigation, a Department of Justice (DOJ) Attorney instructed Squad NS-24 to minimize all non-intelligence information that did not specifically pertain to the subject, and to only maintain intelligence information that directly involved the subject's espionage activities." But the agent went on to note that "contrary to DOJ instructions it is my understanding that the case file contains a significant amount of non-intelligence information." The agent also alleged illegal activity concerning several other "ELSUR operations to collect foreign intelligence and counterintelligence information." The agent believed that the requests for "ELSUR coverage was a subterfuge to collect evidentiary information concerning a public corruption matter."[56] In other words, the more easily obtained FISA warrant was pursued to engage in electronic surveillance of domestic crime—surveillance that should have been subject to the tougher standards of Title III. Considering that NS-24 operates in Washington, D.C., it is possible that targets of electronic surveillance in a public corruption matter could be members of Congress or their staff. Such information could form the basis of other investigations that people would be unaware were spawned by illegally collected communications. Worse, the information could also be used by the executive branch to extort cooperation from members of Congress and other public officials implicated in corrupt activity.

FISA and Executive Power
The Scope of FISA Activity

The use of FISA wiretaps is neither an extraordinary nor an infrequent event. Statements abound in court opinions to the effect that "electronic surveillance is largely governed by Title III," but this is incorrect, at least concerning the federal government.[57] FISA orders are far more frequent than federally authorized Title III wiretaps, but this escapes the notice of most judges since all FISA orders are made by only the eleven specially appointed federal district court judges to the FISC. Since FISA's inception, there have been over 20,000 warrant applications made under the statute. Only four applications, all for the year 2003, have been denied. It has become legend that no FISA application is ever denied or modified by the FISA court. Although such actions are rare, they do occur.

In a recent ten-year period (1995–2004), non-FISA applications for wiretap warrants to federal judges averaged about 560 per year, while for the same period there were, on average, 1,060 FISA applications per year. Each non-FISA wiretap on average intercepted 2,092 separate communications from 153 different people, yielding a per year average of over one million communications intercepted, involving some 85,000 people. FISA wiretaps comprised 65.4 percent of all federal wiretaps for the period, and in the three years following 9/11, FISA wiretaps made up almost 75 percent of all authorized communication surveillance taps.

The information on the number of communications and so on is unavailable for FISA, since the only public reporting required by law is a yearly declaration stating the total number of applications made, denied, and modified during the annual reporting period. Assuming, however, that the numbers of persons and communications intercepted for FISA wiretaps and non-FISA surveillance are similar, and taking into account that FISA taps are usually authorized for 90 or 120 days (more than double the average of 44 days in 2004 under Title III taps), this would yield, at a minimum, that FISA wiretaps intercept nearly five million communications each year, involving about 325,000 people.[58]

These impressive numbers constitute a conservative estimate; for several reasons there is little doubt that they greatly understate FISA activity. First, FISA taps are comprehensive, in that a single warrant usually covers a myriad of devices and places, such as telephones, cell phones, computers, fax machines, homes, offices, automobiles, and copy machines and often allows for placement of video equipment on target properties. Second, it seems that warrants are frequently issued against facilities rather than persons, so they may authorize the intercept of all communications emanating from a building or even a complex of buildings. Third, the specificity requirements normally found in Title III warrants are much less rigorous in FISA warrants, so a broader range of material may be intercepted than is contemplated in Title III wiretaps. Finally, although we estimate FISA numbers using the 90-day benchmark, FISA warrants against foreign nationals are usually authorized for 120 days or, in certain cases, as long as a year. By a substantial margin, the majority of surveillance conducted by the federal government in the United States is performed under FISA warrants. At a minimum, FISA intercepts make up 85 percent of all federally authorized wiretap intercepts.

The FISC consisted of seven members until the Patriot Act increased the court to eleven members in May 2002. Since 2002, each of these judges heard an average of about 150 applications each year, or one application every two and a half days. Each FISA application is a complex of affidavits, assertions of probable cause under FISA, legal explanations of sufficiency of evidence, and certifications by the attorney general and heads of intelligence agencies. Judges are charged with passive supervisory duties in regard to wiretap warrants and normally require reports asserting that the parameters of warrant orders are being adhered to. This means that at any given time the FISA court will have hundreds of active warrants with new warrant applications and requests for extensions on existing warrants coming in at a steady pace.

Wiretap Statistics

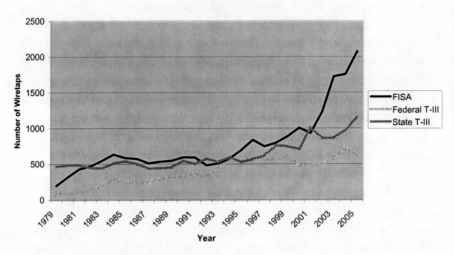

Figure 5.1. Wiretap Statistics, 1979–2005

Each active wiretap, application for warrant, and request for extension of exist-ing authorized surveillance requires close scrutiny and evaluation of the statutory and constitutional rights of targets and potential targets, especially where U.S. citizens are involved. It is clear that the sheer volume of material simply forbids any close judicial supervision of governmental activities concerning authorized surveillance and that the FISC has limited means to assure accountability and discover abuses of the FISA process.

"Legiscide" in One Act

In a purported effort to increase the effectiveness of the FISA process and to create an environment of cooperation, Congress amended FISA in the Patriot Act to increase the FISC to eleven judges and, most importantly, to eliminate the "primary purpose" interpretation and to direct sharing of information between law enforcement and intelligence agencies. The original FISA legislation re-quired that foreign intelligence be "the purpose" of a warrant application. Courts interpreted "the purpose" to mean "primary purpose." This amendment was undertaken at the urging of President Bush and Attorney General Ashcroft in an atmosphere of panic and emergency, and the Bush administration claimed that the changes were necessary to maintain the security of the nation. Congress forwent the normal hearings, discussion, and probing that such sweeping legisla-tion affecting civil rights would normally receive. In the act, Congress now re-quired only that pursuit of foreign intelligence be "a significant purpose" of a FISA warrant.[59]

The DOJ argued that the "significant purpose" language meant that prosecu-tors may now initiate and direct FISA wiretaps, since the new language of the statute indicates that the "primary purpose" of the investigation may be some-thing other than the collection of foreign intelligence. In other words, collection of foreign intelligence may be a "significant purpose" in a particular case, but the primary purpose may be a prosecutorial end or a desire to gather domestic intel-ligence. It is difficult to overestimate the effect that this change has had on elec-tronic surveillance.

Traditionally, intelligence agencies had the last call on whether or not the information they collected would be produced in support of prosecution, and on a number of occasions spies and other lawbreakers have been freed or faced lesser charges rather than put to trial on the basis of classified information. But the amendment to FISA made by the Patriot Act creates a sea change in that it now makes the FISA process prosecution-driven rather than intelligence-driven. This is the very thing that the FISC and the Office of Intelligence Policy and Review (OIPR), the chief accountability office in the DOJ for intelligence matters, feared most: the use of FISA to engage in primarily domestic surveillance for pros-ecutorial purposes. The provisions of the Patriot Act, though, had a significant hurdle to manage in the form of an unprecedented en banc unanimous decision of the FISC that threatened to ignore the new language.

The FISC Ruling

In March 2002, Attorney General Ashcroft proposed new minimization pro-cedures to the FISC and asked that obstacles to information sharing between prosecutors and investigators be dismantled and that the FISC now permit FISA warrants to be controlled and directed primarily for law enforcement purposes. Although the court granted most of what the attorney general requested, it re-fused to adopt certain proposals. The court noted that since the probable cause standard under FISA was less rigorous than that found under Title III and that since FISA warrants did not comply with provisions of the Fourth Amendment, it had a duty "to preserve both the appearance and the fact that FISA surveillances and searches were not being used *sub rosa* for criminal investigations."[60]

Consequently, the court held that "law enforcement officials shall not make recommendations to intelligence officials concerning the initiation, operation, continuation or expansion of FISA searches or surveillances." Additionally, the court directed that "the FBI and the Criminal Division shall ensure that law enforcement officials do not direct or control the use of the FISA procedures to enhance criminal prosecution" and that the process not "result in the Criminal Division's directing or controlling the investigation using FISA searches and surveillances toward law enforcement objectives."[61]

The court completely ignored the Patriot Act amendments to FISA and based its opinion on the rather practical footing of minimization procedures. The court seemed to say that no matter what Congress does to change the "primary purpose" rule, such a rule is still required in practice to achieve the proper minimization of intercepted communications and to protect the privacy of citizens. The argument is that if the "primary purpose" rule were abandoned, prosecutors would use the fig leaf of "foreign intelligence" to obtain FISA wiretaps against criminal suspects in cases where they are not able to meet the requirements of Title III. In the same spirit of concern for privacy and civil liberties, the court described abuses that the FBI and others had taken with the FISA process. In rather pointed language, the court called attention to misuse of previous FISA warrants, noting that scores of applications contained misleading or erroneous information.[62] Most of these "errors" concealed unauthorized communications and collaboration between prosecutors and agents working FISA wires or intelligence officials and criminal investigators, but declassified government documents also show a wider variety of abuses and errors in the FISA process than those discussed by the court.

An internal memorandum from an unnamed FBI official to Marion Bowman, deputy general counsel for national security affairs at the FBI, acidly remarked that "you have a pattern of occurrences which indicate to OIPR an inability on the part of the FBI to manage its FISAs."[63] Other documents reveal "unauthorized searches, incorrect addresses, incorrect interpretation of a FISA order, . . . overruns of ELSUR [electronic surveillance]" as well as the unauthorized video surveillance of citizens. In one case, for example, a FISA target gave up his cell phone and the number was reassigned to a new customer. A language specialist listening to the tapes reported that the user of the cell phone was not speaking the expected language, but no action was taken, and the new user of the cell phone number "was therefore the target of unauthorized electronic surveillance for a substantial period of time."[64]

But declassified documents offer a mere glimpse of what transpires in the FISA process, and it is impossible to estimate the level of abuse or mismanagement associated with FISA orders. The problems were serious enough, though, that "in November of 2000, the Court held a special meeting to consider the troubling number of inaccurate FBI affidavits in so many FISA applications," and the FISC complained that the DOJ explained "what went wrong, *but not why*" and "decided not to accept inaccurate affidavits from FBI agents whether or not intentionally false. . . . One FBI agent was barred from appearing before the Court as a FISA affiant"; the court's concerns helped initiate an investigation into the matter by the DOJ Office of Professional Responsibility. While the court awaited the report of the investigation, in March 2001 OIPR revealed another series of "errors" in FISA warrant applications and interception operations.[65]

Based on its past experience and concerns for abuse of FISA orders, the court had little faith that Ashcroft's proposed guidelines would adequately protect the privacy and rights of citizens. In addition to modifying Ashcroft's new guidelines concerning the execution of FISA warrants and the collection and dissemination of intercepted communications, the court declared that the "2002 procedures appear to be designed to amend the law and substitute the FISA for Title III electronic surveillances." The court declared, "The purpose of minimization procedures as defined in the Act, is not to amend the statute, but to protect the privacy of Americans in these highly intrusive surveillances and searches."[66]

The court was unanimous in its opinion, and it should be noted that the court could hardly be characterized as left-leaning or composed of civil libertarians. All of the judges were appointed to the FISC by William Rehnquist, at the time chief justice of the United States and not known for his liberal sentiments, and five of the seven members were originally appointed to the federal bench by Republican presidents; two each by Presidents Ford and Reagan and one by President George H. W. Bush. After this setback, Attorney General Ashcroft quickly took an appeal of the decision to the judges of the FISCR, who are known as the "Maytag repairmen" of the federal judiciary since, before this appeal, they apparently had never heard a case.

A Case Named "In re [deleted]"

The three-member FISCR, again appointed by the chief justice, presides over a remarkable process, a process that almost guarantees that the government will win any appeal and provides no means for an adversarial hearing. First, the appellate proceeding is *ex parte*, with only the government's position presented to the court. No provisions for incorporating arguments opposed to the government's position were made either in the FISA or in the rules adopted by the

FISCR. Indeed, the FISCR only reluctantly agreed to allow *amicus curiae* briefs to be filed in the case, and then only after Solicitor General Ted Olson raised no objection.

Second, since no party has standing to bring a case to the court except for the DOJ, there may be no appeal taken from a decision rendered in favor of the government. The court considers matters of great importance to the rights of citizens, but a decision adverse to the interests of the people, or even a violation of the Constitution, may not be appealed. The American Civil Liberties Union filed an appeal of the FISCR decision, but it would require a reworking of the standing doctrine by the Supreme Court to accept the ACLU as a proper party to appeal the decision. Indeed, the Supreme Court rejected the appeal without comment.[67] The strange result is that aggrieved parties of FISA abuse, people illegally surveilled, will never know about the violation of their rights and will therefore never be in a position to press a legal claim. Meanwhile, information collected from their communications or their offices and homes may be used for a myriad of purposes and stored in government databases. Such information may even be used to damage reputations, affect business operations, or otherwise hurt people disfavored by the administration in power.

Third, the court conducts proceedings in secret. FISA provides that "proceedings under this Act . . . shall be maintained under security measures established by the Chief Justice in consultation with the Attorney General and the Director of Central Intelligence."[68] Indeed, it is only as a result of an extraordinary event that the public is even aware that an appeal took place at all. Repeated requests by members of Congress for the *unclassified* FISC opinion were finally answered when the FISC chief judge agreed to make the decision public after receiving unanimous support for publication from all judges currently on the FISC or involved in the decision.[69] It is remarkable that it took three senior senators to dislodge an unclassified opinion from a court that deals exclusively with intelligence matters, matters that by law are under direct oversight of congressional committees.[70]

Even the title of the original FISC decision, *In re [deleted]*, though perhaps necessary, is a bizarre testament to the secrecy of the process. Though the transcripts of the hearing have been released and supporting briefs have been made public, it does nothing to square the process with traditional appellate practice. There is nothing to say that future appeals may not remain completely secret and thus unexposed to criticism or examination. Indeed, it is a strange procedure whereby an appellate court may make substantive rulings at law on the constitutional rights of citizens in complete secrecy and without the public or even fellow federal judges being made aware of those rulings. Such a design is inimical to democracy and creates the possibility of a parallel "secret Constitution." Ruling on questions of individual privacy and executive power, the FISCR creates constitutional precedent that remains undisclosed to the bar, the public, Congress, fellow judges, and even the Supreme Court. Regardless of the substance of such jurisprudence, it strains the imagination to conceive of constitutional meaning forged wholly in secret.

Finally, the judges who were appointed to the FISCR have a history of employment and publicly stated positions that indicate bias toward executive power. The chief judge of the court, Ralph Guy, is a former U.S. attorney and argued the government's side at trial in *Keith* for the Nixon administration. Judge Laurence Silberman was a deputy attorney general and testified against FISA at congressional hearings, claiming it to be an unconstitutional restraint on executive power and a violation of the "case or controversy" clause of Article III.[71] In what appears to be a bit of an inside joke, the FISCR opinion makes reference to the testimony of Silberman before Congress, stating that "we do not think there is much left to an argument made by an opponent of FISA in 1978 that the statutory responsibilities of the FISA court are inconsistent with Article III."[72] Additionally, of course, Solicitor General Olson, representing the government in the case, lost his wife in the terrorist attacks on September 11. His personal loss, which arguably resulted from a failure in the FISA process, may have made him, even if understandably, even more zealous in his efforts to enlarge the scope of FISA and presidential prerogative to engage in surveillance.

Given the composition of the FISCR and the nature of the process, reversal of the FISC's decision was a forgone conclusion. DOJ attorneys argued that the FISC had completely overlooked the changes the Patriot Act had made to FISA and that the effect of that legislation was to eliminate the requirement that the primary purpose of a FISA application must be to collect foreign intelligence rather than aid in criminal investigation. They said that Congress was clear that the language change from "the purpose" to "a significant purpose" meant to allow FISA warrants to be directed and managed by criminal investigators and prosecutors.

Despite the setting, the judges deserve credit for asking some very hard questions and shaking the government's arguments around to a fair degree. But questioning from the bench cannot substitute for opposing counsel. It also put the judges in the awkward position of having to fill that role half-heartedly. Indeed, at the end of the hearing, Olson tried to put a good face on it by saying that "I think that this process has been up to this point very very effective. . . . This may be an ex-parte procedure, but the Court and the members of this Court are asking very very difficult, hard questions, the same kind of questions I think that some-one who was an adversary, if there were one, would be asking the Court to ask."[73] Of course, this statement simply emphasizes that the absence of opposing coun-sel deprives the court of perspectives and arguments that cannot, should not, and will not be argued by government counsel. The matters discussed during the hearing posed issues of great importance to citizens and government, and it is unprecedented in our history that constitutional issues and statutory questions about privacy and civil liberties would be settled with only the government's position represented. The types of questions addressed at the hearing without adversarial process were extraordinary, and included:

- Do FISA warrants meet Fourth Amendment requirements?
- Did the FISC violate separation of powers by exerting undue control over executive branch agencies?
- Is the "primary purpose" test constitutionally required or merely a conceit or even mistake on the part of the judiciary and OIPR?
- Does the FISC even have the power to review minimization procedures proposed by the attorney general?
- How far may the FISC go in investigating the underlying motive for an application?

These are not questions to be answered or even addressed without arguments and briefs from opposing counsel. They have important implications for all U.S. citizens, and to decide these matters with only the government's position repre-sented is to give the executive branch the power to create constitutional jurispru-dence favorable to presidential power almost at will.

In its decision reviewing the FISC opinion, the court made several important holdings. First, the FISCR found that "the refusal by the FISA court to consider the legal significance of the PATRIOT Act's crucial amendments was error" and ruled that the act eliminated the "primary purpose" test. Despite denying the government's argument that the FISA contemplates no distinction between for-eign intelligence and law enforcement purposes, the court nevertheless held that "so long as the government entertains a realistic option of dealing with the agent other than through criminal prosecution, it satisfies the significant purpose test."[74] In other words, as long as there is a weak but sustainable claim that a target may be a source of foreign intelligence, the government has met the pur-pose test for obtaining a FISA order.

Second, the court ruled that the imposition of "walls" between law enforcement personnel and intelligence agents was not originally required by FISA and that the Patriot Act was clearly meant to eliminate such obstacles to cooperation. The FISCR held that the "wall" procedure was "unstable because it generates dangerous confusion and creates perverse organizational incentives." Indeed, the FISCR seemed to agree with testimony given before Congress that "the FISA court requirements . . . may well have contributed . . . to the FBI missing opportunities to anticipate the September 11, 2001 attacks." The "wall" procedure, said the court, led the FISA court to assert "authority to govern the internal organization and investigative procedures of the Department of Justice which are the province" of Congress and the president.[75]

Third, the FISCR held that "the government's purpose . . . is to be judged by the national security official's articulation and not by a FISA court of inquiry into the origins of an investigation nor an examination of the personnel involved." This means that any investigation into the purpose of an application is limited to questioning senior agency and department personnel. As the court explains, "the important point is that the relevant purpose is that of those senior officials in the Executive Branch who have the responsibility of appraising the government's national security needs."[76] The result is that FISC judges may only investigate the purpose of a FISA application by asking those people who are furthest removed from the facts of the case and the FISA process itself.

Although the attorney general and the director of the FBI must certify applications for FISA orders, it is unreasonable to believe that these officials possess detailed knowledge of the facts behind any particular application. Determinations of purpose in these cases are necessarily fact-intensive and must rely on the information gleaned from agents familiar with the circumstances of an application. Since FISC judges now may not inquire into purpose by questioning those most knowledgeable of the facts concerning an application, responses to judicial queries on this issue will likely devolve into pro forma declarations. It is naive to assume that operational personnel will not exploit this limitation on FISA judge inquiries to press for applications that are motivated for illicit or questionable purposes or as a means to circumvent Title III requirements.

The FISCR, as may be expected given the experience and backgrounds of its members and the *ex parte* nature of the hearing, used the forum to convey to the attorney general and senior DOJ staff that they read broad presidential authority to engage in national security electronic surveillance and that Congress clearly meant to "amplify" that power in the Patriot Act.[77]

In virtually all respects it is a dream situation for an appellate court and the DOJ. The FISCR, so long as it decides for the government, may make broad conclusions at law without fear that it will be overturned on appeal. Theoretically the Supreme Court could review a decision even decided in favor of the government, but this seems very unlikely. The FISCR judges have no fear that a losing side will test their holdings or that further litigation will call into account the wisdom and felicity of their decisions. Nor do they need to be concerned about condemnation from their colleagues, since the FISCR has sole jurisdiction over appeals from the FISC. This is a process of making law in a bottle; there are no internal or external threats or challenges to the decisions of the FISCR. The FISCR is what amounts to a supreme court on national security surveillance issues—but in a process with no adversarial parties or contested issues.

Without the leavening effects of adversarial parties and potential public review of decisions, foundational elements of American jurisprudence, the court went beyond the needs of the case and produced dicta and rulings at law that turned the FISA on its head. And it should be noted that in practical effect there is no difference between dicta and holding in the FISCR decision; dicta has the force of law because there is no other body or adversary to maintain the distinction between holding and conjecture. Even suggestion or speculation by FISCR concerning what is legally acceptable will translate into action on the part of DOJ.

Completely absent from the hearing is any recognition that the underlying motive for FISA was to delimit presidential prerogative. Solicitor General Olson claimed at the outset of the FISCR hearing that the intent in passing FISA was to prevent the kind of terrorist attacks that occurred on September 11. But that assertion is simply untrue, and he ignores the clear fact that the motivating reason in 1978 for FISA was to limit presidential prerogative to spy on citizens. The Senate Judiciary Committee related that FISA was "in large measure a response to the revelations that warrantless electronic surveillance in the name of national security has been seriously abused."[78] The problem was not that prior to FISA the president had too little power but rather too much power with virtually unlimited discretion. In every hearing held on FISA before and after its passage, the primary concern has been for civil liberties and how to make the president conform to a legal process that will protect the citizenry.

The primary goal of FISA was, as Senator Ted Kennedy said, to "bring national security electronic surveillance under the rule of law" and to limit "whatever inherent power the President may have to engage in such electronic surveillance in the United States."[79] No one doubted that the president had all the power necessary to protect the national security of the nation; FISA was born in an effort to prevent abuse of that power.

Dangers of FISA

FISA poses a number of serious threats to civil rights and liberties, many of which are connected to the secrecy that envelops the process. First, and most obviously, it may have become precisely that alternative to Title III that the FISC feared. With the decision of the FISCR allowing both for sharing of FISA information with law enforcement and prosecutors and for direction of FISA wiretaps by Criminal Division counsel, there is no doubt that government counsel will pursue a FISA warrant over a Title III warrant at every opportunity.

FISA, as we have seen, has a number of advantages over Title III for prosecutors and law enforcement. FISA targets, unlike Title III targets, will never be told that their communications were intercepted by the government or that their houses and offices were searched, bugged, or subjected to video surveillance. Title III surveillance requires that after termination of warrants, targets and (subject to judicial discretion) other intercepted parties must be notified as to the original order and the period for which communications were intercepted, whether or not the intercepted communications lead to prosecution. Additionally, judges under Title III may make the original application, the order, and the intercepted communications available to the target.[80] FISA provides for no disclosure or notice requirement except when surveillance is used in criminal prosecutions and, indeed, assumes that surveillance will remain classified and undisclosable in perpetuity.

Although both FISA and Title III provide for civil damages against unauthorized surveillance, it is almost a certainty that an unauthorized target of a FISA wiretap will never discover that fact or be able to obtain sufficient evidence at discovery to maintain a civil action. Appellate courts have held that federal courts have no power to enjoin FISA surveillance. In theory, under exceptional circumstances in a criminal prosecution where the Constitution requires an adversarial hearing on the lawfulness of a FISA application and order, litigants may be entitled to those materials.[81] But no court has ever required the government to divulge a FISA application or order to any criminal or civil litigant. Additionally, under both FISA and Title III, federal officials and law enforcement personnel hold qualified immunity to suit as well as absolute immunity in defined circumstances. The theoretical possibility of damages under FISA, then, is merely statutory ornamentation of no practical use in checking illegal behavior: no damages have ever been awarded for violations of FISA.

Title III contains a provision authorizing courts or administrative departments

TABLE 5.2
Comparison of FISA and Title III

Feature	FISA	Title III
Must targets and interceptees eventually be notified of surveillance?	No	Yes
Must warrant specify things to be seized?	No	Yes
Probable cause target committing crime?	No	Yes
Probable cause that facility targeted is being used for criminal activity?	No	Yes
May judge reject application even when probable cause exists?	No	Yes
Minimization of intercepts at acquisition stage?	No	Yes
May defendant obtain warrant application?	No	Yes
May defendant obtain electronic surveillance order?	No	Yes
Stringent standard of judicial review of applications?	No	Yes
Procedure for triggering administrative discipline for wilful misbehavior of federal officials?	No	Yes
Liability for unauthorized surveillance?	Yes[1]	Yes
Criminal sanction for unauthorized surveillance?	Yes[2]	Yes

1. But no successful cases.
2. But no cases brought.

to trigger disciplinary administrative proceedings against federal employees who act "willfully or intentionally with respect to . . . violation" of the statute.[82] FISA contains no such provision, though both statutes do contain criminal sanctions for their violation. But on no occasion has any federal official been prosecuted criminally under the provisions of FISA, while a number of officials have been convicted of crimes or found liable for damages under Title III. FISA sanctions are at worst illusory and at best very unlikely ever to be used or to act as an incentive to federal agents to avoid unauthorized activity.

Second, FISA as interpreted by the FISCR reduces the role of the judiciary in the FISA process and prevents adequate judicial oversight of FISA warrants. As noted, after the FISCR decision FISC judges may not inquire into the purpose of an application below the level of senior DOJ personnel, which means that the judge must in all practicality simply accept the statement of the attorney general or deputy attorney general concerning the purpose of any particular application. As a result of this holding, parties with direct involvement and knowledge of the details of the case at hand may not be made to appear; they may be replaced with senior officers who rubber-stamp FISA applications.

No doubt the vast majority of agents are competent and mindful of applicable laws and rules and procedures, but it is a disaster of a process that relies on abusers to report their own abuse and to manage their own accountability. As the first director of OIPR, Kenneth Bass, commented in a statement to the Senate Judiciary Committee in September 2002, "OIPR has played an important role throughout FISA as part of the internal 'checks and balances' to offset features of FISA that depart from the criminal search warrant standards."[83] But "since September 11, 2001, the requirement that OIPR be present at all meetings and discussions between the FBI and Criminal Division involving certain FISA cases has been suspended."[84] This change means that contacts between intelligence agencies and prosecutors may be initiated without authorization or oversight, perhaps even without notification of OIPR. It is difficult to overestimate the importance of these changes, which essentially work to prevent OIPR from fulfilling the oversight function required by the FISC.

The FISC has lost its window into the way FISA orders are carried out and must now, apparently, rely solely on the self-reporting of abuse and error by the very people who seek FISA orders and are responsible for their execution. This circumstance provides the executive branch with the means to use secrecy to cover up embarrassing or illegal activities, since the FISCR decision essentially shields the president and executive branch officials from meaningful inquiry by the FISC.

Third, there is no evidence that the government can be trusted to stay within the bounds of FISA definitions and guidelines. Since the FISCR now allows prosecutors to control FISA orders, it is predictable that they will use the orders in such a way to maximize intercept of non-foreign intelligence targets. Considering that each FISA wiretap intercepts thousands of communications, often from large facilities and through automated recording devices, it is likely that a good deal of information interesting to prosecutors but of no relevance to national security will be intercepted.

And since FISA only requires that a defendant be notified if FISA-intercepted material will be used at trial, it is conceivable that in the past and, now that prosecutors may run wires, even more so in the future that information of criminal activity is passed to investigators with no intention of admitting the intercepts into evidence. Investigators may be informed of detailed information concerning criminal activities that may lead to arrest and prosecution of offenders who will never know, nor will probably even the court, that it was communications intercepted through FISA that sparked the original investigation. If handled strategically, prosecutors could obtain FISA orders that cover large numbers of communications that might yield extensive evidence of domestic crime but bypass the requirements of Title III.

Further, the same Criminal Division prosecutors who must meet the strict requirements of Title III will also be the ones to press for FISA applications. The potential for misuse of the FISA process to obtain warrants for what is essentially domestic surveillance that could not be obtained under Title III is obvious. Now that only a "significant purpose" of the warrant must be to obtain foreign intelligence, prosecutors will no doubt attempt to fit otherwise domestic investigations into the frame of a FISA warrant.

We may also see a rather extended definition of just what constitutes an agent of a foreign power for FISA purposes. In possible harbingers of such definitional extension, in a series of opinions as a judge on the D.C. Circuit Court of Appeals, Antonin Scalia took a rather broad view of executive authority to engage in electronic surveillance. In *Ellsberg v. Mitchell,* a case concerning surveillance of the Black Panther Party, Scalia concluded that the Black Panthers were "known to have had 'contacts with foreign revolutionaries,' which [quoting from a previous appeal], we emphasized, 'provide the clearest justification for a national security exception to Title III.' "[85] The events giving rise to *Ellsberg* occurred before passage of FISA, but it is a legitimate question whether the relaxed standard of "foreign agent" reflected in Scalia's opinion would be adopted by both FISCR and the Supreme Court.

Technology Overtakes FISA

In December 2005, the *New York Times* released a story about warrantless electronic intercept of communications by U.S. citizens by the National Security Agency.[86] Amazingly, whether because of timidity or an attempt to curry favor with the Bush administration, the *Times* sat on the story for over a year. The newspaper had the story in hand before the presidential elections of 2004 but held the story back. Only when it became clear that the newspaper's handling of the matter and the underlying story itself would come out in a different forum did it publish the story. President Bush made at least two requests for the paper not to publish the story, one coming December 5, 2005, in a face-to-face meeting with *Times* publisher Arthur O. Sulzberger Jr. in the Oval Office.[87] Although the revelation contained little detail concerning the nature of the presidentially ordered surveillance, it recollected similar activity by the NSA in the Johnson and Nixon administrations. Under Projects Minaret and Shamrock, thousands of citizens' communications were intercepted by the National Security Agency without warrant and solely on presidential orders between 1967 and 1973.

But that surveillance was different in kind and magnitude than that engaged in by the NSA on the authorization of President Bush. For one thing, the targets of the Nixon-era surveillance were determined beforehand, comprising over a thousand U.S. citizens and organizations and several thousand foreign citizens and organizations. While the reasons may have been irrational or weak or prejudiced, there was consideration given to which organizations and persons should be

placed on the watch list. The NSA worked from the watch list in screening communications, even though they operated a mass approach of sweeping up communications indiscriminately based on technology that recorded conversations
and communications containing certain words or phrases.[88] And of course these
actions were pre-FISA and indeed are the very reason for FISA's enactment,
which was made the "exclusive" process for undertaking foreign intelligence
surveillance.

After the *Times* disclosed the existence of the program, President Bush defended his actions based on inherent presidential authority, authorization by
Congress to engage in all means to wage successful war after 9/11, and, tellingly,
the assertion by Assistant Attorney General William Moschella that "the President determined that it was necessary following September 11 to create an early
warning detection system. FISA could not have provided the speed and agility
required for the early warning detection system."[89] But the claim that FISA is
insufficiently flexible to meet exigent circumstances is difficult to understand; it
provides for *ex post facto* authorization of surveillance and clearly contemplates
that the statute should not tie the hands of presidents when national security is at
stake.[90] What is clear and is at the root of President Bush's failure to meet the
requirements of FISA and the Fourth Amendment is that FISA, like the Fourth
Amendment, requires that there be individualized suspicion, that there be a
target's name on the warrant, that a judge review the nature of the suspicion for
conformance with statutory requirements, and that minimization procedures are
understood.

At least one NSA surveillance program authorized by Bush reverses the process contemplated under FISA and the Fourth Amendment. It starts with massive
amounts of surveillance and hopes that it can distill individualized suspicion out
of a sea of largely irrelevant data. Advances in technology and software allow the
NSA to collate, compare, and analyze sources and patterns of communications
and scan innumerable communications for phrases, intonations, accents, dia-
lects, and device-specific anomalies. Mark Klein, a retired AT&T employee, disclosed documentation and facts concerning special rooms constructed by AT&T
and the NSA to divert communications to surveillance equipment and software.
These rooms were located in communications hubs; Klein's documents revealed
that "AT&T had an agreement with the federal government to systematically
gather information flowing on the Internet through the company's network."[91]

The reason President Bush went outside FISA and resorted to the time-worn
unilateral decision to engage in warrantless surveillance is that it would have been
impossible to meet any warrant standard, FISA or otherwise, without individu-

alized suspicion. Faced with the choice of adhering to the Fourth Amendment and FISA and forgoing a promising avenue of intelligence created by new technologies, President Bush authorized the surveillance, banking that the inherent powers argument would provide a fig leaf of protection if the operation became public.

But much depends on how the operation without FISA approval is conducted. If it is limited to purely foreign communications, then surveillance is simply espionage, and the power of the president to engage in this intelligence gathering has never been seriously questioned. But it becomes highly questionable if it surveils mixed U.S.–foreign-destination communications, and is illegal and unconstitutional if purely domestic communications are subjected to intercept. Indeed, one district judge determined that presidentially ordered warrantless NSA surveillance of the content of communications between U.S. residents and foreigners is unconstitutional and a violation of FISA. Whether or not this ruling stands on appeal, it demonstrates a certain amount of judicial fatigue with the Bush administration's insistence on always pressing for maximum presidential authority. One thing that history shows concerning electronic surveillance is that reliance on self-restraint is misplaced; a program that is unaccountable to judges or the public is most certainly a very tempting vehicle for abuse. But unlike the FISA process, it is a matter that the president must bear politically when it is discovered; there is no shield of process to protect him, so he stands or falls with public scrutiny and judgment of the actions. If he makes the gamble to walk at the edge of constitutional and legal propriety, he suffers the results if he miscalculates and stumbles across the line. The danger may be that such revelations, because of stressful or dangerous times, will win favor with the public and the courts and that longstanding constitutional principles will be jettisoned.

At the beginning of this chapter we indicated that civil liberties and the desires of Congress to denude the presidential prerogative to spy on citizens may have been better served by not passing FISA. We are worse off with FISA than without. It created a vast institutional process that subjects innumerable people to surveillance and insulates the president from responsibility. All told, the legiscide known as FISA destabilized the constitutional balance between Congress and the president, between executive authority to provide for national security and congressional oversight of that authority, and it threatens to ensure the occurrence of precisely that which it originally intended to prohibit.

We take the contrarian view, that it is better to have the president take the risk of embarrassment, investigation, and possible impeachment by leaving the surveillance field open rather than to attempt to limit presidential power through statutory constraints that end up codifying in an established process the very abuses that Congress was attempting to prevent.

Formerly, the possibility that information of abuse might leak to the press clearly made presidents and their attorneys general circumspect when considering whether or not to engage in warrantless surveillance, especially where the targets were U.S. citizens or political organizations. In the very act of authorizing such surveillance, the president was also empowering its participants, arming them with potential material with which to attack the president on an alleged failure to adhere to constitutional requirements. FBI agents engaging in warrantless surveillance of citizens or political organizations under questionable circumstances gained power and leverage within the organization simply because they had information that could be used against superiors worried about leaks or even congressional investigations. Under such circumstances, moreover, the number of people associated with these endeavors necessarily had to be small, thereby reducing the scope of their activities.

The depersonalization of surveillance decisions and the procedures set up in FISA work to diminish executive accountability generally. As Judge Robert Bork noted, "To take a not improbable case, if even one judge proves excessively tolerant, the government can go to him in all doubtful, or even improper cases." There is nothing to prevent DOJ from attempting to run questionable or improper warrant applications through a "cooperative" FISC judge. If an improper warrant is denied and it is felt to be too revealing or doubtful to take on appeal, then DOJ can simply let it die without suffering ill effects. But if it is successful, then the FISA process provides blanket protection for the president and all executive branch officials involved. Any efforts to hold officials criminally or civilly accountable under such circumstances would surely fail. And since there is no party to bring an appeal when the government successfully procures a warrant, as Bork observed, "the 'rule of law' will turn out to be the temper of one district judge, unknown to the other judges and the Supreme Court."[92] Once the executive branch complies with the FISA process, even in bad faith or to procure warrants that should not have been issued, the result is that the statute immunizes all participants from prosecution or civil liability and insulates the president against potential embarrassment. Congress ultimately deprived itself of political leverage by creating a process that, even when abused, will never yield accountability of executive branch officials.

A new constitutional jurisprudence initiated under crisis conditions may be suspect in itself and result in serious damage to privacy rights and other civil liberties, but a jurisprudence forged in secret, permanently unavailable to congressional oversight, and for practical purposes not subject even to Supreme Court review—now that is astounding indeed. This is a secret Constitution that has been created by eleven FISC judges, three FISCR judges, the president, and the attorney general, a Constitution that rearranges Fourth Amendment jurisprudence, rights to privacy, criminal procedure, and First Amendment rights under an impenetrable veil of secrecy. This is a power conveyed to the executive branch by Congress in the mistaken belief that it was reining in presidential authority to engage in intrusive surveillance of American citizens.

CHAPTER SIX

The New Executive Privilege

I think executive privilege means whenever the President feels that
he is threatened, he can simply refuse to comply with a court order.

—*Antonin Scalia*

Executive privilege can be defined most broadly as the executive's "right to withhold information from either Congress or the judicial branch"—and thus, indirectly, from the people. From the beginning of the republic, it has been used by presidents in information disputes ranging from congressional investigation of a military battle with Native Americans to Nixon's White House tape recordings.[1]

In the preceding discussion, we have described various facets or techniques of presidential secrecy, and we have shown how each of them has grown by various means to the point where it stands ready to support and facilitate what we have called the secret presidency. Executive privilege, the topic of this chapter, is the last of those techniques we will discuss. It is distinguishable from anti-terror policy, FISA powers, classification power, and even the state secrets privilege because, unlike those other secrecy-related topics we have covered, it has been thoroughly addressed by other commentators. It is the subject of three major works of presidential scholarship—*The Politics of Executive Privilege* (2004) by Louis Fisher, *Executive Privilege: Presidential Power, Secrecy and Accountability* (2002) by Mark Rozell, and *Executive Privilege: A Constitutional Myth* (1974) by Raoul Berger—as well as numerous journal articles.[2] We intervene, here, in the debate between Berger, who argues that executive privilege has no sound basis in law or political history, and Rozell, who defends executive privilege on constitutional as well as practical grounds. While Berger certainly goes too far in denying any justification for executive privilege, his thorough investigation raises a number of valid questions about the currently prevailing scholarly practice of accepting executive privilege as a legitimate tool of presidential power. Thus we do not agree with Rozell, who maintains that the need for a vigorous executive privilege is beyond question and denies the need for statutory or decisional limitations on that power.

Moreover, the Bush administration has sought to expand dramatically the scope and depth of executive privilege as a cornerstone of the secret presidency. The administration has undertaken specific initiatives with the clear purpose of engineering a new executive privilege, and those initiatives are readily visible as a move to consolidate power. Rozell himself testified before Congress on the dangers of the 2001 executive order expanding the secrecy of presidential records.[3]

The Bush administration's uses and justifications of executive privilege become plain in the context of three legal and political disputes: the expansion of the Presidential Records Directive, the Energy Task Force, and the investigations of the 9/11 terror attacks. Taken together, these examples evince a new conception of executive privilege that sets far wider parameters for its appropriate use than existing court decisions or commentary ever have contemplated. As such, the new executive privilege figures prominently in the expansion of executive secrecy we have been charting throughout this study: an expanded protection for presidential documents enlarges the realm of secrecy surrounding the office. As Rozell has pointed out, that effort is in part a response to the weakening of executive privilege under the Nixon regime: the Bush White House seeks to regain the ground lost after the controversy surrounding Watergate and after the five presidential administrations between Nixon and Bush grappled (unsuccessfully, in Rozell's view) with the problem of recovering some form of the privilege from the disrepute generated by Watergate.[4] We believe, however, that the administration's actions to expand executive privilege represent more than that. For the Bush administration, executive privilege is a key component of an attempt to reshape the institution of the presidency in ways that maximize presidential power and secrecy.

A Constitutional Myth?

In the opening lines of his book, Rozell succinctly states the dilemma of executive privilege: "a presidential administration sometimes needs to conduct the duties of government in secret, yet the coordinate branches and the public need information about the executive branch so that they can fulfill their democratic responsibilities."[5] As we will see, Rozell emphasizes the first part of this formulation more heavily than the second, so the need for executive secrecy is, for him, a starting point from which all further investigation of the dilemma flows. In the end, however, it becomes clear that the executive secrecy he advocates is an either/or choice. The legislature either has control of the executive or it does not.

Rozell articulates the contrary argument, for legislative supremacy, thus: "a chief executive who is subservient to the will of the legislature has no such right"—that is, to withhold information.[6] Additionally, in Berger's view, if the executive serves the people, then the information gathered in the course of that service is not his, and it is obvious that he has no right to withhold information he does not own.[7] Critics of executive privilege warn that citizens and legislators cannot oversee the executive effectively if they do not have access to information.[8] Yet Rozell strongly advocates the opposite view, that the executive has the right and the duty to withhold information from Congress and the public in certain circumstances. Thus, his contribution to presidential studies lines up with those who advocate a strong executive.

While Rozell has unquestionably set the standard for the study of presidential secrecy with his thoroughly researched and closely argued work, we conclude in the end that his prescriptive argument for executive privilege unfettered by statutory or decisional limitations is unpersuasive, for three reasons. First, we believe he relies too much on the purported constitutional foundation he derives from Article II's "executive power" clause. It is one thing to argue that the practical necessities of executing laws requires some form of executive privilege; it is quite another to suggest, as he does, that that practical necessity was recognized and operationalized by the drafters of the original document.

Second, Rozell advocates continued reliance on the president's virtue to determine appropriate and responsible uses of the privilege, rather than constraining it by statute or other rule. This reliance certainly seems misplaced in view of the executive privilege claims he chronicles, some of which he acknowledges to be inappropriate uses of the power. Here, he falls into the trap Berger describes: indulging in a circular argument about the separation of powers. Rozell says that the informal operation of separation of powers rather than any formal rules ought to be the mechanism to solve interbranch executive privilege controversies, but as Berger points out (and as we posit below), we must first define precisely what that separation is (that is, what powers are allotted separately to which branches) before it can be applied to a particular conflict.[9]

Third, Rozell refers repeatedly to national security as a potential justification for executive privilege. The Supreme Court in *United States v. Nixon* drew a clear line between matters that involve national security and those that do not.[10] National security matters are more properly addressed under the state secrets doctrine, which we discussed in chapter 3; executive privilege applies more typically to non–national security cases. We think that this distinction between the two privileges is important to maintain in view of the overreaching that often occurs in state secrets cases, as we have documented. We think that it is important keep the definitions clear so that excessive expansion of privilege does not continue. Also, to infuse executive privilege claims with references to national security is to invoke a "last-resort" power in cases that often fall far short of that level of gravity. In the following section, we will look more closely at some of the claims Rozell advances regarding executive privilege.

With Myths Like That, Who Needs Reality?
Executive Privilege and Constitutional History

One by one, Rozell takes on the attacks on executive privilege made by Berger and others, maintaining that the Constitution can and should be read to authorize the executive to refuse congressional and public requests for information. Thus does he oppose Berger, who denies any constitutional grounding for executive privilege. In his constitutional analysis, Rozell relies principally on two sources of evidence: a reading of Locke and Montesquieu that argues for greater executive discretion and the indisputably general language of Article II, sections 1 and 3.

With regard to the point concerning political philosophy, Rozell cuts against the grain of standard Lockean interpretation when he cites Locke as believing that "in times of emergency, when the legislature is not in session, he [Locke] proposes giving the executive the 'power of doing good without a rule.' "[11] Rozell believes, contrary to standard interpretations, that modern political thinkers saw the need for a strong and efficient executive and argued for that result within a constitutional government. He does not explain fully, however, how he goes from a "strong executive" reading of such canonical texts as Locke's *Second Treatise* to a reading of the United States Constitution in which the executive possesses unlimited secrecy powers. It is undisputed that the drafters of that document were influenced by European political theory of the time, but the "faithfully executed" clause of Article II, section 3 and the "executive power" clause of section 1 say nothing about "doing good without a rule." Thus, it is far from clear that a given idea circulating in the political theory discourse of late eighteenth-century Europe found its way into the governing document of the newly created United States of America. And in any event, even when Rozell cites arguments from the *Federalist* justifying a strong executive, he is relying implicitly on a mode of constitutional interpretation that seeks to base its interpretative conclusions on the imputed intentions of the drafters of the document alone. At the very least, such a claim needs fuller development.

Saikrishna B. Prakash maintains that "much of the English and American history thought to firmly ground executive privilege in our Constitution has been woefully oversold; practices and episodes in England and during the early post-ratification era in America simply do not provide the unambiguous support claimed by proponents of a privilege."[12] He does not find the same evidence Rozell does, detecting no indications that the drafters meant to ensure that the privilege would be available to the newly created executive. In fact, he suggests that the opposite conclusion may be warranted: that the power was deliberately excluded. As he sees it,

> the Constitution seems to lack an explicit reference to anything resembling an executive privilege. As everyone recognizes, the phrase "executive privilege" is nowhere to be found. More importantly, the Constitution is bereft of any obvious references to a power to keep executive proceedings "secret" or to a right "not to be questioned" regarding executive communications. Conceivably, the apparent absence of such authority may indicate a deliberate decision not to cede such power. After all, the presence of certain significant congressional privileges and their notable absence with respect to the President and the judiciary may tempt us to conclude that the Framers and Ratifiers chose to deny these privileges to the magisterial branches.[13]

Similarly, Louis Fisher cites constitutional debates as evidence that the "faithfully executed" clause was not meant to confer on the executive sole or unlimited responsibility for executing the laws. According to Fisher,

> placing the President at the head of the executive branch did not remove from Congress the power to direct certain executive activities and to gain access to information needed for the performance of its legislative duties." At the Convention, Roger Sherman considered the Executive "nothing more than an institution for carrying the will of the Legislature into effect." It was never the purpose to make the President personally responsible for executing all the laws. Rather, he was to ensure that the laws be faithfully executed, including laws that excluded him from some operations in the executive branch.[14]

Although he does not find constitutional support for executive privilege, Prakash nonetheless sees it as a legitimate presidential power, in much the same way that "oxygen" and "movement" are necessary to the executive office: the executive cannot perform any of its proper functions without them.[15] One could also see the judicial review power claimed by the Supreme Court in *Marbury v. Madison* as analogous to executive privilege: neither is granted, explicitly or implicitly, in the Constitution, and yet both have become pragmatically necessary to the performance of the essential duties of the Supreme Court and the executive branch, respectively.

It is undisputed that Article II does not mention privilege or secrecy powers. Rozell points to the fact that Article II contains more vague and non-specific terms than Article I. As Prakash points out, that evidence is at best inconclusive and does not meet the burden of showing that executive privilege is constitutionally based.

"Judge In His Own Cause": A Self-Regulating Executive?

Rozell narrates the history of executive privilege from Nixon to George W. Bush, concluding that Nixon's successors had a difficult time with secrecy because of the lingering taint Nixon's misdeeds had imposed on the phrase "executive privilege". Carter and Ford, he tells us, were reluctant to use the words and almost equally reluctant to antagonize the post-Watergate Congress by withholding information.[16] He criticizes President Reagan, who "went to great lengths to establish secrecy measures [but] was reluctant to make a strong case for executive privilege." Reagan's concessions in specific controversies and general unwillingness to stake a constitutional claim of executive privilege weakened the doctrine unnecessarily, in Rozell's view. He argues that this weakening occurred at a time when executive privilege was most in need of resuscitation as a legitimate and necessary presidential prerogative. While George H. W. Bush used *de facto* executive privilege, he too was reluctant to make an explicit claim. None of these administrations, Rozell says, were "willing to assert [their] rightful constitutional authority to withhold information under the appropriate circumstances."[17]

When he reaches the Bill Clinton and George W. Bush presidencies, Rozell is critical of the specific uses to which they applied executive privilege. Clinton "tried to use executive privilege on several occasions to thwart investigations into allegations of corruption or illegality—exactly the type of circumstances for which executive privilege should never be used." In Bush's case, "the president tried to use executive privilege to vastly expand the scope of the power at the expense of Congress and open information." While their motives may have been different, Rozell says, "the implications of presidential misuse of executive privilege are serious, regardless of the circumstances and personal motives." Both presidents have used the privilege openly rather than secretly and thereby "reignited constitutional debate" over it, but because they misused the power even as they sought to justify it, they lost an opportunity to forge sound and beneficial constitutional standards for the future.[18]

According to Rozell, Clinton asserted executive privilege more often than any president since Eisenhower—a count that excludes the incidences of *de facto* use, where the administration ignored or refused requests for information without an official assertion of privilege. One D.C. Circuit ruling during the Clinton years involved Secretary of Agriculture Mike Espy. Espy was accused of taking illegal gifts from lobbyists, and the independent counsel investigating Espy sought access to documents collected in the White House's own internal investigation.[19]

In the *In re Sealed Case* decision, the D.C. Circuit issued a ruling that further refined the executive privilege doctrine enunciated in *U.S. v. Nixon* by outlining two strands of executive privilege. The presidential communications privilege relates to decision-making and advice, and it derives from the president's Article II powers. According to the court, "communications made by presidential advisers in the course of preparing advice for the President come under the presidential communications privilege, even when these communications are not made directly to the President." It can only be overcome by a strong showing of need satisfying two conditions: "that each discrete group of the subpoenaed materials likely contains important evidence; and second, that this evidence is not available with due diligence elsewhere." Even when misconduct is alleged, the presidential communication privilege requires a "focused showing of need" before documents will be released.[20]

The deliberative process privilege, by contrast, is rooted in the common law. It "belongs to executive officials more generally" and "is much more easily overcome by a showing of need."[21] Unlike the presidential communications privilege, the deliberative process privilege "disappears altogether when there is any reason to believe government misconduct occurred." Clearly, the presidential privilege offers greater protection on this reading: it is constitutional in origin, it applies to post-decisional and factual materials, and it is harder to overcome. After discussing the two strands of privilege at issue in the case, the court decided that the requested information was not protected.[22] Thus, the court rejected the administration's claim of secrecy while defending the secrecy power generally. Crucially, the court reaffirmed the constitutional origin of one strand of privilege (i.e., the presidential communication privilege), but also denied its absolute operation by requiring a balancing test when such claims are at issue.

The Espy case represents a doctrinal advance in the law of executive privilege. There are now two different types of executive privilege that can be claimed;

depending on which one applies, the trial court confronting the privilege claim must undertake a constitutional or common-law analysis to determine the appropriate disposition of the putatively secret materials. Of course, the *Espy* decision is only binding in the D.C. Circuit, but that is where most executive privilege cases arise. In the words of a member of the court, the D.C. Circuit "is committed to preserving the rule of law by ensuring the legality of executive branch actions, even presidential actions." Through its experience, the court has come to "view judicial power to hear cases in which presidential action is directly challenged as a necessary, even if rarely invoked, part of ensuring that the courts play their proper role in preserving the rule of law."[23]

Here, the court did invoke its power, and in the process helped to clarify several points of the law of executive privilege. In addition to delineating the two types of privilege, the court also ruled that the presidential communications strand could be invoked to protect communications not made directly to the president.[24] The court found the same rationale to apply to other communications among executive staff that applies to advice given to the president directly. Also, the court specified that two different showings of need are required, depending on which strand of privilege is involved. Third, the stronger presidential communications strand applies even after the decision in question has been made—which clearly confers additional protection on the advisor-advisee relationship between the president and executive branch staff.

Rozell maintains that it falls to the presidents themselves to use executive privilege appropriately, to refrain from asserting the privilege to conceal illegality or other abuses of power, and he insists that formal legal limits (such as the ones just listed, presumably) are not needed. Clinton used the power improperly; Reagan failed to use it vigorously enough. In the end, though, it must remain up to the president to decide on the limits of the privilege, according to Rozell's view of things. He does not find it necessary to impose legal limits in the form of statutory provisions or court decisions; he believes Congress already has the means to address a recalcitrant executive. While it is true that Congress potentially has retaliatory options available when the president claims executive privilege, it is difficult to assess the adequacy of those options when the nature of the secret information is not known.[25] If the withheld information is damning enough, the executive may choose to face a congressional subpoena or a contempt citation rather than face the consequences of releasing the information. More to the point, a full congressional response cannot occur if all information is not known.

A system that relies on the executive to police and constrain itself—to be, in short, "judge in his own cause"—encourages executive overreaching.[26] Rozell is certainly worried about overreaching and impropriety: he cites that problem repeatedly and criticizes those presidents who indulged in it. Moreover, he criticizes the self-serving statements of Richard Nixon to the effect that executive power is unreviewable. Thus, Rozell is clearly concerned about an unconstrained secrecy power in the executive, but he would rely on the separation of powers dynamic to constrain a president who is unwilling to constrain himself.[27]

Louis Fisher agrees, in a descriptive sense, that most of the executive privilege disputes "are resolved through political accommodations."[28] Fisher catalogs the techniques available to Congress to deal with a recalcitrant executive, and he summarizes their application in specific controversies: threat of impeachment, treaty ratification, withholding action on pending bills or appointments have all been used, at one time or another, as leverage in disputes between the executive and legislative branches over information. He doubts whether "handy cites from judicial opinions will win the day" very often.[29] However, Brian Smith cautions that reliance on these informal mechanisms encourages presidential brinksmanship. The executive will be more likely to push disputes to constitutional crisis and to engage, even prematurely, in dilatory or obstructionist behavior, if a clear judicial resolution is not in sight. Smith notes an inconsistency here in Rozell's position: Rozell criticizes presidents for failing to press privilege claims because their retreat weakens the doctrine, but by "discouraging a legislative solution, he expressly encourages this kind of brinksmanship."[30] To put it somewhat differently, Rozell clearly believes that the doctrine of executive privilege is rooted in the Constitution, but at the same time he does not want to see that doctrine construed or tested by courts or by the legislature. By insisting that informal solutions are virtually the only acceptable means for addressing interbranch information disputes, he would prevent the development of clear precedent or statutory language.

To rely on the separation of powers, *a priori*, to limit the power of one branch is to engage in circular argumentation, as Berger reminds us: if the institutional actors within each branch are unwilling or legally unable to act as a counterforce, then there is no effective separation.[31] We need to know in advance, then, what the institutional relationships are before we can argue for one result or another on separation of powers grounds. To state simply that the governmental functions ought to remain separate and ought to be entrusted to distinct branches is not an adequate articulation of the distribution of powers within a political system. We still need to know how far the power of each governmental division extends.

It is similarly erroneous to assume a pre-given distribution of power among coordinate branches that never changes. Few commentators would posit such a static model, but suggestions that the separation of powers works like some invisible hand to reach a sound resolution of interbranch conflicts works to the same effect. It is necessary to evaluate the state of the power relations among the three branches at a given historical moment before we can know how separation of powers can or should work to further democratic or constitutional values. This point is borne out by the Supreme Court in two recent cases, where Justices Thomas and Scalia echo Nixon to say that executive power is self-legitimating or unreviewable. The Justices articulate a power relationship that privileges the executive. If that is the state of things now, then effective separation and balancing cannot occur.

Appearing before the Senate Judiciary Committee in July 2006, Deputy Attorney General Stephen Bradbury sounded a similar note. When Senator Patrick Leahy asked Bradbury whether the president was right or wrong in his interpretation of a recent Supreme Court decision, Bradbury replied, "The president is always right." That an executive branch official was willing to make this flat assertion in a public statement to Congress, even in jest, shows the confidence with which the administration maintains its view of its own supremacy over the other braches in matters of foreign policy.[32]

The Bush administration's expansive view of executive power can also be seen in its use of "signing statements," that is, statements executed and issued by the president as he signs legislation. These statements are not a new practice, but the American Bar Association (ABA) points out that the Bush administration has issued 800 of them, as compared to less than 600 total issued since the beginning of the republic.[33] What is crucial is the content of these statements: are they merely comments on legislation, or do they amount to a refusal to execute laws that the executive finds objectionable?

The ABA report finds Bush's signing statements to fall frequently in the latter category: they are refusals to execute laws. Reviewing this practice, the report announces that the ABA "opposes, as contrary to the rule of law and our constitutional system of separation of powers, the issuance of presidential signing statements that claim the authority or state the intention to disregard or decline to enforce all or part of a law the president has signed, or to interpret such a law in a manner inconsistent with the clear intent of Congress." The report finds that the Bush administration's signing statements are "ritualistic, mechanical and generally carry no citation of authority or detailed explanation"—an indication, certainly, of their unprecedentedly frequent use.[34] As used by the Bush administration, these statements constitute a challenge to Congress—and, eventually, to the courts—as to whether the legislative power resides exclusively with Congress.

Dissenting from a ruling that requires a due process hearing for an executive detainee (but that also authorizes extra-judicial detention for "enemy combatants") Thomas remarks that "the Court has recognized the President's independent authority and need to be free from interference." According to Thomas, in "certain decisions relating to national security and foreign affairs, the courts simply lack the relevant information and expertise to second-guess determinations made by the President based on information properly withheld."[35] Thomas is writing in dissent, so obviously his view is not legally binding, but we note it here as evidence of a sitting justice's highly deferential stance regarding executive power.[36]

Justice Scalia offered a similarly deferential view, this time in a case that did involve executive privilege. The following statement is not a prepared text, but rather an informal statement, which accounts for its somewhat rambling nature. Nonetheless, it clearly indicates Scalia's view, and so we have included it here:

> I think executive privilege means whenever the President feels that he is threatened, he can simply refuse to comply with a court order. And the same thing with Congress. And it ends up in a, you know, a struggle of the two branches. I don't view that as some legal doctrine that enables him to withhold certain documents. He is, he has the power as an independent branch to say, no, this intrudes too much on my power, I will not do it. And after that, it's a, it's a struggle between two branches. And if you view executive privilege that way, forcing him to assert executive privilege is really pushing things to an extreme that should not very often occur in this Republic.[37]

Scalia's statement is strikingly similar to the assertion made by counsel for the president in *United States v. Nixon*. Counsel said that although the matter was being submitted to the Court for decision, "the President also has an obligation to carry out his constitutional duties." As Rozell puts it when summarizing this exchange, Nixon believed that "although the Court could declare the law, the President still had the final word."[38]

When the Court evinces the kind of deference voiced by Thomas and Scalia to the executive, it is simply not functioning as a check on executive power. On this view of things, courts merely ask, but cannot ultimately command, the litigant-executive to surrender documents for inspection. And at that point we are no longer operating in what Judge Patricia Wald and Jonathan Siegel call the "judicial model of dispute resolution," which assumes that "the President's duty to release information is governed by law, and, second, that the law is susceptible of judicial enforcement." To abandon this model seriously undermines the rule of law, for "if the courts cannot compel the President to disclose information, they cannot compel the President to obey other legal requirements either, and if they cannot compel the President, they cannot compel any executive official, because the courts ultimately depend on the President for enforcement of their orders."[39] In short, we must take into account the willingness of courts to perform their role in executive privilege disputes. If the courts are unwilling to uphold the rule of law as Wald and Siegel articulate that role, then effective oversight is wanting, and separation of powers not protected but imperiled.

Additionally, the executive has an array of techniques available to evade oversight and defeat document review. Executive privilege must be viewed in aggregation with other such mechanisms. Rep. Henry Waxman of the House Committee on Government Reform released a report in September 2004 detailing the Bush administration's record on secrecy by showing the multiple techniques that it has been employing: document classification and resistance to FOIA, secret detention operations, and evading statutory oversight mechanisms, among others.[40] We have addressed the various techniques of presidential secrecy throughout this book; the point here is that such an array of potential—and actually used—secrecy mechanisms renders belief in executive self-regulation unrealistic.

This arsenal of secrecy techniques not only throws out of balance the previously existing balance of powers among the branches by giving the executive multiple avenues to avoid oversight, but it also reduces greatly the likelihood that the executive will opt for openness. To take one example detailed in Waxman's report, the administration has evaded the oversight requirements of the Federal Advisory Committee Act, a 1972 law designed to make public all relationships between the federal government and private entities furnishing advice to government.[41] The publicity requirements of FACA apply when an advisory group "has at least one member that is not a federal employee."[42] The Bush administration, however, has found various ways to narrow the applicability of FACA. The Homeland Security Act, for example, authorizes the secretary of homeland security to exempt any advisory group from FACA.[43] Waxman also notes a tactic that turns certain private entities into federal employees while they advise the government, thus placing them outside FACA supervision.[44]

This example shows the commitment of the Bush administration to secrecy, but it also illustrates the way that secrecy techniques work cumulatively to defeat oversight. In some instances executive privilege need not be asserted because other protective mechanisms are available; in other cases the privilege will be asserted more vigorously when the executive knows that the information will be harder to get by other means (for example, by using FOIA or FACA). In short, there are simply too many incentives for withholding information, so that the executive cannot be relied on to use executive privilege responsibly or restrainedly.

Blurring the State Secrets/Executive Privilege Distinction

The third problem with Rozell's conception of executive privilege is his repeated reference to "national security" as a justification for executive privilege. Arguing in defense of a strong executive privilege in chapter 2, for example, he notes that "in the national security realm, an important matter of presidential concern is the potential effect of public revelations of policy discussions. Such openness, for example, could lead to demands for the executive to act before it is prepared to do so." He continues by saying that "courts have generally provided broad discretionary authority to the president in national security and foreign affairs." Similarly, when criticizing the Bush administration for its choice of cases in which to invoke executive privilege, he notes that "none of these cases concerned national security." This was important because "with the nation at war abroad and fighting terrorism domestically, it is not hard to imagine circumstances in which the Administration might stake a claim to executive privilege to protect national security and the public interest."[45]

Rozell also cites the *Reynolds* case as a source of support for strong executive privilege.[46] *Reynolds,* however, is the precedent-setting case in which the state secrets privilege in the United States was applied for the first time. Here again, he underemphasizes important differences between national security and non–national security matters. The state secrets privilege is typically raised in cases of national security. It is possible that presidential advice could involve national security and that therefore executive privilege could be used to protect that advice. In such a case, both privileges would potentially be available to the executive. But the arguments for each privilege are distinct. Protection of national security, obviously, can be a valid basis for withholding information, as we reviewed in chapter 3.

The problem here, however, is that national security–related arguments can confuse matters in executive privilege cases. The Supreme Court in *United States v. Nixon* rejected the president's attempt to unify executive privilege and state secrets privilege, holding that they are distinct in source and function. The Nixon court ruled that

> neither the doctrine of separation of powers, nor the need for confidentiality of high-level communications, without more, can sustain an absolute, unqualified Presiden-

tial privilege of immunity from judicial process under all circumstances. The President's need for complete candor and objectivity from advisers calls for great deference from the courts. However, when the privilege depends solely on the broad, undifferentiated claim of public interest in the confidentiality of such conversations, a confrontation with other values arises. Absent a claim of need to protect military, diplomatic or sensitive national security secrets, we find it difficult to accept the argument that even the very important interest in confidentiality of Presidential communications is significantly diminished by production of such material for in camera inspection with all the protection that the district court will be obliged to provide.[47]

The Court clearly distinguished executive, or "presidential," privilege from state secrets privilege. President Nixon's attempt to obtain absolute privilege protection without asserting a national security interest was explicitly rejected by the Court. Nixon could not avail himself of the absolute protection of the state secrets privilege because he could not reasonably claim that national security issues were involved in the disclosure of the Watergate tapes.

We believe that it is important for the two privileges to remain definitionally separate. By referring repeatedly to national security in the executive privilege context, Rozell sometimes pairs the term *national security* with the term *public interest*, offering both as justifications for executive secrecy.[48] Taken together, the two terms form an endlessly expansive justificatory category: the executive should be accorded discretion (and perhaps absolute protection from disclosure of information) whenever national security or public interest so requires, but when would a president ever acknowledge acting neither in the public interest nor to protect national security? If the president were permitted to defeat congressional inquiry by claiming either of the two justifications, he would be likely to do so in virtually every case. Moreover, he would be able to avoid even *in camera* inspection of documents by a trial judge. In short, the reintroduction of national security into executive privilege analysis creates a doctrinal dilemma: we risk losing the distinction between state secrets and executive privilege, expanding the scope of presidential privilege beyond meaningful limitation, or both.

Recent Cases
The Presidential Records Act Expansion

The Presidential Records Act was passed in 1978 in the wake of the continuing litigation over Nixon's presidential records after he resigned, and it established that "the records of a president relating to his official duties belong to the American people." Under the PRA, for the first five years after a president leaves office, only Congress and the courts generally have access to his records; restrictions on access can be extended to twelve years in cases of sensitive records. After twelve years, the FOIA governs access to the records, and executive privilege also potentially applies.[49] At the end of his second term, Ronald Reagan issued Executive Order 12667, which established procedures for current and former presidents claiming executive privilege.[50] George W. Bush replaced Reagan's order with E.O. 13233, which "establishes a process that generally operates to block the release of presidential papers."[51] Under Bush's order, a former president can unilaterally assert executive privilege over his records, which, as Rozell points out, is problematic for two reasons. First, the interest of a former president in maintaining confidentiality of advice is far weaker than that of a sitting president. Second, the burden "will shift from those who must justify withholding information to fall instead on those who have made a claim for access to information." Thus, "the Bush Administration actions on executive privilege dramatically shift the burden away from where it belongs."[52]

Bush's order allows for indefinite delay in the release of records, even without an assertion of executive privilege. Vice presidents, current and former, can claim privilege over their records, and representatives of deceased presidents can assert privilege on the president's behalf.[53] The regulations promulgated under the PRA, and the case law established by *In re Sealed Case*, are clearly contravened by the order. For one thing, the official archivist of the United States has statutory power to decide claims of privilege concerning archived records, but Bush's order simply eliminates that grant of power.[54]

These provisions baldly advance secrecy over public access without any reasonable relationship to the underlying policy rationale for executive privilege, that is, the president's need for candid advice. Even if national secrecy is at issue, "executive privilege may actually be frivolous in [that] case because there are already other secrecy protections in place for national security purposes."[55] The state secrets privilege, discussed in chapter 3, protects national security–related matters; thus, national security is not a plausible reason for the expanded secrecy protections of Bush's order—particularly regarding former presidents. In short, Bush's order is an unwarranted expansion of presidential secrecy via executive privilege, and although Rozell is an advocate for vigorous, constitutionally grounded executive privilege, even he has gone on record opposing this particular use of it.

The Energy Task Force

President Bush's formation of the National Energy Policy Development Group (NEPDG) provoked criticism for its inclusion of energy industry representatives in closed-door White House advisory meetings. Early in his first term, the president established the NEPDG under Vice President Cheney and charged it with the mission of "developing . . . a national energy policy designed to help the private sector, and government at all levels, promote dependable, affordable and environmentally sound production and distribution of energy for the future."[56] Formally, the NEPDG was comprised of government members, so the oversight requirements of the FACA would therefore, at first blush, appear not to apply.[57] However, the presence of high-level industry executives at the otherwise secret meetings led some critics to argue that those private members' role in the group was virtually the same as that of the formal government members.[58] The implication, obviously, was that the interests of large energy corporations were being promoted at these secret sessions at the expense of the larger public good. And the administration's secrecy about the process heightened fears of improper industry influence—and even direction—of national energy policy.

Controversy swelled following the White House's refusal to provide any information to the public about these confidential meetings. The ensuing litigation included *Walker v. Cheney*, a suit brought by the comptroller general to compel production of records, and *Sierra Club v. Cheney*, a second suit for document production that reached the Supreme Court as *Cheney v. U.S. District Court*. Both of these cases were resolved in favor of the administration.[59]

Significantly, both cases were decided without the assertion of executive privilege. Thus, Vice President Cheney never had to invoke that privilege and submit to the courts' adjudication of it. In *Walker*, the district court ruled that the plaintiff, Comptroller General David Walker, lacked standing to bring the suit; the court applied an especially rigorous standing analysis in order to avoid, if possible, the "constitutional clash" that an executive privilege dispute would bring.[60] The vice president benefited, clearly, from the narrower analysis the court applied, because he never had to await the result of *in camera* inspection of materials that invocation of executive privilege usually involves.

In other words, if the case had not been dismissed and executive privilege had been raised, the court would have examined the purportedly confidential materials and subjected them to the balancing test that the law of executive privilege requires. The court turned separation of powers on its head by allowing the concern itself to foreclose any analysis of what the separation of powers might actually work out to be in the case. Rather than applying the doctrine of executive privilege to resolve an interbranch dispute, the court conceptualized executive privilege as a threat to separation of powers. This approach reflects both a static conception of separation of powers and a profound solicitude for the interests of executive secrecy at the expense of openness and accountability.

In the *Sierra Club* litigation, the Supreme Court similarly eliminated the necessity of an executive privilege claim, albeit by different means. In that case, the vice president had sought a writ of mandamus compelling the district court to vacate its pre-trial discovery orders. The court of appeals denied the mandamus petition, requiring the vice president–petitioner to assert executive privilege prior to seeking such mandamus relief. The Supreme Court disagreed, holding that it was not necessary to assert the privilege before seeking mandamus relief.[61]

The Court was chary, once again, of confronting executive power. The majority noted, first, that the case was a civil matter, unlike *Nixon*. Thus, in the Court's view, the public interest in disclosure was already weaker in *Sierra Club* than in *Nixon*. In one sense, that may be true—criminal allegations involving the executive are more serious than civil claims in terms of possible ultimate consequences. However, civil matters may ultimately lead to criminal charges, particularly when Congress is investigating the conduct of executive branch members. Second, while the Sierra Club case is civil in nature, there is nonetheless a weighty constitutional matter involved, as the Court notices.

"The Executive Branch, at its highest level, is seeking the aid of the courts to protect its constitutional prerogatives," the majority opinion states.[62] Once again, the Court turns separation of powers on its head by allowing the mere invocation of the idea of separation of powers to defeat any counterbalancing function the judiciary could perform. The Court itself assumes the role of "protecting" the executive rather than overseeing or constraining executive power. Just as the courts have declined to confront executive power in state secrets cases, so do they appear to retreat in the face of executive privilege controversies. Moreover, in *Sierra Club*, there was not even a claim of executive privilege: the Court relieved the vice president from the burden of even claiming privilege—it was enough for the vice president to claim merely that the discovery orders interfered with his constitutional duties. If the vice president had been required to assert executive privilege, as the Court of Appeals ruling required, then the trial court would have been the arbiter of that claim, performing an oversight role by inspecting the documents in chambers and deciding whether the public interest required release.

During the litigation, counsel for the vice president suggested that there could have been an informal resolution of the controversy. He argued that Congress had "plenty of practical leverage" to obtain release of the NEPDG documents: for example, they could have refused to act on the administration's energy proposal. "There can be a give and take," he opined, "there can be a process of accommodation between the branches . . . which is the way that Congress has gotten information for over 200 years."[63] In theory, that is precisely the approach to resolving executive privilege disputes that Rozell favors: an informal, transactional process rather than rule creation or rule application. However, the institution of the presidency has grown stronger over the course of those 200 years, and, as we have demonstrated throughout this book, vast growth in secrecy powers has occurred over the past thirty years, both despite and as a result of the collapse of the Nixon presidency.

The strengthened institutional configuration we see now, with its arsenal of secrecy-related powers, is far less susceptible to the give and take of legislative-executive relations that would balance power between the two. For one thing, the reluctance of the courts to get involved works much the same way as it would in any potential legal dispute: when one party has an ultimate advantage in court, that advantage will shape, and even distort, the informal negotiations taking place before adjudication. The litigant facing greater risk at trial has a clear incentive to settle for less, for a "least worst" outcome short of trial. In the same way, when the executive knows that the courts will not act to compel disclosure, the executive has far less reason to bargain or compromise. Of course, the legislative checks mentioned above, such as delaying confirmation of executive appointments, are exercised independently of the courts, but the two kinds of checks on executive power are not unrelated. It is easier to resist the executive when one has a clear basis in law for doing so, and it is more difficult when the law is unfavorable. Moreover, the biggest executive privilege controversy we have seen was in fact resolved by the courts, and it was the Supreme Court's decision that ended not only the controversy but also the presidency in that case.

Whatever one thinks of the reasoning in *U.S. v. Nixon*, it is accepted that the Court's intervention determined the outcome.[64] Perhaps better than the other two controversies cited in this chapter, the NEPDG dispute demonstrates the inadequacy of informal means to resolving executive privilege disputes in the age of the secret presidency, despite the administration counsel's protestations to the contrary.

The NEPDG litigation terminated when the case was returned to the D.C. Circuit, and that court directed the District Court to dismiss the complaints. The court had to determine what constitutes membership on a federal advisory committee, and it saw this task as a possible encroachment on the presidential advise-ment process. "In light of severe separation-of-powers problems," the court ex-plained, "we must construe the statute strictly."[65] "Strict construal" in this case meant a reading favorable to the executive: the definition of membership was held to include only voting members, so industry representatives were not considered members (and therefore not subject to FACA publicity requirements). Thus, all the remaining challenges to the energy group process were disposed of by the D.C. Circuit, and the disposition was once again based on a solicitude for execu-tive control of information.

The 9/11 Investigations

Two investigative bodies studied and produced reports on the devastating terror attacks of September 11, 2001: a select congressional committee, and the private 9/11 Commission. The full congressional report was not released to the public; large portions were classified. The private commission's work was hin-dered and delayed by the Bush administration, as indicated below. In the end, Congress voted to give the commission more time to complete its report.

The White House refused to permit the full 9/11 panel to view notes of presi-dential briefings taken by four of its own panel members: the four note-taking members had to keep their notes from the other members.[66] The president and vice president also proposed strict limits on their own interviews with the com-mission: they would be questioned for only one hour each, and only the chair and vice chair would ask questions.[67] The administration also refused initially to permit National Security Advisor Condoleezza Rice to testify, and these disagree-ments led Congress to pass an extension of the deadline for the commission's report.[68] Rice stated that "it would be improper under separation of powers for an incumbent national security adviser to testify at a public hearing."[69] The Bush administration finally changed its position, allowing Rice to testify, under oath, before the commission.

At the same time, the administration agreed to permit the full panel to ques-tion the president and vice president without a time limit, although they would not be under oath.[70] The administration insisted that their appearance "should not be considered official testimony."[71] The reversal on Rice's testimony followed public criticism about Rice's numerous appearances on TV talk shows, where she discussed anti-terror policy: her frequent discussions of that topic undercut the rationale for withholding her testimony.[72] Similarly, one panel member pointed out that the president had given a three-hour interview to Bob Woodward in preparation for Woodward's book, so that a shorter time limit for the commission hearings was unseemly.[73]

The next dispute arose a week later, when the commission "identified 69 documents from the Clinton era that the Bush White House withheld from investigators and which include references to al Qaeda, Osama bin Laden and other issues relevant to the panel's work." In response to the commission's request, the White House produced twelve of the documents, and failed to produce, at that time, the remaining fifty-seven.[74] The lengthy *9/11 Commission Report* was finally produced in July 2004.

Before evaluating the executive privilege issues arising in the course of the 9/11 investigations, it is necessary to clarify why executive privilege is relevant at all in an area—investigating an attack on the United States—with such obvious national security implications. In other words, shouldn't the 9/11 investigations be analyzed under the "state secrets" rubric instead? The answer is simple: the administration does not appear to have raised state secrets privilege in the course of the investigations. Instead, their demurrals have sounded more like executive privilege claims, especially with regard to the dispute over Rice's testimony. The administration repeatedly phrased its objections in terms of Rice's status as a close advisor to the president.[75] Thus, the 9/11 investigations are significant to our analysis of executive privilege development.[76]

Throughout the 9/11 investigation process, the administration guarded secrecy quite closely, often in ways that seemed unconnected to the recognized justifications we have discussed in this chapter. For example, the president attempted to limit questioning of himself and the vice president to one hour, as noted above. It is difficult to discern a nexus between the interview time limit and the preservation of candid advice within the executive—and to our knowledge, no one has ever tried to articulate any such nexus. Similarly, Bush and Cheney's statements to the commission were not made under oath. Once again, an oath does not preserve confidential communications—although unsworn testimony does carry less legal weight, and that is the likelier reason for the refusal to testify under oath. These two examples suggest that the administration sought to preserve secrecy for reasons other than those traditionally accepted in executive privilege cases. The furor over whether or not Condoleezza Rice would testify is similarly notable for the lack of a coherent, consistent administration position. While persisting in her refusal to testify, she repeatedly defended the administration on television talk shows. The predictable justification for refusal—that Rice was a close presidential advisor who needed to continue providing candid advice to the president on critical matters—became unavailable to the administration as Rice discussed those same matters on national television, presumably with White House approval.

It is significant for a sitting president to become involved in an ongoing investigation that involves his own administration, and the stakes were certainly high in this case, where the nation had suffered a horrible attack with great loss of life. Interestingly, though, the administration failed to exploit the opportunities for the public acceptance of secrecy in the investigation. The administration undercut its own position in the Rice dispute and imposed seemingly arbitrary conditions on the statements and information it provided. To some extent, the 2004 presidential election was certainly a factor, as the president would soon receive a public response to his handling of this matter of great public interest and concern. Total refusal to cooperate with the investigations would have been even more politically risky than usual, with an election mere months away.

However, there were legal justifications for secrecy available that the administration never used. It is difficult to say why things proceeded in such an *ad hoc* manner instead of as an orderly dispute over law with clear and consistent positions. Perhaps the administration chose not to attune itself closely to the law of executive privilege but rather opted to emphasize informal actions and procedures. In any event, the interaction with the 9/11 investigative bodies contrasts sharply with the Bush administration's advancement of anti-terror initiatives, discussed in chapter 4. With its anti-terror policy, the administration used public cooperation—and, not incidentally, fear—to the fullest extent in order to work major changes in the federal government. In the end, though, the administration emerged from the 9/11 investigations to win reelection, so the management of the potential scandal must be judged to be largely successful.

The New Executive Privilege

We submit that a convincing case for a constitutionally based executive privilege has not yet been made. There is no explicit textual support for the privilege, and the arguments from constitutional history and the drafters' implicit intent are speculative. That is not the end of the matter, however. We concur with Prakash that there are appropriate governmental powers not rooted in the Constitution. Certain incidents of governmental power are necessary, even if not inherent in a definitional sense, in order for the branches to carry out the functions that have been explicitly assigned to them. Judicial review is one such power: it was not conferred by the Constitution but rather claimed by the Supreme Court on its own initiative, and it has become an established feature of our government of separate powers, in which each branch checks the others.

Though some would argue how, precisely, it ought to be used, the continued existence of judicial review is not seriously in question. Similarly, executive privilege, defined as the executive's "right to withhold information from either Congress or the judicial branch"—and thus, indirectly, from the people—is a necessary component of executive power.[77] It facilitates the passage of candid advice to the president from his advisors, and without it such advice would be far more difficult to obtain. Thus, we argue that the continued existence of executive privilege, albeit one not rooted in the Constitution, is an enduring and unavoidable feature of our governmental system. However, the privilege must be properly limited.

First, executive privilege is cabined by the state secrets privilege. At times, Rozell's analysis seems to risk conflating the two, when in fact they are distinct: state secrets relate to national security and are protected by absolute privilege, while executive privilege relates to non–national security matters and is a qualified privilege, capable of being overcome upon a proper showing of need. To raise issues of national security is to move out of the executive privilege realm entirely and to operate under a different calculus. Thus, national security concerns should not be raised to buttress executive privilege claims: they belong in a different domain and are bound by different rules.

One thing that this classificatory move accomplishes is to make clear just what counts in executive privilege analysis. Once the layer of "national security" issues is peeled away, it is easier to focus on the true competing interests in play: the executive's need to receive candid advice on the one hand and the people's right to know (or the legislature's constitutional responsibilities) on the other. Unlike the state secrets area (at least as the law now stands), executive privilege cases require courts to weigh these interests; the executive's interest in secrecy does not always or automatically trump the public's interest in openness.

Once we have established that executive privilege is not constitutionally grounded and that it exists in a more limited form, the next question is how it is to be construed or managed. Rozell maintains that informal processes of inter-branch negotiation are the best way for information disputes involving the executive to be resolved. He is not alone in this position: Louis Fisher has analyzed the various means available to Congress to obtain information the executive does not want to release, including the subpoena power, delaying passage of bills, and even impeachment. Fisher, in fact, worries that establishment of decisional rules of executive privilege might cede too much power to the executive rather than limiting executive power. He suggests that that was what occurred in the *Nixon* case, where the Supreme Court discussed national security even though that was not an issue in the case.[78] Thus, Fisher is concerned that courts may construct unwieldy rules that make executive privilege even harder to control. To be sure, though, there are some cases in which "federal courts [apply] the necessary pressure" to settle the information dispute between the executive and legislative branches, such as *United States v. AT&T*.[79] And in some cases, the "message from federal judges is that an agreement hammered out between the two branches is better than a directive handed down by a court."[80]

The problem we see with exclusive reliance on informal settlement mechanisms to the exclusion of court action is that the institution of the presidency has grown stronger and more secretive in the post-Watergate period, and the separation of powers dynamic cannot possibly remain unaffected by that growth. Thus, for example, the executive's ability to fend off congressional oversight that would otherwise occur under FOIA and FACA changes the playing field on which Congress and the president interact. Similarly, an aggressive use of secrecy under FISA and vastly expanded powers under the anti-terror laws confer advantages on the executive that did not exist previously.

To see separation of powers as a dynamic concept is to appreciate that both daily interbranch struggles and larger institutional changes affect the field, sometimes creating imbalances that threaten democratic and constitutional values. We argue that just such an imbalance has occurred with regard to secrecy and that Congress and the courts must act to correct it. There have been judicial decisions on executive privilege, most recently in the energy group litigation. As we argued in the state secrets context, courts must be willing to confront the secret presidency and to fashion rules that resolve competing claims of secrecy and openness. The courts must help to establish what the separation of powers is, rather than using that phrase itself as a justification for staying out of the fray altogether. Under *United States v. Nixon*, courts are directed to weigh and decide competing claims in the executive privilege area. It would be easier if Congress codified the privilege, but in the absence of legislation the courts will have to continue refining executive privilege law.

The most crucial aspect of executive privilege law is the principle that the law applies at all. We have seen in the energy group cases that courts can be reluctant to apply or enforce the law by requiring assertion of executive privilege. We think that that reluctance is a disturbing phenomenon, one that possibly indicates a dangerous trend—rather than questioning the scope of executive privilege, courts may be retreating to a stance that avoids executive privilege altogether. If that is indeed what is happening, then executive privilege is becoming a "dirty word" in a sense quite opposite its connotation during the post-Nixon years. Back then, it was a dirty word because it evoked Nixon's lawbreaking; now, it suggests an unwarranted intrusion on executive power. It would be ironic indeed if we came full circle to the point where a "hands off" approach to executive privilege engendered the same kind of executive overreaching that provoked the executive privilege decision in *Nixon* in the first place.

Finally, we submit that it is a mistake to view law and informal negotiation in isolation from one another. It is well known that the legal field, in areas as diverse as civil rights, antitrust, and environmental law, structures the course of private interaction. What the courts have done and are likely to do in a given case has bearing on negotiated settlements, conferring advantage and enabling outcome prediction. Thus, in interbranch disputes over information, decisional precedent and even positive law set the bounds within which the parties will negotiate. Law does not stifle private negotiation but rather facilitates and structures it. The courts can help to restore a balance to the area of executive privilege that has been lost during the secret presidency.

A Secret Presidency for the New Millennium?

The President is there in the White House for you, it is not you who are here for him.

— Walt Whitman

We have traced the development of secrecy-related powers in the American presidency, mostly over the past thirty-five years. We made descriptive claims about the ways secrecy has grown during this time, and we made two kinds of normative arguments: one a political theory argument against secrecy, the other a constitutional argument against secrecy.[1] The political theory claim essentially condemns practices of secrecy by the executive because such practices threaten democracy. The constitutional claim is that Article II does not authorize the secrecy-related practices that the contemporary executive has at hand. It is worth asking, at this point, how these three arguments might be made to, or about, future presidents. Given the state of development of presidential secrecy as we have documented it here, the institution now has structures facilitating secrecy built into it, and the office has grown more powerful in one particular aspect, like a plant whose parts are unevenly exposed to light. What might future presidents do with the office in its new configuration, and should we be concerned?

The Growth of Institutionalized Secrecy

We began this book by describing a meeting during the Ford administration in which top-level administration officials bemoaned the lack of greater secrecy capabilities and complained that they could not accomplish all that they wished to do without those greater powers. Thirty years later, some of those same officials were present to witness the arrival of those very conditions, in a new administration that had made secrecy its watchword. But what has changed in the intervening years, between the 1970s and the beginning of the new millennium?

We have described the historical and institutional threads of change, noting where those threads cross. It is well known that Watergate and the fall of Richard Nixon led to widespread distrust of the presidency and to resounding calls for limiting presidential power. What is less known is the repeated occurrence, post-Watergate, of a process called "legiscide": the congressional ceding of power, through legislation, to the executive. Lowi cited the War Powers Resolution as one instance, and we have described others here (see chapter 1). On the surface, those acts appear to be assertions of congressional power to limit the executive branch, but they actually create a semi-secret space in which the president can pursue policy goals shielded from criticism (even from view) by a cloak of legality. War Powers is one example: the president can commit troops to a conflict and dare the Congress to call them back.

More pertinent to secrecy, however, are the state secrets privilege (legalized by the Supreme Court and left unrestrained by Congress for fifty years), the intelligence surveillance power (legalized by FISA in 1978), and the post-9/11 anti-terror initiatives (legalized by unusually rapid congressional acceptance of the Patriot Act and related laws). Through a combination of action and inaction, Congress has created a legalized space for the executive to operate in secrecy, so that actions that might have been viewed as paranoid overreaching in the 1970s is now lawful behavior. Representative Peter Hoekstra, Republican Congressman from Michigan and chairman of the House Intelligence Committee, broke with this trend, though, when in 2006 he criticized the president, publicly and privately, over warrantless surveillance.[2]

If some secrecy powers in the presidential arsenal were forged with the help of Congress, others were surely facilitated by the federal courts. Executive privilege, we have seen, gains such endlessly expansive interpretation that Justice Scalia sees a right in the executive to defy judicial process.[3] Similarly, decisions regarding interpretation of the anti-terror laws show great deference to the executive; when district courts balk at excessive secrecy, the circuits often overrule them, as did the D.C. Circuit on the military tribunals issue and the Second Circuit on the material witness question (see chapter 4). Of course, the Supreme Court's June 29, 2006, decision in *Hamdan*, discussed in chapter 4, is an important exception.

An obvious question is how the office of the presidency will look when future leadership changes take place. In Skowronek's terms, how will the conditions in both political and secular time be structured for the next administration? Our concern is that even a president with a less pronounced affinity for a secretive administration will confront structures that are, at the very least, efficacious to the pursuit of political goals, and he or she will be strongly encouraged to utilize them. Will presidents in the near future forgo the institutional advantages that have accrued during the post-Watergate period? One way to approach this question is to look at both political and secular conditions specific to the current situation. There is little or no indication that the threat of further terror attacks will diminish in the near future, and that "secular-time" condition will likely continue to foster a war mentality with respect to intelligence and law enforcement. Future presidents might inherit military deployments in Iraq, Afghanistan, and elsewhere, with those deployments a commitment to completing the missions in some sense. The creation of the Department of Homeland Security in 2002 accelerated research efforts on security technologies, in part by generating federal funding support for such research.[4]

With regard to power, we can look first at the growth of the secrecy-related bureaucracy that stands ready for use. We have shown that Democratic presidents Carter and Clinton used state secrets, executive privilege, and FISA more than occasionally. It would therefore be a mistake to say that the trend toward increased secrecy and opacity in the presidency is a trait of Republican presidents only.

Mark Rozell has pointed out, though, that the Bush administration moved to institutionalize further both executive privilege (by resolving information disputes without ever asserting the privilege formally) and presidential records secrecy (by vastly expanding protection of those records beyond what Reagan had done). If a new administration sought to repudiate, in Skowronek's terms, the political order left by Bush, he or she would need to decide first, whether or not to repudiate the culture of secrecy, and second, how to confront the secrecy bureaucracy that comes with the job. A president wishing to repudiate the massive and expanding structures of executive branch secrecy may alienate large swaths of the bureaucracy and seriously hamper his policy initiative or reelectibility.

An appraisal of presidential power must also address interbranch relationships, and we have tried to do so here. A half-century ago, Robert Dahl wrote a landmark article addressing the question of policymaking by the U.S. Supreme Court.[5] Dahl reported that the Court unquestionably makes policy (and thereby poses a potential problem for democracy); however, the threat does not materialize because the Court consistently votes in line with dominant national alliances, broadly speaking. But what if the Court acts to facilitate executive actions, covering them with a protective mantle of Court-legitimated secrecy? We have cited statements from Justices Thomas and Scalia and others signaling the possible emergence of just that sort of jurisprudence. The Patriot Act reauthorization debates defy easy categorization in terms of alliances or even party allegiances: as we note above, Republicans as well as Democrats have expressed concern and frustration about the difficulty of obtaining information related to anti-terror activities from the Bush administration.[6]

What, then, is the dominant national alliance on that issue? It may be that the Court is not implementing an existing alliance but rather aiding in the promotion of secrecy irrespective of the contours of any such alliance. We would then face a threat to democracy quite different from the potential threat noted by Dahl: not a judiciary too out-of-step with dominant understandings of the political branches but rather a judiciary too complicit in the expansion of executive power at the expense of the power of the people and their legislative representatives.

With regard to Congress, one could well ask why it has repeatedly given away power to the president over the past thirty years while appearing outwardly to limit presidential power. Two separate dynamics are worth noting here. First, it is problematic to ascribe unitary intentions to a group as diverse and complex as a legislature in a large nation such as the United States. It is one thing to build support for particular legislation. Lawmakers may support a bill and form a majority for different reasons, including compromises among factions and individual agreements. Particular provisions draw support from particular lawmakers, and party- and constituent-related pressures come into play. When votes fall along party lines, it is likely that at least some in the majority voting bloc were responding to organizational pressures. The result may come in the form of unintended consequences: long-term changes in institutional structures and power relations were not part of the calculus individual legislators performed before voting. The Patriot Act, for example, passed Congress in record time, with barely a pause for discussion. There was far more argument the second time around, when it came up for reauthorization. The effects, nonetheless, are all too real.

James Sundquist has pointed out that Congress may suffer from an institutional tendency to give away power as well. Seen in this light, passage of the Patriot Act and FISA are not simply miscalculations or short-sighted mistakes but rather the result of "the nature of the congressional animal." Congress, he continues,

> is a creature compelled to nurture its relationship with the state or district that determines, at two- or six-year intervals, whether it lives or dies. The demands of the constituency are so urgent and incessant so as to lead the members of Congress— House members in particular but senators as well—to concentrate on the role of

representative of their areas, to deal with local and peripheral matters, avoid broader responsibility, and leave basic national decisions to the president. If that view is correct, the will to govern, the necessary guts, will not be regained—or acquired in the first place—without radical change in the nature or the behavior, or both, of the members themselves.[7]

This piece of the puzzle helps to explain why Congress might repeatedly step back from confronting the growing secrecy of the presidency and sometimes even facilitate the process. If Congress doesn't want to lead in general and if secrecy issues often implicate important matters of national security, then we can expect members to be even less likely to lead on those matters. Of course, that vacuum of leadership is problematic from our perspective, but it is nonetheless easier to understand in view of Sundquist's comments.

We have argued throughout this book that institutional changes to the presidency wrought since Watergate have resulted in part from the actions of individual presidents and in part from larger forces, such as the widespread public impulse to restrain presidential power in response to Watergate itself. The threat of terror attacks following 9/11 helped to catalyze institutional change in an administration already committed to increasing executive power. The Bush administration consolidated several powers that rely on and are defined by secrecy, and in view of that development it is necessary to study the presidency with a focus on secrecy in subsequent years. We hope that this book is an aid to such efforts, so that transparency in American government may eventually be regained.

Secrecy and Democracy

In a recent essay, Robert Dahl considered the institutions necessary to support a robust democracy. Among those he found to be indispensable were free expression, alternative sources of information, and independent associations. These institutions, in turn, help to bring about enlightened understanding, effective participation, and influence on the national political agenda—political goods that come about through civic participation.[8] When Dahl's crucial democratic institutions are viewed alongside the secret presidency as we have described it in the preceding pages, the effect is striking: we see at once the greater importance of safeguards when institutionalized secrecy threatens as well as the ways in which excessive secrecy can render those very safeguards ineffective. In the everyday dynamic of the balance of powers, the freedoms of expression, information, and association help to keep the separate branches of a representative democracy in balance.

Dahl might have added transparency to his list of conditions that nurture democracy. To some extent, our institutions draw their vitality from a political culture of transparency. Transparency brings the obvious benefit of subjecting governmental actions to scrutiny and oversight: by the other branches, by the media, and by the public generally. Free expression is enhanced when citizens can speculate and form opinions on matters of public concern, and that process in turn depends on the availability of information from multiple sources, which relies on independent associations to help keep channels of information open. If government operates not with transparency but with opacity, all three democracy-sustaining institutions are in peril.

With transparency as the norm, exceptions stand out as unusual and must be justified. Legitimate secrets, which usually have to do with intelligence gathering or other national security concerns, require accommodation into democratic practice, because members of a democracy operating under the rule of law will tend to view such deviations with suspicion. What we have increasingly seen instead, in Athan Theoharis's terms, is a "culture of secrecy," which marks as deviant precisely the opposite kind of phenomenon: questions about increased executive power or calls for openness. In a culture of secrecy, congressional investigations such as the Waxman Report or even a Republican lawmaker's recent complaints about the White House withholding information begin to look deviant and therefore suspect.[9] It goes almost without saying that incremental increases in secrecy are far easier to achieve when secrecy is the norm.

In the U.S. political system, much of what is done in secret comes to public awareness late (or not at all), so that the effect of publicity on presidential action is blunted. Obviously, unknown actions cannot be challenged, and even when such actions cannot be hidden from view permanently, delay is the next best course of action. As discussed in chapter 4, the Bush administration delayed revelations about the Valerie Plame affair, about the manipulation of prewar intelligence on alleged Iraqi WMDs, and about the torture of prisoners in Abu Ghraib and elsewhere long enough that none of these scandals affected the outcome of the 2004 presidential election. The point is not the effectiveness of presidential scandal damage control but rather the ways in which secrecy functions to obscure problems that call, at the very least, for full and vigorous investigation.

In his book on presidential lying, Eric Alterman writes, "Excessive secrecy, a close cousin of lying and frequently its handmaiden and inspiration, has been a key facet of American governance since literally before the nation's founding."

He notes that "keeping a secret is not the same as telling a lie, just as refusing a comment is not the same as intentionally misleading. But it takes a brave politician to risk attack for honestly doing the former, when he can just as easily dispose of the problem with an easy resort to the latter."[10] However, in a system where secrecy is so deeply entrenched, the opposite may be true: why risk being caught in a lie when there is little chance that the matter will ever come to light? In many cases, if secrets are guarded carefully enough, the public will not even know what to ask. Alterman condemns presidential deception in part because it sets in motion a causal chain over which presidents have no control.[11]

Perhaps the best way to understand the relationship between lying and hiding things is to think of them working in tandem. Sometimes a lie works to hide unpopular facts, sometimes secrecy is more protective than lying, and sometimes they work together to create an impenetrable wall around the executive. Alterman mentions the Office of Strategic Intelligence, which was to be used "for the purposes of distributing deliberate misinformation to foreign media."[12] The Bush administration announced in 2002 that the office would be closed, but in a political version of Cartesian radical doubt, the very mention of such a project in the first place vitiates any assurance that it was cancelled: the announcement of cancellation could, in itself, be a product of the disinformation campaign. The operation of lies and concealment, then, work more harm together than separately, and they erode public confidence in the operation of government in general and the executive in particular.

Secrecy and Constitutionalism

We have argued throughout this book that the Constitution does not authorize the varieties of presidential secrecy currently in use. The state secrets privilege and executive privilege are creations of politics ratified by the courts. They arose out of political conflict, the executive claimed them, and the courts agreed. FISA, the classification power, and the array of anti-terror laws passed post-9/11 are statutory in nature, but all three of these matters raise constitutional problems as well. There is a strand of critique based on constitutionalism, then, running through our study of presidential secrecy.

Constitutionalism can be defined restrictively, as the belief that "constitutional meaning and legitimate constitutional practice are fixed in a text and made authoritative through the practice of judicial review."[13] Adherents of this view are likely to believe, in the words of Steven Griffin, that "the Constitution has come through American history unscathed."[14] But there are, of course, other ways to understand "constitutionalism" that are less restrictive and more inclusive of institutions other than the courts. For example, scholars can study the extent to which "constitutional meaning and practice are forged in, and contested by, non-judicial institutions."[15] Thus, the range of meanings of constitutionalism is broad, and one does not have to follow a narrow interpretation in order to assign enduring meaning to the Constitution.

In the last instance, though, there is a core belief that all versions of constitutionalism must share, that is, that "constitutional texts are interpretable and binding." Constitutionalism cannot be reduced beyond that basic understanding without changing the American system of government drastically. "Once members of a constitutional system give up on the idea that constitutional provisions are authoritative and directive," Howard Gillman warns, "or that certain institutions deserve the final say in questions of constitutional interpretation, then by definition there can be no text-based practice; there can only be conventional politics that is masked as constitutional politics."[16] Perhaps this is what political actors sensed during the Nixon presidency, the Iran-Contra scandal, the McCarthy hearings, and the Bush administration's domestic spying program. Sometimes claims of constitutional authority (or actions taken in the absence of such claims) strike a note that is so badly out of tune with the general sense of how the Constitution structures political power arrangements that we sense a threat to even the thinnest notion of constitutional fidelity.

Here, though, secrecy presents yet another unique form of danger, because we cannot always evaluate how presidential actions fit with constitutional norms, even broadly defined ones, if we do not know exactly what is happening. When a president claims an implied constitutional warrant for a new kind of action and then warns that the other branches should not question the existence of such a warrant, the claim begins to look exactly like "conventional politics masked as constitutional politics." The move is doubly dangerous, because it obfuscates the "conventional politics" of the situation while using the Constitution in a way that enlarges constitutionalism beyond any sensible understanding of the term.

When we say that secrecy imperils constitutionalism, we mean that the interpretative act of trying to derive a constitutional basis for the secrecy powers we describe is a fruitless endeavor that does harm to a political system governed by a functioning constitution. In other words, by appealing to the Constitution for powers clearly not found there, presidents diminish the role of the Constitution in political life: the appeal becomes, indeed is, an empty and cynical gesture. In the starkest terms, one could set up a field of political action with constitutional limits on one end and the unimpeded play of political forces on the other. Either we respect constitutional constraints, or we admit that political action is simply the play of power. Of course, a constitutional basis for the exercise of power is the best thing the executive can have, so it is unsurprising that presidents try such arguments so frequently. However, fidelity to the text requires courts and others to say, sometimes, that the text does not permit this or that action, so the action cannot be taken.

As Justice Black famously remarked in the 1952 steel seizure case, "The President's power, if any, to issue the order must stem either from an act of Congress or from the Constitution itself."[17] By virtue of this principle, presidents are obliged to try to ground their actions in one or the other; when the claim is weak or even disingenuous, presidents often find it preferable to make the claim anyway rather than holding back from acting. One of the harms that results from this dressing-up of weak or nonexistent constitutional warrants is damage to the very notion of constitutionalism—the commitment to a belief that the Constitution means something and is binding. In a political system that has held together under constitutional structures for so long, the peril of such a path is threatening indeed.

Introduction • The Secret Presidency

Epigraphs: Gaillard Hunt, ed., *The Writings of James Madison*, vol. 9 (New York: Putnam's, 1910), 103; interview of Maxwell D. Taylor, *CBS Morning News*, June 17, 1971.

1. "Semi-Annual Review of Intelligence Community," National Security Council Meeting, Cabinet Room, White House, January 13, 1977, 2–4.

2. *Terminiello v. Chicago*, 337 U.S. 1, 37 (1949 dissenting).

3. Roy P. Basler, ed., "Message to Congress in Special Session of July 4, 1861," *The Collected Works of Abraham Lincoln*, vol. 4 (New Brunswick, NJ: Rutgers University Press, 1953), 430.

4. Clinton L. Rossiter, *Constitutional Dictatorship: Crisis Government in the Modern Democracies* (Princeton: Princeton University Press, 1948), 314.

5. Theodore J. Lowi, "Afterword: Presidential Power and the Ideological Struggle Over Its Interpretation," in Martin L. Fausold and Alan Shank, eds., *The Constitution and the American Presidency* (New York: State University of New York Press, 1991), 227, 234.

6. Ibid., 237.

7. Jeffrey K. Tulis, "The Constitutional Presidency in American Political Development," in Fausold and Shank, eds., *The Constituion and the American Presidency*, 133–46, at 134.

8. Lowi, "Afterword," 238.

9. *United States v. Curtiss-Wright Export Corp.*, 299 U.S. 304, 320 (1936).

10. *Youngstown Sheet and Tube v. Sawyer*, 343 U.S. 579, 634 (1952).

11. Harold Hongju Koh, *The National Security Constitution: Sharing Power after the Iran-Contra Affair* (New Haven: Yale University Press, 1990), 134.

12. Kenneth E. Collier, *Between the Branches: The White House Office of Legislative Affairs* (Pittsburgh: University of Pittsburgh Press, 1997), 1.

13. Lowi, "Afterword," 238–39.

14. Richard Neustadt, *Presidential Power: The Politics of Leadership from FDR to Carter* (New York: John Wiley and Sons, 1980), 25, 30, 33, 35, emphasis in original.

15. Ibid., 15, 16, emphasis in original.

16. Gordon Silverstein, *Imbalance of Powers: Constitutional Interpretation and the Making of American Foreign Policy* (New York: Oxford University Press, 1997), 156.

17. Military Order, "Detention, Treatment, and Trial of Certain Non-Citizens in the War Against Terrorism," 66 Fed. Reg. 57833–57836, November 13, 2001.

18. Michael Creppy, Chief Immigration Judge of the United States, "Memorandum: Cases Requiring Special Procedures," September 21, 2001.

19. U.S. Department of Justice, Office of the Inspector General, *The September 11 Detainees: A Review of the Treatment of Aliens Held on Immigration Charges in Connection with the Investigation of the September 11 Attacks*, April 2003.

20. Ibid.; see also *Hamdi v. Rumsfeld*, 542 U.S. 507 (2004) and *Padilla v. Rumsfeld*, 432 F.3d 582 (4th Cir. 2005).

21. For example: temporary refusal to reveal the members of the Presidential Foreign Intelligence Advisory Board, even though board membership is public information, see Federation of American Scientists, *Secrecy News*, vol. 2002, no. 77, August 15, 2002, www.fas.org/sgp/news/secrecy/2002/08/081502.html; limiting disclosure of information to Congress, see George W. Bush, "Memorandum: Disclosures to Congress," October 5, 2001; pressing executive privilege in unprecedented contexts, see, for example, George W. Bush, "Memorandum for the Attorney General: Congressional Subpoena for Executive Branch Documents," December 12, 2001; *Cheney v. United States Dist. Court*, 542 U.S. 367 (2004).

22. Executive Order 13233, "Further Implementation of the Presidential Records Act," 66 Fed. Reg. 56025–56029 (November 1, 2001).

23. See, for example, U.S. Congress, House Government Reform Committee, "Hearing on Justice Department Document Policies," December 13, 2001, where Representative Dan Burton noted that Bush officials "enthusiastically embrace secrecy . . . [and operate] as if they had no reason to be accountable to the public or to the Congress. . . . And the Justice Department has recently indicated that it will no longer comply with congressional requests for deliberative documents pertaining to criminal investigations, whether open or closed. Such a move signals a troubling and arguably unconstitutional shift in policy between the executive and legislative branches of our government."

24. See, for example, David Cunningham, "Squelching Dissent in the Name of Security," *Boston Globe*, December 15, 2003, A19; Eric Lichtblau, "F.B.I. Scrutinizes Anti-War Rallies," *New York Times*, November 23, 2003, A1.

25. Department of Education, Office of Inspector General, *Review of Formation Issues Regarding the Department of Education's Fiscal Year 2003 Contract with Ketchum, Inc. for Media Relations Services*, April 2005, www.ed.gov/about/offices/list/oig/aireports/a19f0007.doc, accessed April 23, 2006.

26. Robert Y. Shapiro, Martha Joynt Kumar, Lawrence R. Jacobs, eds., *Presidential Power: Forging the Presidency for the Twenty-First Century* (New York: Columbia University Press, 2000), 4. See also, in the same volume, Lyn Ragsdale, "Personal Power and Presidents," 39.

27. Richard Neustadt, "The Constraining of the President: The Presidency after Watergate," *British Journal of Political Science* 4, no. 4 (October 1974): 383–97, at 384, 396, 397.

28. Ibid., 383.

29. Tom C. Clark, untitled memorandum to President, July 17, 1946, reproduced in Appendix A in *Zweibon v. Mitchell*, 516 F.2d 594 (D.C. Cir. 1975).

30. Shapiro et al., George C. Edwards, "Neustadt's Power Approach to the Presidency," ch. 2, 11.

31. U.S. Senate, *Report of the Commission on Protecting and Reducing Government Secrecy,* 105th Cong., 2nd Sess., Senate Doc. 105-2, 1997, 5.

32. John Ashcroft, "Remarks of Attorney General John Ashcroft: Attorney General Guidelines," May 30, 2002, www.fas.org/irp/news/2002/05/ag053002.html, accessed April 23, 2006.

33. Neil A. Lewis, "Bush Claims Executive Privilege in Response to House Inquiry," *New York Times,* December 14, 2001, A26.

34. Glen Johnson, "Bush Denies Congress Papers for FBI: Probe Panel Denounces Claim of Executive Privilege," *Boston Globe,* December 14, 2001, A2.

35. Warren Bates, "Attorney: U.S. Trying to Seize Groom Lake Lawsuit Files," *Las Vegas Review Journal,* June 17, 1995, www.reviewjournal.com/webextras/area51/1995/lawsuits/groomfiles.html, accessed April 23, 2006; *Maxwell v. First National Bank of Maryland,* 143 F.R.D. 590 (Dist. Maryland 1991).

36. Theodore Lowi, "Presidential Democracy in America: Toward the Homogenized Regime," *Political Science Quarterly* 109, no. 3 (1994): 401–15, at 403.

37. Raoul Berger, *Executive Privilege: A Constitutional Myth* (Cambridge: Harvard University Press, 1974).

38. *United States v. Reynolds,* 345 U.S. 1, 10 (1953).

One • The Secret Presidency in Historical-Theoretical Perspective

Epigraph: Neustadt, *Presidential Power,* 161.

1. James D. Barber, *The Presidential Character: Predicting Performance in the White House* (New York: Prentice Hall, 1992), 3, 399.

2. Ibid., viii–x, 4.

3. Ibid., 6.

4. Ibid., 227.

5. Ibid., 85.

6. Ibid., 4.

7. James L. Sundquist, *The Decline and Resurgence of Congress* (Washington, D.C.: Brookings Institution Press, 1981).

8. Ibid., 4, 460.

9. Sundquist states that the decline of party influence can be measured by "the proportion of voters who do not identify with any party, who call themselves independents, and who split their tickets with abandon." Also, "it is manifested in the decay and disappearance of old-style party organizations and the failure of new-style structures to fill the vacuum. It is reflected in the rise of individualism within the Congress." Ibid., 475.

10. Ibid., 460–83.

11. See, for example, Jeremey Brecher and Brendan Smith, "The Limits of Power: Questions for Alito," *The Nation,* January 6, 2006, www.thenation.com/doc/20060123/questions_for_alito, accessed April 25, 2006.

12. John Yoo, "The President's Constitutional Authority to Conduct Military Operations

against Terrorists and Nations Supporting Them," Memorandum Opinion for the Deputy Counsel to the President, Deputy Assistant Attorney General, September 25, 2001, available at www.usdoj.gov/olc/warpowers925.htm, accessed August 15, 2006.

13. On the importance of party attachments, see Martin P. Wattenberg, *The Decline of American Political Parties, 1952–1984* (Cambridge: Harvard University Press, 1986).

14. Theodroe Lowi, *The Personal President: Power Invested, Promise Unfulfilled* (Ithaca, NY: Cornell University Press, 1985).

15. Stephen Skowronek, *The Politics Presidents Make: Leadership from John Adams to George Bush* (Cambridge: Belknap Press, 1993).

16. Neustadt, *Presidential Power*, 176.

17. Lowi, The *Personal President*.

18. Neustadt, *Presidential Power*, 135, 161.

19. Richard Neustadt, "The Constraining of the President: The Presidency after Watergate," *British Journal of Political Science* 4 (1990), 383–97, at 383.

20. Neustadt, *Presidential Power*, xi, 15.

21. G. W. Bush press conference, November 4, 2004, available at www.whitehouse .gov/news/releases/2004/11/20041104–5.html, accessed July 31, 2006.

22. Ibid., 16.

23. Ibid., 22.

24. Ibid., 43.

25. Skowronek, *The Politics Presidents Make*, 31.

26. *USA Today*, "Bush Was Satisfied on Pre-9/11 Probes," April 11, 2004, www.usatoday .com/news/sept11/2004–04–11-bush-pre911-probes_x.htm, accessed April 23, 2006.

27. Lyn Ragsdale, "Personal Power and Presidents," in Shapiro, Kumar, and Jacobs, eds., *Presidential Power: Forging the Presidency for the Twenty-First Century* (New York: Columbia University Press, 2000), 38.

28. Harvey Mansfield, *Taming the Prince: The Ambivalence of Modern Executive Power* (New York: Free Press, 1989).

29. *Bush v. Gore*, 531 U.S. 98 (2000).

30. Neustadt, *Presidential Power*, 33.

31. Skowronek, *Politics*, 5.

32. Neustadt, *Presidential Power*, 139, 140, 142.

33. Dana Milbank and Vernon Loeb, "Bush Utters Taunts about Militants: 'Bring 'Em On,'" *Washington Post*, July 3, 2003, A1.

34. Mike Allen, "Bush's Isolation from Reporters Could Be a Hindrance," *Washington Post*, October 8, 2004, A9. Martha Joynt Kumar has long studied presidential communication in the modern White House, and she notes that there is some dispute as to what constitutes a press conference. For example, a reporter once caught President Bush walking to Air Force One and asked him a single question. Then the reporter asked, "Does this constitute a press conference?" Bush replied, "You bet." Kumar relies on the official reports and records to determine what counts. Martha Joynt Kumar, "Does This Constitute a Press Conference? Defining and Tabulating Modern Presidential Press Conferences," *Presidential Studies Quarterly* 33, no. 1 (March 2003), 1.

35. Mike Allen, "Bush Administration Officials Admit That Press Conference Was

Rigged," www.informationclearinghouse.info/article1922.htm, March 7, 2003, accessed April 23, 2004.

36. Ken Auletta, "Fortress Bush: How the White House Keeps the Press under Control," *New Yorker*, January 19, 2004, 53–65, at 53.

37. On Kennedy, see Neustadt, *Presidential Power*, 154.

38. Lowi, *Personal President*, 20, 182.

39. Lowi, *American Presidential Democracy*, 403.

40. Lowi, *Personal President*, 56.

41. Theodore Lowi, "American Presidential Democracy: Toward the Homogenized Regime," *Political Science Quarterly* 109, no. 3 (Summer 1994): 401–15, at 413n14.

42. Lowi, *Personal President*, 179.

43. Lowi, "American Presidential Democracy," 404, 412.

44. Lowi, *Personal President*, 175.

45. Ibid., 174.

46. Louis Fisher, "The Way We Go to War," in Gary L. Gregg II and Mark J. Rozell, eds., *Considering the Bush Presidency* (New York: Oxford University Press, 2004), 118.

47. Skowronek, *Politics*.

48. J. G. A. Pocock, *Politics, Language, and Time: Essays on Political Thought and History* (Chicago: University of Chicago Press, 1989).

49. Skowronek, *Politics*, 10.

50. Ibid., 15, 20, 22.

51. Ibid., 27.

52. Ibid., 31.

53. Ibid.

54. Lowi, *Personal President*, 182.

55. Mark Crispin Miller, *The Bush Dyslexicon: Observations on a National Disorder* (New York: Norton, 2002).

56. Eccles. 1:9–10.

57. Skowronek, *Politics*, 441.

58. Ibid., 409.

Two • The Classified President

Epigraphs: U.S. Senate, *Report of the Commission on Protecting and Reducing Government Secrecy*, 105th Cong., 2nd Sess., Senate Doc. 105-2, 1997, xxxvi; *Congressional Record*, June 20, 1966, p. 13654.

1. Theodore J. Lowi, "Afterword: Presidential Power and the Ideological Struggle Over Its Interpretation," in Martin L. Fausold and Alan Shank, eds., *The Constitution and the American Presidency* (New York: State University of New York Press, 1991), 238.

2. Ibid., 239.

3. Ibid.

4. U.S. Congress, House of Representatives, *Iran-Contra Investigation: Joint Hearings Before the House Select Committee to Investigate Covert Arms Transactions with Iran and the Senate Select Committee on Secret Military Assistance to Iran and the Nicaraguan Opposition,*

100th Cong., 1st Sess., 1988, 349, quoted in Brad Rockwell, "Domestic Covert Actions and the Need for National Security Qui Tam Prosecutions," *American Journal of Criminal Law* 16 (1988–1989): 207–67, at 212.

5. Federation of American Scientists, "Central Intelligence Agency Refuses to Release Oldest U.S. Classified Documents Sought in Litigation," www.fas.org/sgp/news/jmpoldest.html, March 30, 1999, accessed April 20, 2006.

6. See *Gravel v. United States*, 408 U.S. 606 (1972).

7. U.S. Congress, House Committee on Government Operations, *U.S. Government Information Policies and Practices. Part 1: The Pentagon Papers*, 92nd Cong., 1st Sess., 1975, 20.

8. U.S. Senate, *Report of the Commission on Protecting and Reducing Government Secrecy*, xxi.

9. "Cissel 44CD42M 100lb Shipboard Steam Heated Laundry Dryer Service Manual," www.navy-nex.com/ship_stores_CD/PDF/Laundry/MAN434.PDF, accessed December 18, 2002. This manual and others once cited in Federation of American Scientists, *Secrecy News*, vol. 2002, no. 124, December 18, 2002, have since been removed from the Internet by the U.S. Navy.

10. For a vivid visual example of this tightening-up process, visit the National Security Archives website for a side-by-side comparison of a biographical document on Augusto Pinochet released unredacted by the Clinton administration in 1999 and the same document heavily redacted as released by the Bush administration in 2003. See www.gwu.edu/nsarchiv/NSAEBB/NSAEBB90/index2.htm, accessed April 21, 2006.

11. First Amendment Center, "Defense Department Keeps Wraps on FOIA Video," February 14, 2003, www.firstamendmentcenter.org/news.aspx?id=6295, accessed April 20, 2006. The video, a Humphrey Bogart–themed production entitled "The People's Right to Know," has become a symbol of secrecy after 9/11. The Department of Defense explained that the denial was required to protect intellectual property rights, since the video made unauthorized use of clips from movies and news broadcasts. This is a disturbing justification for denial of a FOIA request, since it creates an incentive to place such material in documents in order to defeat requests for information. Eventually, the video was released in redacted form, with scenes blacked out.

12. H. Gerth and C. Wright Mills, eds., *From Max Weber* (New York: Oxford University Press, 1967), 233.

13. Shaun Waterman, "Pentagon Probed on Torture Memo Secrets," UPI, July 8, 2004.

14. Erwin Griswold, "Secrets Not Worth Keeping: The Courts and Classified Information," *Washington Post*, February 15, 1989, A25.

15. U.S. Senate, *Report of the Commission on Protecting and Reducing Government Secrecy*, xxi.

16. Ibid., xxxix.

17. Information Security Oversight Office, *Report to the President, 2003*, www.fas.org/sgp/isoo/2003rpt.pdf, accessed April 21, 2006.

18. Patrick Leahy and Chuck Grassley, letter of August 13, 2002, to Attorney General John Ashcroft; *A Review of the FBI's Actions in Connection With Allegations Raised by Contract Linguist Sibel Edmonds*, unclassified summary, January 2005, www.usdoj.gov/oig/special/0501/final.pdf, accessed April 21, 2006.

19. U.S. Senate, *Report of the Commission on Protecting and Reducing Government Secrecy*, 29.

20. "Code Names: Author Q and A," www.codenames.org/qanda.html, accessed April 21, 2006.

21. Louis Fisher, *The Politics of Shared Power: Congress and the Executive*, 4th ed. (College Station: Texas A&M University Press, 1998), 132.

22. Richard Gid Powers, "Introduction" in Daniel Patrick Moynihan, *Secrecy: The American Experience* (New Haven: Yale University Press, 1998), 18.

23. Christopher Schmitt and Edward T. Pound, "Keeping Secrets: The Bush Administration Is Doing the Public's Business Out of the Public Eye," *U.S. News and World Report*, December 22, 2003, www.usnews.com/usnews/news/articles/031222/22secrecy.htm, accessed April 23, 2006.

24. Brief for the Appellees, *American Foreign Serv. Ass'n v. Garfinkel*, 488 U.S. 923 (1988) (no. 87-2127), 42. The Department of Justice under President Clinton reaffirmed this view through a memorandum analyzing congressional power to authorize disclosure of classified information to members of Congress by executive branch employees without first seeking permission. "Access to Classified Information: Memorandum Opinion for the General Counsel, Central Intelligence Agency," Office of Legal Counsel, November 26, 1996, 4.

25. *Payne v. National Security Agency, ex parte in camera*, "Classified Declaration of Gary W. Winch," civil action no. 97-0266 SC/DJS (New Mexico, 1997). Document in the authors' possession.

26. One of the authors worked in signals intelligence collection for eight years and has extensive experience in handling information classified by the National Security Agency.

27. For a fascinating discussion of the attack on the USS *Liberty* and the micromanagement of Eisenhower concerning the U2 flights, see James Bamford, *Body of Secrets* (New York: Doubleday, 2001), 43–62, 187–239.

28. *Security Classification of Information: Volume 2: Principles for Classification of Information*, prepared by the Oakridge K–25 site for the Department of Energy (April 1993), ch. 2, www.fas.org/sgp/library/quist2/chap_2.html, accessed April 20, 2006.

29. Ibid.

30. Codified at 50 U.S.C. 403(d)(3).

31. U.S. Senate, *Report of the Commission on Protecting and Reducing Government Secrecy*, 8.

32. George W. Bush, "Statement on Signing the Department of Defense Appropriations Act, 2004," September 30, 2003.

33. "2003 Report on Cost Estimates for Security Classification Activities," Information Security Oversight Office, July 2004, www.archives.gov/isoo/reports/2003_cost_report.html, accessed January 3, 2005.

34. Ibid., 1.

35. Information Security Oversight Office, *Report to the President, 2003*, 17.

36. Ibid., 6.

37. 47 Fed. Reg. 14874, 5.2.

38. Ibid., 5.5.

39. Executive Order 13292, "Further Amendment to Executive Order 12958, as Amended, Classified National Security Information," 68 Fed. Reg. 15315, 5.2(b)(7).

40. U.S. Congress, House of Representatives, *Treasury, Postal Service, and General Government Appropriations Bill, 1995,* 103rd Cong., 2nd Sess., H. Rept. 103-534, May 26, 1994.

41. Information Security Oversight Office, *Report to the President,* 2004, 15, www .archives.gov/isoo/reports/2004-annual-report.pdf, accessed April 21, 2006.

42. The data in this paragraph and the one following is extracted or calculated from ISOO's *Report to the President, 2004.*

43. J. William Leonard, Director, Information Security Oversight Office, "The Importance of Basics," National Classification Management Society Annual Training Seminar, Reno, Nevada, June 15, 2004, 1–2.

44. Investigation of Major General Antonio Taguba, *Article 15-6 Investigation of the 800th Military Police Brigade,* May 2, 2004, news.findlaw.com/cnn/docs/iraq/tagubarpt .html#ThR1.1, accessed April 21, 2006.

45. Leonard, "The Importance of Basics," 1.

46. The authors wish to thank Professor Thomas Price for the example presented here concerning *The Fourth Protocol.*

47. Executive Order 13292, 1.7.

48. The authors asked Director Leonard in a January 13, 2005, e-mail: "Are you aware of any occasion when a government employee was subjected to administrative sanctions under executive order or agency policy for over-classifying or improperly classifying material? I have searched Lexis and Westlaw and other venues, but have not found such a case." Director Leonard responded: "From my perspective, as well as that of the staff who predate me at ISOO, we are not aware of any instances."

49. U.S. Senate, *Report of the Commission on Protecting and Reducing Government Secrecy,* xxvi, xxvii.

50. *Security Classification of Information: Volume I—Introduction, History and Adverse Impacts,* www.fas.org/sgp/library/quist/, accessed April 20, 2006. See esp. ch. 2.

51. *Documents Illustrative of the Formation of the Union of the American States,* "Resolution of Secrecy Adopted by the Continental Congress, November 9, 1775," 69th Cong., 1st Sess., 1927, H. Doc. no. 398, 18.

52. Morris R. Franklin et al., *Memorandum of Correspondence of the United States, Vol. II: Correspondence,* February 5, 1775–January 1, 1779, 152.

53. Quoted in *Halperin v. Central Intelligence Agency,* 629 F.2d 144, 157 (D.C. Cir., 1980).

54. James Madison, *Notes of Debates in the Federal Convention of 1787* (1787; repr. New York: Norton, 1987), 433–34.

55. Clinton Rossiter, ed., *The Federalist Papers* (New York: New American Library, 1961), 392.

56. Charles T. Cullen, ed., *The Papers of Thomas Jefferson,* vol. 23 (Princeton: Princeton University Press, 1990), March 11, 1792.

57. Ibid., "Memoranda of Consultations with the President," entry for March 31, 1792, at 262.

58. Cullen, ed., *The Papers of Thomas Jefferson,* April 2, 1792.

59. U.S. Congress, House of Representatives, "British Treaty," doc. no. 114, Foreign Relations, 4th Cong., 1st Sess., March 30, 1796.

60. U.S. Senate, Committee on the Judiciary, Subcommittee on Constitutional Rights, *The Power of the President to Withhold Information From the Congress, Memorandums of the Attorney General*, 85th Cong., 2d Sess., 1958.

61. Office of Legal Counsel, U.S. Department of Justice, *History of Refusals by Executive Branch Officials to Provide Information Demanded by Congress; Part I—Presidential Invocations of Executive Privilege vis-à-vis Congress*, 6 *U.S. Op. OLC* 751, 758, December 14, 1982.

62. *A Compilation of the Messages and Papers of the Presidents, 1789–1897*, Message of April 20, 1846, to House of Representatives, vol. 4 (1897): 431–36, at 432.

63. Ibid., 433, 434.

64. Ibid., 435.

65. 11 *Op. Atty. Gen.* 137, 142–43 (1865).

66. *A Compilation of the Messages and Papers of the Presidents, 1789–1897*, May 1, 1862, at 3275.

67. 36 Stat. 1085.

68. U.S. Senate, *Report of the Commission on Protecting and Reducing Government Secrecy*, xxii.

69. Ibid., part I, 5.

70. 42 U.S.C. 2014.

71. Moynihan, *Secrecy: The American Experience*, xv.

72. U.S. Senate, *Report of the Commission on Protecting and Reducing Government Secrecy*, 5.

73. Ibid., xvi.

74. Section 2(a).

75. *Goldstein v. United States*, 258 F. 908 (1919).

76. *United States v. Nagler*, 252 F. 217 (1918).

77. Quoted in Harold C. Relyea, "National Security and Information," *Government Information Quarterly* 4, no. 1 (1987): 11–28, at 13.

78. Sidney W. Souers, "Policy Formulation for National Security," *American Political Science Review* 43, no. 3 (June 1949): 534–43, at 535.

79. "Remarks at the Detroit Edison Monroe Plant in Monroe, Michigan," *Public Papers of the Presidents* 39, no. 28, September 22, 2003.

80. 67 Fed. Reg. 1601 (2003).

81. Mark Shulman, "The Progressive Era Origins of the National Security Act," *Dickinson Law Review* 104 (Winter 2000): 289–330, at 295.

82. "Policy Formulation," 534.

83. Shulman, "The Progressive Era Origins," 289–90.

84. Ibid.

85. 52 Stat. 3 (1938).

86. *Security Classification of Information*, volume 1, ch. 3, at 45, www.fas.org/sgp/library/quist, accessed July 25, 2006.

87. 15 Fed. Reg. 597 (1950).

88. 62 Stat. 737–38 (1948).

89. 16 Fed. Reg. 9795 (1951).

90. Thomas L. Burns, *The Origins of the National Security Agency*, United States Cryptologic History, ser. 5, vol. 1 (Ft. George Mead, MD: Center for Cryptologic History, National Security Agency, 1990), 49.

91. Ibid., 54, 97.

92. 15 Fed. Reg. 598 (1950).

93. 16 Fed. Reg. 9795 (1951).

94. 18 Fed. Reg. 7049 (1953).

95. 25 Fed. Reg. 1583 (1960).

96. 10 C.F.R. 25.5.

97. 35 U.S.C. 181.

98. *United States v. The Progressive*, 467 F. Supp. 990, 995 (W.D. Wis. 1979).

99. 68 Stat. 919 (1954).

100. See *United States v. The Progressive, Inc.*

101. Executive Order 11652, "Classification and Declassification of National Security Information and Material," 37 Fed. Reg. 5209, March 8, 1972.

102. 5 U.S.C. 552 *et seq.*

103. 50 U.S.C. 1801 *et seq.*

104. 115 Stat. 272 (2001).

105. U.S. Senate, *Report of the Commission on Protecting and Reducing Government Secrecy*, xlix.

106. *Department of the Navy v. Egan*, 484 U.S. 518, 527, 529 (1988).

107. Ibid., 530.

108. Louis Fisher, *National Security Whistleblowers*, Congressional Research Service, RL33215, December 30, 2005, 24, 25, emphasis in original.

109. 5 U.S.C. 2302.

110. The authors have interviewed numerous whistleblowers who report that inspector general offices tried to get them to drop complaints, investigated them for wrongdoing, and were otherwise intimidating and abusive. Some of those interviews involve whistleblowers whose cases have become public, such as those of Sibel Edmonds, Michael German, and Jesselyn Radack.

111. Project on Government Oversight, "Homeland and National Security Whistleblower Protections: The Unfinished Agenda," April 28, 2005, www.pogo.org/p/government/go-050402-whistleblower.html, accessed April 27, 2006.

112. *Lachance v. MSPB*, 174 F.3d 1378, 1381 (1999).

113. For an excellent account of the law concerning national security whistleblowers, see Fisher, *National Security Whistleblowers.*

114. See, for example, Harold Hongju Koh, *The National Security Constitution: Sharing Power after the Iran-Contra Affair* (New Haven: Yale University Press, 1990).

115. Christopher v. Harbury, 536 U.S. 403, 417 (2002).

116. *Haig v. Agee*, 453 U.S. 280, 293–94 (1981).

117. *Chicago & Southern Air Lines, Inc. v. Waterman S.S. Corp.*, 333 U.S. 103, 111 (1948).

118. *United States v. Nixon*, 418 U.S. 683, 710 (1974).

119. 5 U.S.C. 552(b)(1)(A).

120. 410 U.S. 73, 81 (1973).

121. 88 Stat. 1562 (1974).

122. *Center for National Security Studies v. United States,* 331 F.3d 918, 927, 937 (D.C. Cir. 2003).

123. *Arabian Shield Development Company v. CIA,* no. 3–98–CV–0624–BD, 11–12 (N.D. Texas 1999), *cert. denied* at 531 U.S. 872 (2000).

124. *Phillippi v. CIA,* 546 F.2d 1009, 1011 (D.C. App. 1976).

125. *Bassiouni v. CIA,* 392 F.3d 244, 246 (7th Cir. 2004). The panel consisted of Judges Richard Posner, Frank Easterbrook, and Diane Sykes. Posner and Easterbrook are intellectual leaders of the conservative judiciary.

126. See, for example, *Hidalgo v. FBI,* 344 F.3d 1256 (D.C. App. 2003); *Jefferson v. Department of Justice,* 284 F.3d 172 (D.C. App. 2002); *Office of the Capital Collateral Counsel v. Department of Justice,* 331 F.3d 799 (11th Cir. 2003); *Nation Magazine v. United States Customs Serv.,* 71 F.3d 885 (D.C. App. 1995); *Oguaju v. United States Marshal's Service,* 288 F.3d 448 (D.C. App. 2002); *Students Against Genocide v. Dep't of State,* 257 F.3d 828 (D.C. App. 2001).

Three • State Secrets and Executive Power

Epigraphs: Remarks at the Virginia Ratifying Convention, June 9, 1788; Scott Armstrong, "Do You Wanna Know a Secret?" *Washington Post,* February 16, 1997, C1.

1. Jonathan Turley, "Through a Looking Glass Darkly: National Security and Statutory Interpretation," *Southern Methodist University Law Review* 53 (Winter 2000): 205–49, at 212.

2. *Kasza v. Browner,* 133 F.3d 1159, 1163–64 (9th Cir. 1998).

3. Richard Leiby, "Secrets Under the Sun," *Washington Post,* July 20, 1997, F4.

4. George Washington University Press Release, March 15, 1995, www.ufomind.com/area51/articles/1995/gwu_950315.txt, accessed April 22, 2006.

5. Turley, "Through a Looking Glass Darkly," 210.

6. Neely Tucker, "Judge Orders White House Papers' Release," *Washington Post,* October 18, 2002, A6.

7. *Int'l Action Ctr. v. United States,* Civil Action no. 01-72 (GK) (D.D.C. 2002).

8. *United States v. Reynolds,* 345 U.S. 1, 10 (1953).

9. Rejected Federal Rule of Evidence 509.

10. *Halkin v. Helms,* 598 F. 2d 1 (D.C. Cir. 1979).

11. Agriculture: 67 Fed. Reg. 61465, September 30, 2002; Health and Human Services: 66 Fed. Reg. 64347, December 12, 2001; Environmental Protection Agency: 67 Fed. Reg. 31109, May 9, 2002; OSTP: 68 Fed. Reg. 55257, September 17, 2003.

12. *United States v. Nixon,* 418 U.S. 683 (1974). Quotation from Charles Alan Wright and Kenneth W. Graham, *Federal Practice and Procedure: Federal Rules of Evidence,* vol. 26 (St. Paul, MN: West Publishing, 2001), 498.

13. Louis D. Brandeis, *Other People's Money* (New York: F.A. Stokes, 1914), 92.

14. Kenneth Culp Davis, *Discretionary Justice: A Preliminary Inquiry* (Baton Rouge: Louisiana State University Press, 1969), 98–120.

15. Francis E. Rourke, "Secrecy in American Bureaucracy," *Political Science Quarterly* 72, December (1957), 542.

16. Quoted in *Jencks v. United States*, 353 U.S. 657, 681–82 (1957).

17. William E. Leuchtenburg, ed., *The New Freedom* (New York: Prentice-Hall, 1961), 84.

18. *Halkin v. Helms*.

19. *Barlow v. United States*, Cong. Reference no. 98-887X (Court of Federal Claims 2000).

20. *Patterson v. FBI*, 893 F.2d 595 (3rd Cir. 1990).

21. *Maxwell v. First National Bank of Maryland*, 143 F.R.D. 590 (Dist. Maryland 1991).

22. *Molerio v. Federal Bureau of Investigation*, 749 F.2d 815 (D.C. Cir. 1984); *Sterling v. Tenet* Civil Action no. 01–CIV–8073 (S.D. New York 2002); *Tilden v. Tenet*, 140 F. Supp 2d 623 (E.D. Virginia 2000).

23. *Doe v. United States*, no. 96-397C (Court of Federal Claims 1997); *Guong v. United States*, 860 F.2d 1063 (Federal Cir. 1988).

24. *Black v. United States*, 62 F.2d 1115 (8th Cir. 1995).

25. Lawrence E. Walsh, *Final Report of the Independent Counsel for Iran/Contra Matters: Volume 1: Investigations and Prosecutions* (Washington, D.C.: U.S. Government Printing Office, 1993), 122.

26. See Scott Armstrong, "The War Over Secrecy: Democracy's Most Important Low-Intensity Conflict" in Athan Theoharis, ed., *A Culture of Secrecy: The Government Versus the People's Right to Know* (Lawrence: University Press of Kansas, 1998).

27. On the Federal Records Act, see 44 U.S.C. 3310 *et seq.*, 160.

28. Brian Z. Tamanaha, "A Critical Review of the Classified Information Procedures Act," *American Journal of Criminal Law* 13 (Summer 1986), 318.

29. *United States v. Curtiss-Wright Export Corp.*, 299 U.S. 304, 318 (1936).

30. See Charles Alan Wright and Kenneth W. Graham, "Rejected Rule 509," in *Federal Practice and Procedure*, 5611–72, vol. 26 (Minneapolis: West Publishing, 2002).

31. For example, John R. Stevenson and William H. Rehnquist, "The President's Executive Privilege to Withhold Foreign Policy and National Security Information," Department of State and Department of Justice, Office of Legal Counsel Memorandum, December 8, 1969.

32. *United States v. Burr*, 25 F. Cas. 30, 37 (Cir. Court of Virginia, 1807).

33. Ibid.

34. Letter of Jefferson to George Hay, June 17, 1807, press-pubs.uchicago.edu/founders/documents/a2_1_1s21.html, accessed April 22, 2006.

35. *United States v. Burr*, 37.

36. For a detailed discussion of *United States v. Burr* in relation to the state secrets privilege, see Louis Fisher, *In the Name of National Security: Unchecked Presidential Power and the Reynolds Case* (Lawrence: University Press of Kansas, 2006), ch. 7.

37. See, for example, *Edmonds v. Department of Justice*, 323 F.Supp 2d 65, 70 (D.D.C. 2004); *In re United States*, 872 F.2d 472, 474–75 (D.C. Cir. 1989); *Jabara v. Kelley*, 75 F.R.D. 475, 483 (D. Michigan 1977).

38. U.S. Senate, Committee on the Judiciary, Subcommittee on Constitutional Rights, *The Power of the President to Withhold Information*, 36.

39. 11 *Op. Atty. Gen.* 137, 142–43.

40. 25 *Op. Atty. Gen.* 326, 330–31.

41. *Totten v. United States*, 92 U.S. 105, 106 (1875).

42. *Tenet v. Doe*, 125 S.Ct. 1230, 1233 (2005).

43. *Doe v. Tenet*, 329 F.3d. 1135, 1146 (9th Cir. 2003).

44. *Tenet v. Doe*, 1236, 1237.

45. *Weinberger v. Catholic Action of Hawaii*, 454 U.S. 139 (1981); *Tenet v. Doe*, 1237.

46. *Weinberger*, 140.

47. *Firth v. Bethlehem Steel Co.*, 199 F. 353 (E.D. Pennsylvania 1912).

48. As discussed above, the Supreme Court in *Tenet v. Doe* expressly rejected the idea that *Totten* was a state secrets privilege case. But until the *Doe* decision, most commentators considered *Totten* not merely as a decision about a rule of contracts but also as a decision in the state secrets line of jurisprudence.

49. Randall K. Miller, "Congressional Inquests: Suffocating the Constitutional Prerogative of Executive Privilege," *Minnesota Law Review* 81 (February 1997): 631–91, at 635.

50. Stevenson and Rehnquist, "The President's Executive Privilege," 1.

51. *United States v. Reynolds*, 7.

52. 35 U.S.C. 181–88.

53. *District of Columbia v. Bakersmith*, 18 App. D.C. 574 (D.C. Cir. 1901); *King v. United States*, 112 F. 988 (5th Cir. 1902).

54. *District of Columbia v. Bakersmith*, 577.

55. *King v. United States*, 996.

56. J. W. Ehrlich, ed., *Blackstone's Commentaries on the Laws of England* (San Carlos, CA: Nourse, 1959), 62.

57. *Trial of Maha Rajah Nundocomar*, 20 State Trials 923, 1057 (1775).

58. *Beatson v. Skene*, 5 Hurlst. & N. 838, 853 (1860).

59. *Duncan v. Cammell, Laird and Co., Ltd.*, [1942] A.C. 624, 641 (1942).

60. See, for example, *Carey v. Queen* [1986] 2 S.C.R. 637 (1986); *Commonwealth of Australia v. Northern Land Council*, 30 F.C.R. 1 (1991); *Conway v. Rimmer* [1968] A.C. 910 (1968); *Kain v. Farrer* 37 L. T. 469 (1877); *Leven v. Board of Excise*, 17 F.D. 586 (1814); *Queensland Pine Co. v. The Commonwealth of Australia*, 1920 St. R. Qd. 121 (1920); *Robinson v. State of South Australia* [1931] A.C. 704 (1931); *Steven v. Dundas* (1727), in William Maywell Morison, *Dictionary of Decisions: The Decisions of the Court of Session from its Institution to the Present Time*, vol. 19 (Edinburgh: Bell and Bradfute, 1804), 7905.

61. *Glasgow Corporation v. Central Land Board*, 1956 S.C. (HL) 1, 11.

62. *Conway v. Rimmer*, 954, 977.

63. *United States v. Reynolds*, 8.

64. Ibid., 10.

65. *Reynolds v. United States*, 192 F.2d 987 (3rd Cir., 1951), at 995, 997.

66. The Supreme Court refused to entertain a *coram nobis* filed by relatives of the *Reynolds* victims (*In re Herring*, 539 U.S. 940 (2003)). The plaintiffs then filed an action in district court and lost (*Herring v. United States*, Civil Action no. 03–CV–5500–LDD (E.D. Pennsylvania 2004)), and the district court's decision was upheld by the Third Circuit Court of Appeals (*Herring v. United States*, 424 F.3d 384 (3rd Cir. 2005)). These courts held

that the government's actions in asserting the state secrets privilege did not rise to the level of an "unconscionable plan or scheme to improperly influence the court or interfere with the judicial machinery performing a task of impartial adjudication" (*Herring v. United States*, Civil Action no. 03–CV–5500–LDD, 10 (E.D. Pennsylvania 2004)).

67. Louis Fisher, *In the Name of National Security*.

68. *United States v. Reynolds*, 10.

69. U.S. Senate, Committee on the Judiciary, Subcommittee on Constitutional Rights, *The Power of the President to Withhold Information*, 75.

70. Editors, "Separation of Powers and Executive Privilege: The Watergate Briefs," *Political Science Quarterly* 88 (December 1973), 606.

71. *Landmark Briefs and Arguments of the Supreme Court of the United States: Constitutional Law*, vol. 79 (Washington, D.C.: University Publications of America, 1975), 718.

72. *United States v. Nixon*, 418 U.S. 683, 706, 711 (1974).

73. *United States v. Reynolds*, 345 U.S. 1, 9–10 (1953).

74. *Haig v. Agee*, 453 U.S. 280, 292 (1981).

75. *Republic Steel v. United States*, 3 C.I.T. 117 (1982); *U.S. Steel v. United States*, 6 C.I.T. 182 (1982).

76. *Yang v. Reno*, 157 F.R.D. 625 (M.D. Pennsylvania 1993).

77. *Halpern v. U.S.*, 258 F.2d 36 (2nd Cir. 1958).

78. U.S. Senate Select Committee on Intelligence, *Disclosure of Classified Information to Congress*, S. Hrg. 105-729, 105th Cong., 2nd Sess., 1998, 54.

79. *Tilden v. Tenet*, 627.

80. Ibid.

81. Christopher Schmitt and Edward T. Pound, "Keeping Secrets: The Bush Administration Is Doing the Public's Business Out of the Public Eye," *U.S. News and World Report*, December 22, 2003, www.usnews.com/usnews/news/articles/031222/22secrecy.htm, accessed April 23, 2006.

82. *Arar v. Ashcroft*, 414 F. Supp. 2d 250 (E.D. New York 2006).

83. *Memorandum in Support of the United States' Assertion of State Secrets Privilege*, Civil Action no. 04–CV–249–DGT–VVP, January 18, 2005, 2–3.

84. *Frost v. Perry*, 919 F.Supp. 1459 (Dist. of Nevada 1996).

85. *Kasza*, 1166.

86. *CIA v. Sims*, 471 U.S. 159, 179 (1985).

87. Presidential Determination 95-45, September 29, 1995. This determination has been renewed yearly by presidents since 1996.

88. *Maxwell v. First National Bank of Maryland*, 598.

89. For an excellent discussion of the A. Q. Khan network, see Christopher O. Clary, "The A. Q. Khan Network: Causes and Implications," Master's thesis, Naval Post Graduate School, December 2005, www.fas.org/irp/eprint/clary.pdf, accessed April 27, 2006. Clary, an employee of the U.S. Navy, claims that "the A. Q. Khan nuclear supplier network constitutes the most severe loss of control over nuclear technology ever. For the first time in history all of the keys to a nuclear weapon—the supplier networks, the material, the enrichment technology, and the warhead designs—were outside of state oversight and control," 1; on the links to Al Qaeda, see 90n268.

90. The Pressler-Solarz Amendment acknowledged that "Soviet forces occupying Afghanistan pose a security threat to Pakistan [and] that an independent and democratic Pakistan with continued friendly ties with the United States is in the interest of both nations" but required the president to certify to Congress that "Pakistan does not possess a nuclear explosive device and that the proposed United States military assistance program will reduce significantly the risk that Pakistan will possess a nuclear explosive device." 22 U.S.C. 2375.

91. Cong. Reference no. 98-887X.

92. *Barlow v. United States*, 21–22.

93. *In re United States*, 872 F.2d 472, 480 (D.C. Cir. 1989).

94. Wallace Notestein, Frances Relf, and Hartley Simpson, eds., *Commons Debates: 1621* (New Haven: Yale University Press, 1935), at 195.

95. 60 Fed. Reg. 19825, April 17, 1995.

96. U.S. Senate, *The Power of the President to Withhold Information*, 58.

97. U.S. Congress, House Committee on Government Operations, *U.S. Government Information Policies and Practices. Part 8: Problems of Congress in Obtaining Information from the Executive Branch*, 92nd Cong., 2nd Sess., May 23, 1972, 3138.

98. Janet Reno, "Memorandum for Heads of Departments and Agencies: Subject: The Freedom of Information Act," Department of Justice, October 4, 1993, www.usdoj.gov/oip/foia_updates/Vol_XIV_3/page3.htm, accessed April 5, 2006.

99. John Ashcroft, "Memorandum for Heads of All Federal Departments and Agencies: The Freedom of Information Act," October 12, 2001, www.usdoj.gov/04foia/011012.htm, accessed April 5, 2006.

100. Office of the Inspector General/Office of Oversight and Review, Department of Justice, *A Review of the FBI's Actions in Connection With Allegations Raised By Contract Linguist Sibel Edmonds*, January 2005, 10, 31, 34.

101. Department of Justice, "Statement of Barbara Comstock, Director of Public Affairs, Regarding Today's Filing in *Sibel Edmonds v. Department of Justice*," Release 02-605, October 18, 2002.

102. *Edmonds v. Department of Justice*, 323 F.Supp. 2d 65, 81 (D.D.C. 2004), *cert. denied*, 126 S. Ct. 734 (2005).

103. *Burnett v. Al Baraka Inv. and Dev. Corp.*, 325 F.Supp. 2d 82 (D.D.C. 2004).

104. Memorandum, "Sibel Edmonds Allegations," June 23, 2004, www.fas.org/sgp/news/2004/06/grassley062304.html, accessed August 15, 2006.

105. *Burnett v. Al Baraka Inv. and Dev. Corp.*, 84, and "Proposed Questions for Sibel Edmonds Deposition" appendix.

106. *Sierra Club v. Cheney*, "Memorandum Opinion," Civil Action no. 01-1530 (D.D.C. 2002), 56, 64–65. But note that higher courts were less concerned about these matters. In *Cheney v. U.S. District Court*, the Supreme Court held that Vice President Cheney need not formally assert executive privilege to support a position that discovery orders interfere with the operation of the Vice President's duties. 542 U.S. 367 (2004).

107. See, e.g., *ACLU v. Bush*, 06-CV-10204 (E.D. Mich. 2006); *Burnett et al. v. Al Baraka Investment & Dev. Corp.*, 04-MS-203 (D.D.C. 2004) www.justacitizen.com/articles_documents/Court_Order_to_Quash_Deposition.pdf; *Crater Corp. v. Lucent*, 423 F.3d

1260 (Fed. Cir. 2005); *Edmonds v. Department of Justice*, 405 F.Supp. 2d. 23 (D.D.C. 2005); *Edmonds v. Department of Justice*, 323 F.Supp. 2d 65 (D.D.C. 2004); *El-Masri v. Tenet*, 05-CV-1417 (E.D. Vir. 2006); *Global Relief Foundation v. O'Neill*, 02-C-674 (N.D. Ill. 2002); *Horn v. Huddle* (D.D.C. 2004; under seal, but order by Judge Royce Lamberth upholding assertion of the privilege was leaked), www.fas.org/sgp/jud/statesec/horn072804.pdf; *McDonnell Douglas Corporation v. United States*, 323 F.3d 1006 (Fed. Cir. 2003); *Monarch Assurance P.L.C. v. United States*, 244 F.3d. 1356 (Fed. Cir. 2001); *Schwartz v. TRW*, 211 F.R.D. 388 (C.D. Cal. 2002); *Sterling v. Tenet*, 416 F.3d 338 (4th Cir. 2006, *sub nomine Sterling v. Goss*); *Tennenbaum v. Simonini*, 372 F.3d 776 (6th Cir. 2004); *Trulock v. Wen Ho Lee*, 66 Fed. Appx. 472 (4th Cir. 2003). The only failures of the privilege so far in the Bush administration are in *Hepting v. AT&T*, C-06-672 (N.D. Calif. 2006) and *ACLU v. National Security Agency*, 06-CV-10204 (E.D. Mich. 2006). In *Hepting*, where the court found that a ruling on the state secrets privilege would be premature since no classified information had yet been put in jeopardy of disclosure. In *ACLU*, a district court judge found one of President Bush's NSA surveillance programs unconstitutional and found that the state secrets privilege did not apply to the program because its existence had been publicly acknowledged by the government. Of course, these rulings are subject to being overturned on appeal.

108. *Int'l Action Ctr.*, 7.

109. 66 Fed. Reg. 56025, November 1, 2001, 2(a), 3(d)(1)(ii).

110. *Nixon v. Administrator of General Services*, 433 U.S. 425, 440 (1977).

111. George W. Bush, "Remarks following Discussions with President Olusegun Obasanjo of Nigeria and an Exchange With Reporters," *Public Papers of the Presidents* 37, no. 44, November 5, 2001, 2.

112. See Joan Hoff, "The Endless Saga of the Nixon Tapes," in Theoharis, ed., *A Culture of Secrecy*, ch. 7.

113. Page Putnam Miller, "We Can't Yet Read Our Own Mail: Access to the Records of the Department of State," in Theoharis, ed., *A Culture of Secrecy*, ch. 9, 191, 192.

114. Military Order, "Detention, Treatment, and Trial of Certain Non-Citizens in the War Against Terrorism."

115. Department of the Navy, Office of the Judge Advocate General, "Asserting the State Secrets Privilege in United States Claims Court and Board of Contract Appeals Cases," February 3, 1992.

Four • The Shadow President

Epigraph: New York v. United States, 342 U.S. 882, 884 (1951).

1. Pub. L. No. 107-56, 115 Stat. 272 (2001); Pub. L. No. 107-296, 116 Stat. 2135 (2002).

2. Pub. L. No. 107-173, 116 Stat. 543 (2002).

3. 8 U.S.C. 1372(a) (1996).

4. Section 16, Judiciary Act of 1789, U.S. Statutes 1:73; 28 U.S.C. 511, 512 (September 24, 1789).

5. Haywood Jefferson Powell, *The Constitution and the Attorneys General* (Durham, NC: Carolina Academic Press, 1999), xv.

6. Kenneth Culp Davis, *Discretionary Justice: A Preliminary Inquiry* (Baton Rouge: Louisiana State University Press, 1969), 15.

7. 5 U.S.C. 553.

8. Davis, *Discretionary Justice*, 146.

9. Attorney General John Ashcroft, Senate Judiciary Committee testimony, December 6, 2001, www.usdoj.gov/ag/testimony/2001/1206transcriptsenatejudiciarycommittee.htm, accessed April 28, 2006.

10. Arlen Specter, Chuck Grassley, *U.S. Senate Roll Call*, June 9, 2003.

11. 50 U.S.C. 421 prohibits the disclosure of the identities of covert intelligence operatives.

12. Amy Goodman and Jeremy Scahill, "Conflict of Interest? White House Rejects Call for Independent Counsel On CIA Leak Despite Longtime Rove-Ashcroft Ties," *Democracy Now!*, www.democracynow.org/article.pl?sid=03/10/01/1435242&mode=thread&tid=13, accessed April 28, 2006.

13. Attorney General John Ashcroft, press conference, October 31, 2001, www.usdoj.gov/archive/ag/speeches/2001/agcrisisremarks10_31.htm, accessed April 28, 2006.

14. 18 U.S.C. 2510–20 (1968).

15. 50 U.S.C 1801–29.

16. 115 Stat. 272, 291, amending 50 U.S.C. 1804(a)(7)(B).

17. Ibid.

18. Ibid., 278–90.

19. Ibid., 288–92.

20. 50 U.S.C. 403-3(c)(6) (Supp. 2002).

21. *United States v. Johnson*, 319 U.S. 503, 515 (1943).

22. *United States v. Calandra*, 414 U.S. 338, 348 (1978).

23. *Pittsburgh Plate Glass Co. v. United States*, 360 U.S. 395, 398 (1959).

24. *United States v. Sells Engineering, Inc.*, 463 U.S. 418, 427 (1983).

25. 115 Stat. 279.

26. The Intelligence Reform and Terrorism Prevention Act of 2004 further expands both the capacity for information sharing and the control of the attorney general over the process. 118 Stat. 3638, 3760 (2004).

27. 115 Stat. 367.

28. Christopher Newton, "Scientist in Anthrax Probe Fired," *Washington Post*, September 4, 2002, www.anthraxinvestigation.com/wp020904.html, accessed April 28, 2006.

29. "Statement of Deborah Daniels, Assistant Attorney General for the Office of Justice Programs," September 4, 2002, www.usdoj.gov/opa/pr/2002/September/02_crm_506.htm, accessed April 28, 2006.

30. 115 Stat. 287.

31. Ibid., 286.

32. *Congressional Record*, July 22, 2003 (House), at H7284–H7311.

33. David Cole, "Enemy Aliens," *Stanford Law Review* 54 (2002): 953–1004, at 966.

34. Ibid., 968.

35. Ibid.

36. Pub. L. No. 108-458, 118 Stat. 3638 (2004).

37. 118 Stat., 3761.

38. 92 Stat. 1790; 50 U.S.C. 1805(a)(3).

39. 118 Stat. 3684.

40. "Events Related to Torture," www.harpers.org/Torture.html, accessed April 28, 2006.

41. Michael Creppy, "Memorandum: Cases Requiring Special Procedures," September 21, 2001, 2.

42. *North Jersey Media Group v. Ashcroft*, 205 F.Supp. 2d 288, 290 (D.N.J. 2002).

43. For a discussion of the mosaic theory in the "state secrets" context, see chapter 3.

44. *North Jersey Media Group, Inc. v. Ashcroft*, 308 F.3d 198, 200 (3rd Cir. 2002).

45. Ibid.

46. Attorney General John Ashcroft, "Prepared Remarks," July 17, 2002, www.usdoj .gov/archive/ag/speeches/2002/071702agawardspreparedremarks.htm, accessed April 28, 2006.

47. Charles Lewis and Adam Mayle, "Justice Department Drafts Sweeping Expansion of Anti-Terrorism Act," *Washington Post*, February 7, 2003, A1.

48. Draft of "Domestic Security Enhancement Act," 14, 59, www.public-i.org/report .aspx?aid=94&sid=200, accessed April 28, 2006.

49. *Kasza v. Browner*, 133 F. 3d 1159 (9th Cir. 1998).

50. Draft legislation, 17, 30.

51. Lewis and Mayle, "Justice Department Drafts Sweeping Expansion."

52. 115 Stat. 350.

53. Draft legislation, 23.

54. *Handschu v. Special Services Division*, 605 F.Supp. 1384 (S.D.N.Y. 1984).

55. *Handschu v. Special Services Division*, 71 Civ. 2203 (CSH) (S.D.N.Y. 2003).

56. Amy Goodman, "13,000 Arabs and Muslims in U.S. Face Deportation and John Ashcroft Attempts to Expand Patriot Act," June 9, 2003, www.democracynow.org/article .pl?sid=03/06/09/1652214&mode=thread&tid=27, accessed April 28, 2006.

57. "Detainee Report," issued June 2, 2003, www.usdoj.gov/oig/special/03-06/index .htm, accessed June 1, 2005.

58. Susan Schmidt, "Ashcroft Wants Stronger Patriot Act," *Washington Post*, June 6, 2003, A11.

59. Draft legislation, 14, 15–23.

60. "Final Report of the Commission on the Terrorist Attacks Upon the United States," www.gpoaccess.gov/911, accessed April 25, 2006.

61. Sheryl Gay Stolberg, "Patriot Act Renewal Passes House, Sending Measure to President," *New York Times*, March 7, 2006, A20.

62. "Bush Signs Homeland Security Bill," November 26, 2002, www.archives.cnn .com/2002/ALLPOLITICS/11/25/homeland.security, accessed April 25, 2006.

63. 116 Stat. 2142.

64. Ibid., 2144, 2149, 2152.

65. David Walker, "9/11: The Implications for Public Sector Management," *Public Administration Review* 62 (2002): 94–97, at 97.

66. 8 U.S.C. 1372(a) (as amended).

67. Ibid.

68. Vernon Loeb, "When Hoarding Secrets Threatens National Security," *Washington Post*, January 26, 2003, foi.missouri.edu/terrorintelligence/whenhoarding.html, accessed April 28, 2006.

69. "Homeland Office Is Told to Answer Queries on Its Role," *Washington Post*, January 3, 2003, A2. Aside from that litigation, the Electronic Privacy Information Center (EPIC) has sued the federal government over anti-terror–related privacy issues numerous times since 9/11. For example, *EPIC v. Department of Justice*, Civ. No. 05-845 (D.D.C. 2005); *EPIC v. Department of Justice*, Civ. Nos. 04-1736, 04-2164 (D.D.C. 2004); *EPIC v. DOC*, Civ. No. 04-1625 (D.D.C. 2004); and *EPIC v. Department of Homeland Security*, Civ. No. 04-0994 (D.D.C. 2004).

70. Scott Armstrong, "The War over Secrecy: Democracy's Most Important Low-Intensity Conflict," in Athan Thoeharis, ed., *A Culture of Secrecy: The Government Versus the People's Right to Know* (Lawrence: University Press of Kansas, 1998), ch. 8.

71. Michael W. Spicer, "The War on Terrorism and the Administration of the American State," *Public Administration Review* 62 (2002): 63–68.

72. Ibid.

73. "Bush Signs Homeland Security Bill."

74. Lisa Nelson, "Protecting the Common Good: Technology, Objectivity, and Privacy," *Public Administration Review* 62 (2002): 69–73.

75. Rachel Clarke, "Ashcroft Trumpets Anti-Terror Laws, BBC News online in Washington," October 7, 2003, www.news.bbc.co.uk/1/hi/world/americas/3164785.stm, accessed April 25, 2006. In defense of administration anti-terror policy, Ashcroft pointed out in a press conference that there have been no new terror attacks in the United States since fall of 2001. This is a classic example of the "false cause" logical fallacy: we do not have any basis for attributing the effect to the cause he cites, that is, administration policy. Moreover, there had been attacks against Americans and others around the world: in Bali, Riyadh, Yemen, and Iraq.

76. William Waugh Jr. and Richard Sylves, "Organizing the War on Terrorism," *Public Administration Review* 62 (2002): 81–89.

77. Ibid.

78. "Terrorism Index," *Foreign Policy*, July/August 2006, webo.foreignpolicy.com/issue_julyaug_2006/TI-index/, accessed August 15, 2006.

79. 18 U.S.C. 3144 (1984). Release or detention of material witnesses.

80. Laurie Levenson, "Material Witnesses and the War on Terrorism," *Loyola of Los Angeles Law Review* 35 (2002): 1217–26, at 1223.

81. *United States v. Awadallah*, 202 F.Supp. 2d 82 (S.D.N.Y. 2002).

82. *United States v. Awadallah*, 349 F.3d 42, 49 (2d Cir. 2004), cert. den. 125 S.Ct. 861 (2005).

83. Christine Haughney, "A Sept. 11 Casualty: 'Radio Man' Jailed for a Month, Then Freed," *Washington Post*, March 11, 2003, A3.

84. *Hijazy v. United States*, 214 F.Supp. 2d 356, 360 (S.D.N.Y. 2002).

85. *Supra*, notes 108, 109.

86. Haughney, "A Sept. 11 Casualty."

87. *Supra,* note 66.

88. 115 Stat. 276.

89. See Amnesty International, *2005 Report on the United States of America,* web .amnesty.org/report2005/usa-summary-eng, accessed April 28, 2006.

90. Ibid., 351.

91. T. Alexander Aleinkoff, "Detaining Plenary Power: The Meaning and Impact of *Zadvydas v. Davis,*" *Georgetown Immigration Law Journal* 16 (2002): 365–89; 121 S.Ct. 2491 (2001).

92. Ibid., 378, 381.

93. Ibid., 382.

94. *Marbury v. Madison,* 1 Cranch 137 (1803).

95. Davis, *Discretionary Justice.*

96. National Public Radio, "INS Registration Tagets Middle Eastern Immigrants," January 11, 2003, www.npr.org/templates/story/story.php?storyId=915471, accessed April 28, 2006.

97. Ibid.

98. John Paden and Peter Singer, "America Slams the Door (On Its Foot): Washington's Destructive New Visa Policies," *Foreign Affairs* (May/June 2003).

99. Testimony of Ali Al-Maqtari on Due Process, AILA InfoNet Doc. No. 23TS1001, http://www.aila.org/Content/default.aspx?docid=2138, posted December 6, 2001, accessed August 15, 2006.

100. Human Rights Watch Report on Arbitrary Detention, www.hrw.org/reports/2002/us911/USA0802-05.htm, accessed April 28, 2006.

101. Cole, "Enemy Aliens," 959, 990, 995.

102. William Rehnquist, *All the Laws But One: Civil Liberties in Wartime* (New York: Vintage Books, 2000).

103. Cole, "Enemy Aliens," 959.

104. Ibid. See also Charles and Mary Beard, *A Basic History of the United States* (New York: Doubleday, Doran, 1944), 168.

105. Military Order, "Detention, Treatment and Trial of Certain Non-Citizens in the War Against Terrorism," 66 Fed. Reg. 57835–36, sec. 7.

106. Cole, "Enemy Aliens," 977.

107. Ibid., 984; *Ex Parte Quirin,* 317 U.S. 1 (1942).

108. *Hamdi v. Rumsfeld,* 543 U.S. 507 at 592, 601, 603 (2004).

109. *Hamdan v. Rumsfeld,* 344 F.Supp 2d 152, 158 (D.D.C. 2004), *petition den.* U.S. App Lexis 2474 (D.C.Cir. 2005), *cert. den.* 125 S.Ct. 972 (2005).

110. *Hamdan v. Rumsfeld,* No. 04-5393 (D.C. Cir. July 15, 2005), slip opinion, at 19.

111. 344 F.Supp. 163–64; D.C. Cir. slip opinion, 10–13.

112. Ibid., 15.

113. Louis Fisher, *Nazi Saboteurs on Trial: A Military Tribunal and American Law* (Lawrence: University Press of Kansas, 2003), 159.

114. *Hamdan v. Rumsfeld,* No. 05-184, decided June 29, 2006, slip opinion at 1–73.

115. Ibid., slip op., 72.

116. *Quirin*, 172.

Five • *The President and National Security Surveillance*

Epigraphs: Quoted in Daniel Patrick Moynihan, *Secrecy: The American Experience* (New Haven: Yale University Press, 1998), 89; *Olmstead v. United States*, 277 U.S. 438 (1928), 476.

1. Theodore J. Lowi, "Presidential Power: Restoring the Balance," *Political Science Quarterly* 100, No. 2 (1985): 185–213, at 186.

2. Ibid., 187.

3. Theodore J. Lowi, "Presidential Democracy in America: Toward the Homogenized Regime," *Political Science Quarterly* 109, no. 3 (1994): 401–15, at 403.

4. Lyn Ragsdale and John J. Theis III, "The Institutionalization of the American Presidency, 1924–1992," *American Journal of Political Science* 41 (October 1997): 1280–1318, at 1281, 1302, 1314.

5. 50 U.S.C. 1801 et seq. (1978).

6. For example, *United States v. Brown*, 484 F.2d 418 (5th Cir. 1973); *United States v. Buck*, 548 F.2d 871 (9th Cir. 1977); *United States v. Butenko*, 494 F.2d 593 (3rd Cir. 1974); *United States v. Hung*, 629 F.2d 908 (4th Cir. 1980).

7. 807 F.2d 197 (D.C. Cir. 1986).

8. *Hepting v. AT&T*, Amended Complaint of February 22, 2006.

9. 277 U.S. 438, 465, 478 (1928).

10. Ibid., 470.

11. Guidance of Attorney General Mitchell discussed in Americo R. Cinquegrana, "The Walls (and Wires) Have Ears: The Background and First Ten Years of the Foreign Intelligence Surveillance Act," *University of Pennsylvania Law Review* 137 (January 1989): 793–828, at 796–97.

12. Alan Westin, "The Wiretapping Problem: An Analysis and a Legislative Proposal." *Columbia Law Review* 52 (February 1952): 165–208, at 166.

13. For example, U.S. House of Representatives, H.R. 4139. 71st Cong., 1st Sess., 1929; U.S. Senate, S.1396. 72nd Cong., 1st Sess., 1932.

14. 73 P.L. 416.

15. Edwin J. Bradley and James E. Hogan, "Wiretapping: From *Nardone* to *Benanti* and *Rathbun*," *Georgetown Law Journal* 46 (1958): 418–42, at 419.

16. *Nardone v. United States*, 302 U.S. 379 (1937).

17. Ibid., 383.

18. *Nardone v. United States*, 308 U.S. 338, 340, 341 (1939).

19. Ibid., 340.

20. *Goldman v. United States*, 316 U.S. 129 (1942).

21. Westin, "The Wiretapping Problem," 173.

22. U.S. Senate, *Final Report of the Select Committee to Study Governmental Operations With Respect to Intelligence Activities: Supplementary Detailed Staff Reports on Intelligence*

Activities and the Rights of Americans, Book III, 94th Cong., 2nd Sess., Sen. Rep. 94-755, pt. 3, 1976, 280.

23. Franklin D. Roosevelt, "Memorandum for the Attorney General," May 21, 1940, reproduced in Appendix A in *Zweibon v. Mitchell* 516 F.2d 594 (D.C. Cir. 1975).

24. U.S. Congress, House of Representatives, H.J.R.553. 76th Cong., 3rd Sess., 1940.

25. See Appendix A in *Zweibon v. Mitchell*.

26. Athan Theoharis, "FBI Wiretapping: A Case Study of Bureaucratic Autonomy," *Political Science Quarterly* 107 (1992): 101–22, at 105–6, 115, 116.

27. U.S. Senate, *Supplementary Detailed Staff Reports on Intelligence Activities and the Rights of Americans, Book III*, 280.

28. Ibid., 280–81.

29. Ibid., 281.

30. "Ex-Agent Says He Bugged Room of Mrs. Roosevelt," *New York Times*, November 1, 1965, 1.

31. Tom C. Clark, untitled, July 17, 1946, reproduced in Appendix A in *Zweibon v. Mitchell*.

32. Gordon Silverstein, *Imbalance of Powers: Constitutional Interpretation and the Making of American Foreign Policy* (New York: Oxford University Press, 1997), 67.

33. U.S. Congress, House of Representatives, *Providing for the Admissibility in Certain Criminal Proceedings of Evidence Obtained by Interception of Communications*, 83rd Cong., 2nd Sess., Rep. 1461, 1954.

34. Lyndon B. Johnson, "Memorandum for the Heads of Executive Departments and Agencies," June 30, 1965, reproduced in Appendix A in *Zweibon v. Mitchell*.

35. Ramsey Clark, "Memo No. 493," November 10, 1966, reproduced in Appendix A in *Zweibon v. Mitchell*.

36. *United States v. U.S. District Court for the Eastern District of Michigan* (*Keith*), 407 U.S. 297 (1972).

37. U.S. Senate, Select Committee on Intelligence, Subcommittee on Intelligence and the Rights of Americans, *Electronic Surveillance Within the United States for Foreign Intelligence Purposes*, 94th Cong., 2nd Sess., June 29, 1976, 25.

38. Richard M. Nixon, speech of August 15, 1973, www.watergate.info/nixon/73-08-15watergate-speech.shtml, accessed April 19, 2006.

39. On Roosevelt and Truman, see Theoharis, "FBI Wiretapping," 109–11; on the surveillance of Martin Luther King, see *Supplementary Detailed Staff Reports on Intelligence Activities and the Rights of Americans, Book III: Dr. Martin Luther King, Jr., Case Study*, pt. 4, 111–30; on Kennedy's use of wiretaps on sitting legislators, see *Electronic Surveillance Within the United States for Foreign Intelligence Purposes*, 21.

40. U.S. Senate, *Final Report of the Select Committee to Study Governmental Operations With Respect to Intelligence Activities: Intelligence Activities and the Rights of Americans, Book II*, 94th Cong., 2nd Sess., Sen. Rep. 94-755, at 37, 205–6.

41. *Katz v. United States*, 389 U.S. 347, 358n23 (1967).

42. 82. Stat. 213 (1968).

43. Silverstein, *Imbalance of Powers*, 96.

44. *Keith*, 301.

45. Ibid., 299, 303, 308.

46. Edward Levi, *Guidelines for Domestic Security Investigations*, Department of Justice, 1976, I(A), II(G), II(J)(3).

47. University of Chicago, "Edward H. Levi, former U.S. Attorney General, President Emeritus of the University and the Glen A. Lloyd Distinguished Service Professor Emeritus in the Law School, Dies at 88," University of Chicago News Office, March 7, 2000, www-news.uchicago.edu/releases/00/000307.levi.shtml, accessed April 18, 2006.

48. National Security Council Meeting, *Minutes: Semiannual Review of the Intelligence Community*, January 13, 1977.

49. The rules survived longer than many would have expected, being jettisoned only in 2003 by Attorney General John Ashcroft.

50. U.S. Congress, House of Representatives, Committee on the Judiciary, Subcommittee on Courts, Civil Liberties, and the Administration of Justice, *Foreign Intelligence Surveillance Act*, 95th Cong., 2nd Sess., 22 June, 1978, 1.

51. *Zweibon*, 614, emphasis added.

52. U.S. Congress, House of Representatives, Committee on the Judiciary, *Foreign Intelligence Surveillance Act*, 94th Cong., 2nd Sess., April 12, 1976, 2.

53. U.S. Senate, Intelligence Committee, *Foreign Intelligence Surveillance Act of 1978*, S. Rep. 95-701, 95th Cong., 2nd Sess., 7.

54. 92 Stat. 1797; U.S. Senate, *Foreign Intelligence Surveillance Act of 1978*, 72.

55. Interview with FBI agent wishing to remain anonymous, May 2005.

56. Memo to the Office of the Inspector General, Department of Justice, April 2, 2002. Document in possession of the authors.

57. The example comes from *United States v. Andonian*, 735 F.Supp. 1469, 1471 (C.D. Calif. 1990).

58. The FISA portion of the figures is calculated using annual reports required under the FISA statute. The reports state only the total number of applications and the number of applications approved, modified, or denied. Non-FISA reports for warrants for electronic eavesdropping are more detailed and issued annually. The statistics concerning non-FISA warrants are based on the annual *Report of the Director of the Administrative Office of the United States Courts on Applications for Orders Authorizing or Approving the Interception of Wire, Oral, or Electronic Communications*.

59. 115 Stat. 291.

60. *In re All Matters Submitted to the Foreign Intelligence Surveillance Court*, 218 F.Supp. 2d 611, 620 (U.S. Foreign Intell. Surveil. Ct. 2002).

61. Ibid., 626, 627.

62. Ibid., 620–21.

63. Anonymous, untitled memorandum, Federal Bureau of Investigation, April 5, 2000, 1.

64. Counterterrorism Division, "Caution on FISA Issues," Federal Bureau of Investigation, April 21, 2000, 2.

65. *In re All Matters*, 621, emphasis in original court release of opinion, not reflected in the case as it appears in Lexis.

66. Ibid., 623, 625.

67. *ACLU v. United States*, 538 U.S. 920 (2003).

68. 1803(c).

69. Judge Colleen Kollar-Kotelly, untitled letter, August 20, 2002, http://www.epic .org/privacy/terrorism/fisa/fisc_ltr_08_2002.html, accessed August 15, 2006.

70. Patrick Leahy, Charles Grassley, and Arlen Specter, letter to The Honorable Colleen Kollar-Kotelly, presiding judge, U.S. Foreign Intelligence Surveillance Court, July 31, 2002.

71. U.S. Congress, House of Representatives, Permanent Select Committee on Intelligence, Subcommittee on Legislation, *Foreign Intelligence Electronic Surveillance: Hearings on H.R. 5794, 9745, 7308, and 5632*, 95th Cong., 2nd Sess., February 8, 1978, 221.

72. *In re Sealed Case*, 310 F.3rd 717, 732 (For. Int. Sur. Ct. of Rev. 2002) (note 19).

73. United States Foreign Intelligence Court of Review, hearing on docket No. 02-001, September 9, 2002, at 103.

74. *In re Sealed Case*, 732, 735.

75. Ibid., 731, 743, 744.

76. Ibid., 736.

77. Ibid., 742.

78. U.S. Senate, *Foreign Intelligence Surveillance Act of 1978*, 95th Cong., 1st Sess., S. Rep. 95-604, 7–8.

79. U.S. Senate, Committee on the Judiciary, Subcommittee on Criminal Laws and Procedures, *Foreign Intelligence Surveillance Act of 1977*, 95th Cong., 1st Sess., June 13, 1977, 1–2.

80. 18 U.S.C. 2518(8)(d).

81. *ACLU v. Barr*, 952 F.2d 457 (D.C. Cir. 1990).

82. 18 U.S.C. 2520(f).

83. U.S. Senate, Judiciary Committee, *The USA PATRIOT Act In Practice*, testimony of Kenneth Bass, "The Delicate—and Difficult—Balance of Intelligence and Criminal Prosecution Interests in the Foreign Intelligence Surveillance Act," September 10, 2002, judiciary.senate.gov/testimony.cfm?id=398&wit_id=941, accessed April 20, 2006.

84. *In re All Matters*, 619.

85. *Ellsberg v. Mitchell*, 807 F.2d 204, 207 (D.C. Cir. 1986).

86. James Risen and Eric Lichtblau, "Bush Lets U.S. Spy on Callers Without Courts," *New York Times*, December 16, 2005, A1.

87. Suzanne Goldenberg, "Media: Bush Gets Personal with Troublesome U.S. Editors," *The Guardian* (London), January 2, 2006, 7.

88. *Halkin v. Helms*, 690 F.2d 977, 983–84 (D.C. Cir. 1982).

89. Untitled letter from Assistant Attorney General William E. Moschella, Department of Justice office of Legislative Affairs, to Chairman Pat Roberts and Vice Chairman John D. Rockefeller of the Senate Select Committee on Intelligence and Chairman Peter Hoekstra and Ranking Minority Member Jane Harman of the House Permanent Select Committee on Intelligence, December 22, 2005, 5.

90. 50 U.S.C. 1805(f).

91. John Markoff and Scott Shane, "Documents Show Link Between AT&T and Agency in Eavesdropping Case," *New York Times*, April 12, 2006, A17.

92. Committee on the Judiciary; Subcommittee on Criminal Laws and Procedures, *Foreign Intelligence Surveillance Act of 1977*, 134.

Six • The New Executive Privilege

Epigraphs: Oral argument transcript at 28. Docket No. 3-475, argued April 27, 2004. See www.supremecourtus.gov/oral_arguments/argument_transcripts.html, accessed April 27, 2006. This remark was made during a colloquy that ensued during oral argument, so Justice Scalia is to be excused for his less than total clarity. The conception of executive power lying behind his comment, however, is unmistakable.

1. Mark Rozell, *Executive Privilege: Presidential Power, Secrecy, and Accountability* (Lawrence: University of Kansas Press, 2002), 1–5.

2. Ibid.; Raoul Berger, *Executive Privilege: A Constitutional Myth* (Cambridge: Harvard University Press, 1974); Louis Fisher, "Executive Privilege and the Bush Administration: Essay: Congressional Access to Information: Using Legislative Will and Leverage," *Duke Law Journal* 52 (November 2002): 323–401; Louis Fisher, "Executive Privilege and the Clinton Presidency: Invoking Executive Privilege: Navigating Ticklish Political Waters," *William and Mary Bill of Rights Journal* 8 (April 2002): 583–629; Saikrishna Bangalore Prakash, "A Comment on the Constitutionality of Executive Privilege," *Minnesota Law Review* 83 (May 1999): 1143–89; Patricia Wald and Jonathan Siegel, "The D.C. Circuit and the Struggle for Control of Presidential Information," *Georgetown Law Journal* 90 (March 2002): 737–78; Brian D. Smith, "A Proposal to Codify Executive Privilege," *George Washington Law Review* 70 (June 2002): 570–612; Marcy Lynn Karin, "Note: Out of Sight, But Not Out of Mind: How Executive Order 13,233 Expands Executive Privilege While Simultaneously Preventing Access to Presidential Records," *Stanford Law Review* 55 (November 2002): 529–70.

3. Congressional Testimony of Mark Rozell, November 6, 2001, www.fas.org/sgp/congress/2001/11601_rozell.html, accessed August 2, 2006.

4. Ibid.

5. Ibid.

6. Ibid.

7. Berger, *Executive Privilege*, 37.

8. Fisher, "Executive Privilege and the Clinton Presidency," 605.

9. Berger, *Executive Privilege*, 11, 45.

10. *United States v. Nixon*, 418 U.S. 683, 706 (1974).

11. Rozell, *Executive Privilege*, quoting John Locke, 21.

12. Prakash, "Constitutionality of Executive Privilege," 1143.

13. Ibid., 1144.

14. Fisher, "Executive Privilege and the Clinton Presidency," 605.

15. Prakash, "Constitutionality of Executive Privilege," 1149.

16. Congressional Testimony of Mark Rozell.

17. Rozell, *Executive Privilege*, 105, 119, 121.

18. Ibid., 122, 123.

19. Ibid., 124, 129.

20. *In re Sealed Case*, 121 F.3d 729, 751, 752 (D.C. Cir. 1998).

21. Rozell, *Executive Privilege*, 130.

22. *In re Sealed Case*, 746, 750, 762.

23. Wald and Siegel, "Struggle for Control," 737.

24. *In re Sealed Case*, 752.

25. Rozell, *Executive Privilege*, 161.

26. James Madison, *Federalist No. 10*, www.jmu.edu/madison/center/main_pages/madison_archives/constit_confed/federalist/federalist_papers/federalist10.htm, accessed April 27, 2006. The phrase is quoted in Berger, *Executive Privilege*, 9.

27. Rozell, *Executive Privilege*, 64, 65, 122, 157, 158.

28. Fisher, "Executive Privilege and the Bush Administration," 304. For a thorough treatment of the range of congressional options for responding to executive recalcitrance, see Louis Fisher, *The Politics of Executive Privilege* (Durham, NC: Carolina Academic Press, 2004).

29. Fisher, "Executive Privilege and the Bush Administration," 323.

30. Smith, "A Proposal to Codify Executive Privilege," 601.

31. Berger, *Executive Privilege*, 11, 45.

32. Dana Milbank, "It's Bush's Way or the Highway on Guantanamo Bay," *Washington Post*, July 12, 2006, A2.

33. American Bar Association, "Task Force On Presidential Signing Statements and the Separation of Powers Doctrine," 14. Available at www.abanet.org/op/signingstatements, accessed August 16, 2006.

34. Ibid., 1, 17.

35. *Hamdi v. Rumsfeld*, 542 U.S. 507, 631, 632 (2004).

36. Cf. Louis Fisher, who writes that "these attitudes have long since been superseded by statutory grants of power to the courts, inviting them to exercise independent judgment on matters of national security." Fisher, "Executive Privilege and the Bush Administration," 609.

37. See epigraph note.

38. Rozell, *Executive Privilege*, 64.

39. Wald and Siegel, "Struggle for Control," 742, 754.

40. U.S. Congress, House of Representatives, Committee on Government Reform, "Minority Staff Report: Secrecy in the Bush Administration" (Waxman Report), September 14, 2004, www.democrats.reform.house.gov, accessed April 26, 2006, iii.

41. 5 U.S.C. App. 2.

42. Ibid.; Waxman Report, 36; 5 U.S.C. App. 3(2).

43. Ibid., 37; 116 Stat. 2243; 6 U.S.C. 871.

44. Waxman Report, 37.

45. Rozell, *Executive Privilege*, 45, 155.

46. Ibid., 45; *United States v. Reynolds*, 345 U.S. 1 (1953).

47. *United States v. Nixon*, 418 U.S. 683, 706 (1974), emphasis added.

48. Rozell, *Executive Privilege*, 135.

49. Waxman Report, 31; 44 U.S.C. 2201–7.

50. 54 Fed. Reg. 3403, January 18, 1989.

51. Waxman Report, 32; 66 Fed. Reg. 56025, November 1, 2001.

52. Rozell, *Executive Privilege*, 7, 33.

53. Waxman Report, 33.

54. Karin, "Out of Sight, But Not Out of Mind," 559.

55. Ibid.

56. *Sierra Club v. Cheney*, 219 F.Supp. 2d 20, 24 (D.D.C. 2002).

57. 5 U.S.C. App. 2.

58. *Sierra Club v. Cheney*, 25.

59. *Walker v. Cheney*, 230 F.Supp. 2d 51 (D.D.C. 2002); *Sierra Club v. Cheney*, 20, 24; *Cheney v. District Court*, 542 U.S. 367, 124 S.Ct. 2576 (2004). See also Jeffrey Carlin, "Note: Walker v. Cheney: Politics, Posturing, and Executive Privilege," *Southern California Law Review* 76 (November 2002): 235.

60. Fisher argues that the *Walker* court decided as it did because there had been no formal congressional demand for the NEPDG information, so the comptroller general "found himself, politically and institutionally, isolated." Fisher, "Executive Privilege and the Bush Administration," 329. It is true that the GAO was at the forefront of the dispute, but there was support, at least at times, for their investigation among lawmakers. Moreover, Fisher's explanation does not insulate the court from criticism for making a legally weak decision. To rule on the legal question of standing based on shifting configurations of political forces gets the matter somewhat backwards: the courts are charged to act, based on the law, when informal mechanisms of settlement are unavailing.

61. *Cheney v. District Court*, 2592.

62. Ibid., 2589.

63. *Walker v. Cheney*, 68n12.

64. Akhil Reed Amar, "In Nixon's Shadow," *Minnesota Law Review* 83 (May 1999): 1405–20, at 1411.

65. *In re Cheney*, 406 F.3d 723, 728 (D.C. Cir. 2005).

66. Dan Eggen, "White House Holding Notes Taken by 9/11 Commission: Panel May Subpoena Its Summaries of Bush Briefings," *Washington Post*, January 31, 2004, A2.

67. Philip Shenon, "Panel Rejects White House Limits on Interviews," *New York Times*, March 3, 2004, A12.

68. Dan Eggen, "White House vs. 9/11 Panel: Resistance, Resolution," *Washington Post*, March 9, 2004, A2.

69. Elisabeth Bumiller and Philip Shenon, "Political Memo: Threats and Responses: No Public Appearance by Person Panel Wants Most," *New York Times*, March 26, 2004, A26.

70. *Supra*, note 65.

71. Elisabeth Bumiller and Philip Shenon, "Bush-Cheney 9/11 Interview Won't be Formally Recorded," *New York Times*, April 27, 2004, A18.

72. "Of Privilege and Policy," *New York Times*, March 31, 2004, A22.

73. *Supra*, note 69.

74. Dan Eggen, "9/11 Panel: Bush White House Withheld Papers," *Washington Post*, April 8, 2004, A4.

75. See, e.g., *supra*, note 65.

76. Significantly, the classified portions of the congressional report apparently received some exposure beyond the highest-level U.S. security establishment. *Harper's Magazine* reported shortly after the Congressional report was released that the Saudi government

sought to rebut allegations contained in the redacted portion. This information would appear to contradict national security rationales for the redaction. See www.harpers.org/HomelandSecurity.html, accessed April 26, 2006.

77. Rozell, *Executive Privilege*, 1.

78. Fisher, *The Politics of Executive Privilege*, 258.

79. Ibid., 246; 567 F.2d 121 (D.C. Cir. 1977).

80. Fisher, *The Politics of Executive Privilege*, 134.

Conclusion • *A Secret Presidency for the New Millenium?*

Epigraph: Walt Whitman, *Leaves of Grass* (New York: Penguin Books, 1981), 92.

1. We are grateful to David Plotke for this formulation.

2. Eric Lichtblau and Scott Shane, "Congressman Says Program Was Disclosed by Informant," *New York Times*, July 10, 2006, A6.

3. Oral argument transcript at 28. Docket No. 3-475, argued April 27, 2004. See www.supremecourtus.gov/oral_arguments/argument_transcripts.html, accessed April 27, 2006.

4. See, for example, "Safety Specification for the Pulsed Fast Neutron Analysis (PFNA) Inspection System at Ysleta Port of Entry Commercial Cargo Facility," www.dhs.gov/dhspublic/interweb/assetlibrary/Mgmt_NEPA_PFNA_Safety_Spec.pdf, accessed April 28, 2006.

5. Robert Dahl, "Decisionmaking in a Democracy: The Supreme Court as National Policymaker," *Journal of Public Policy* 6 (1956): 279–95.

6. Arlen Specter, Chuck Grassley, *U.S. Senate Roll Call*, June 9, 2003.

7. James Sundquist, *The Decline and Resurgence of Congress* (Washington, D.C.: Brookings Institution Press, 1981), 441.

8. Robert Dahl, "What Political Institutions Does Large-Scale Democracy Require?" *Political Science Quarterly* 120, no. 2 (Summer 2005): 187–97, at 188, 196.

9. Larry Abramson, "House Passes USA Patriot Act Extension," *National Public Radio*, July 21, 2005, www.npr.org/templates/story/story.php?storyId=4765076, accessed April 24, 2006.

10. Eric Alterman, *When Presidents Lie: A History of Official Deception and Its Consequences.* (New York: Penguin, 2004), 15.

11. Ibid., 20. Alterman acknowledges this problem by quoting Mill, who asks how the public can "check or encourage what they were not permitted to see?" See 14.

12. Ibid., 14.

13. Howard Gillman, "From Fundamental Law to Constitutional Politics—and Back," *Law and Social Inquiry* 23, no. 1 (1998): 185–202, at 186.

14. Quoted in ibid., 186.

15. Ibid.

16. Ibid., 198.

17. *Youngstown Sheet and Tube v. Sawyer*, 343 U.S. 579, 585 (1952).

Abu Ghraib, 54, 58, 222
accountability, executive, 5, 9
Adams, President John Q., 43
Administrative Procedure Act, 123
Afghani resistance, 112
Afghanistan: Northern Alliance in, 132; seizure of prisoners from, 153; war in, 36
African National Congress, 132
Agriculture, Department of, 87
Air Force, Secretary of, 84, 85, 102
Aleinikoff, T. Alexander, 148
Algiers, 62
aliens, detention of, 125, 136, 147, 155
Al-Qaeda, 151, 212
Alterman, Eric, 222
American Bar Association, 202
American Civil Liberties Union, 180
anthrax, 130
Arar v. Ashcroft, 109
Area 51, 84, 85, 87, 110, 111, 135
Aristotle, 33
Arkin, William, 49
Arms Export Control Act, 47
Ashcroft, Attorney General John, 21, 57, 115, 116, 124, 125, 130, 133, 134, 138, 143, 177, 178
AT&T, 189
Atomic Energy Act, 67, 75, 76
Attorney General, 15, 122, 135, 140, 155, 171, 181

Baker, Edward, 64
Ball's Bluff, Battle of, 64
Barber, James D., 24, 26
Bass, Kenneth, 186
Beatson v. Skene, 102

Berger, Raoul, 19, 193, 195, 201
Biddle, Attorney General Francis, 163, 165
"Big Secret," 52, 53
Bill of Rights, 2
Black, Justice Hugo, 224
Black Panther Party, 188
Blackstone, William, 101
Bork, Judge Robert, 191
Bradbury, Stephen, 202
Brandeis, Justice Louis, 88, 159
Brennan, Justice William, 118
Bridges, Harry, 163
British Intelligence, 59
British law, 19
Brownell, Attorney General Herbert, 164, 165
Bureau of Customs and Immigration Services, 140
bureaucracy, executive, 30
Burke, Charles, 113
Burr, Aaron, 95
Burton, Representative Dan, 15
Bush, President George H. W., 1, 24, 39, 43, 91, 105, 169, 179
Bush, President George W., 3, 15, 22, 42, 43, 54, 114, 118, 136, 142–44, 176, 188–90, 198, 211–12; classification of documents by, 50; and commitment to secrecy, 46; and expansion of executive privilege, 193; and FOIA, 47; foreign relations power, 80; and issuance of military order, 151; leadership claims of, 41; and military action, 39; and military tribunals, 11; and presidential expertise, 35; and presidential records, 207; press conferences by, 35; and 2004 election, 32; and unitary

Bush, President George W. (*continued*)
  presidency, 27; and warrantless surveillance,
  21, 52, 109, 158, 218
Bush v. Gore, 34

Cambodia, bombing of, 52
capitalism, globalization of, 43
Carter, President Jimmy, 25, 85, 106, 117, 169,
  198, 219
Cartesian doubt, 223
Central Intelligence Agency, 55, 71, 72, 91, 96,
  97, 108–12, 167; director of, 138; and Home-
  land Security Act, 141–42; leak of agent's
  identity, 124
Central Intellence Group, 71
character, as focus of presidential studies, 24
Cheney, Vice President Richard, 1, 116, 135, 208,
  212
Cheney v. U.S. District Court, 208
civil libertarians, impeding security, 1
civil liberties, 182; sacrifice of, 134
Clark, Attorney General Ramsey, 164
Clark, Attorney General Tom, 163–65
Clark, Justice Tom, 89
classification, of documents, 46, 87, 192
Clements, William, 169
Clinton, President Bill, 29, 39, 44, 92, 111, 112,
  198–200, 212, 219
Code of Federal Regulations, 74
Coke, Lord, 114
Cold War, 19, 50, 59, 77, 81, 142
Cole, David, 131–32, 151–52
Collier, Kenneth, 8
Combest, Larry, 77
Commerce, Department of, 106
Commission on Protecting and Reducing Gov-
  ernment Secrecy, 47
Committee of Secret Correspondence, 61
common law, 86, 94
Communications Intelligence Board, 72
Continental Congress, 61
Congress, U.S., 3, 17, 22, 23, 30, 53, 55, 57, 71,
  79, 89, 113, 167, 169, 171, 181, 191, 210, 211,
  213, 220–21, 225; and ability to challenge
  president, 1, 2; ceding power to president, 44;
  and classification laws, 45; and classified
  information, 48; control of presidential discretion, 158; delegations of power by, 37; dis-

closures to, 51; early history of, 95; elections
  for, 39; and executive secrecy, 86; and hearings before, 194; and information disputes
  with president, 200–201; legislative intent of,
  202; majority party in, 27; obtaining information from, 99; and nadir of power, 26; oversight responsibilities of, 18, 67, 106; and passage of Espionage Act, 66; post-Watergate,
  198; Republicans in, 124; withholding information from, 16, 195
consent decrees, invalidation of, 136–37
Constitution, U.S., 4, 22, 25, 27, 51, 72, 73, 87,
  224; Amendment 1 of, 115, 133, 192; Amendment 4 of, 21, 158–59, 164–67, 182, 189–92;
  and appointment power, 31; Article II, 18, 21,
  80, 153, 195–99, 217; Article III, 17, 88, 108;
  changes to, 18; and Congressional secrecy, 61;
  executive privilege in, 197, 201; veto power,
  31; violation of, 90
constitutionalism, 142, 223–25
contras, Nicaraguan, 92
Conway v. Rimmer, 102
Coolidge, President Calvin, 25
Cost of Living Council, 115
Creppy, Michael, 133
crown privilege, 101, 102

Dahl, Robert, 219, 221–22
Davis, Kenneth Culp, 88, 122–23, 149
Defense, Department of, 47, 55, 72, 151
deliberative process privilege, 99, 199
Department of the Navy v. Egan, 77–78
Detainee Treatment Act, 154
detention, presumptive, 136
disaster planning, 135
discretion, administrative, 122–23
discrimination, racial and sexual, 20
District of Columbia v. Bakersmith, 100
documents, confidential, 51
Duncan v. Cammel Laird and Co., Ltd.,
  102–4

Ecclesiastes, 42
Edmonds, Sibel, 48, 57, 76, 77, 115, 116
Edwards, George, 13
efficiency/secrecy nexus, 124
Eisenhower, President Dwight, 25, 32, 34, 36,
  73, 164, 199; and wiretaps, 13

Ellsberg v. Mitchell, 188
Electronic Privacy Information Center, 141
Enemy Alien Act, 151
Energy, Department of, 75
Enhanced Border Security and Visa Entry
   Reform Act, 121, 140
Environmental Protection Agency, 87
EPA v. Mink, 81
Espionage Act, 65–68, 76
Espy, Mike, 199, 200
Executive Office of the President, 55
executive orders, 41, 56, 70–76, 81, 114, 117, 119,
   207
executive privilege, 22, 28, 93, 98, 99, 193–
   200, 207, 209, 212, 215–18
ex parte hearings, 76
Ex parte Quirin, 153–54

Faubus, Orval, 32
Federal Advisory Committee Act, 204, 208, 211,
   215
Federal Bureau of Investigation, 48, 72, 82, 91,
   138, 149, 162–63, 178–79, 183, 187; "Alien
   Radical" activities of, 151; and Homeland
   Security, 141, 143; Language Services Section
   of, 115–16
Federal Communications Act, 159, 161, 166
Federal Communications Commission, 159
Federal Register, 71, 75
Federal Rules of Civil Procedure, 128, 129
Federal Rules of Evidence, 94
Federal Tort Claims Act, 167
federalism, 137, 142
Federalist, 61, 63, 196
Federation of American Scientists, 47
Field, Justice Stephen, 96
Fine, Glenn, 138
Firth v. Bethlehem Steel, 98
Fisher, Louis, 39, 49, 78, 104, 107, 154, 193, 197,
   201, 214, 215
Ford, President Gerald, 2, 168, 171, 179, 198,
   217
Foreign Assistance Act, 112
Foreign Intelligence Surveillance Act (FISA),
   20–21, 38, 76, 126, 128, 132, 157–58, 164,
   167, 171–91, 193, 218–20
Foreign Intelligence Surveillance Court, 172,
   175, 176, 179, 182–83, 187, 191, 192

Foreign Intelligence Surveillance Court of
   Review, 173, 179–86
Foreign Policy magazine, 144
foreign power, agent of, 126, 132
Foreign Relations of the U.S., 119
Foreign Student Monitoring Program, 121, 140,
   141
Forrestal, James, 72
Forsyth, Frederick, 59
Frankfurter, Justice Felix, 160
Freedom of Information Act, 47, 50, 75, 81–82,
   115, 135, 138, 204, 207, 215
Frost, Robert, 84
Frost v. Perry, 110

General Services Administration, 57
Geneva Conventions, 154–55
Gerry, Elbridge, 61
Gillman, Howard, 224
Ginsberg, Judge Douglas, 113
Glomar doctrine, 82
Goldman v. United States, 160
Goldstein v. United States, 68
grand jury, secrecy of, 128
Grassley, Senator Chuck, 116
Gravel, Senator Mike, 47
Great Britain, secrecy in, 103
Griffin, Steven, 223
Griswold, Erwin, 47–48
Guantanamo Bay detention facility, 152
Gulf of Tonkin, 39
Guy, Judge Ralph, 181

Haig v. Agee, 105
Halkin v. Helms, 87, 109–10
Hamas, 132
Hamdan v. Rumsfeld, 152, 154, 218
Hamdi v. Rumsfeld, 152
Hamilton, Alexander, 33
Handschu litigation, 137
Hastert, Dennis, 135
Hastings, Warren, 101
Hatfill, Steven, 130
Health and Human Services, Department of, 87
heroism, and the presidency, 3, 4
Hijazy, Abdallah, 146
Hoekstra, Representative Peter, 218
Holmes, Oliver W., 159

Homeland Security, Department of, 15, 139–42, 155, 219; and privacy, 143
Homeland Security Act, 18, 121, 125, 139, 204
homogenized regime, 38
Hoover, J. Edgar, 88, 151, 162, 164–65
Hoover, President Herbert, 25
House of Representatives, U.S., 161; Committee on Government Reform of, 15, 204
Huntington, Samuel, 157
Hyland, William, 169

Immigration and Naturalization Service, special "registry" program of, 138
in camera document review, 81, 208
independent counsel, 91
information: classification of, 19; sharing of, 126
Information Security Oversight Office, 55–60
In re Sealed Case, 199, 207
In re United States, 113
institutions, as focus of presidential studies, 24, 26
integration, racial, 35
intelligence, processing of, 1
Intelligence Advisory Board, 71
intelligence community, legislative control of, 17
Intelligence Reform and Terror Prevention Act, 132
Interagency Classification Review Committee, 56
Invention Secrecy Act, 74–76, 99–100
Iran, 149; hostages in, 92
Iran-Contra scandal, 39, 52, 91, 92, 224
Iraq, 149; detention centers in, 133; intelligence on, 36; war vote on, 39; war with, 5, 35, 36; weapons of mass destruction in, 222
Irish Republican Army, 132
Izard, Senator Ralph, 62

Jackson, President Andrew, 63
Jackson, Attorney General Robert, 161–62
Jackson, Justice Robert, 2, 6, 7
Jefferson, President Thomas, 43, 62, 95–98
Jencks v. United States, 89
John Doe orders, 74
Johnson, President Lyndon, 25, 164, 165
Joint Chiefs of Staff, 47
Jordan, 109

judicial acquiescence, 6
judicial review, 142
judiciary, federal, 76
Judiciary Act, 122
Justice, Department of, 15, 48, 82, 122, 124, 129–30, 161, 164, 168, 170, 173, 177; Inspector General of, 115

Kastenmeier, Representative Robert, 172
Kasza v. Browner, 110
Katz v. United States, 166, 170
Kennedy, Attorney General Robert, 164
Kennedy, President John F., 25, 36, 157, 164–65
Kennedy, Senator Ted, 184
King, Rev. Martin Luther, 165
King v. United States, 100
Kissinger, Henry, 168
Klein, Mark, 189
Kobach, Chris, 150
Koenig, Louis, 45
Koh, Harold Hongju, 7, 8
Koran, 146
Korean War, 6, 38, 72

labor, organized, 35
law enforcement, and secrecy, 89
Leahy, Senator Patrick, 202
Leonard, J. William, 58, 60
Levi, Attorney General Edward, 168–69
liberal-democratic political tradition, 90
Libya, 149
Lincoln, President Abraham, 1, 2, 39, 64, 134
literary theory, and constitutional interpretation, 34
Locke, John, 33, 196
"lone wolves," 132
Lowi, Theodore, 4, 18, 28–30, 36–39, 44–46, 156–57, 218; and "domestic necessity" model, 3, 5; and "legiscide," 18, 37–39, 157, 191, 218; and two tracks of presidential power, 9, 14; and "war model," 3
lying, presidential, 222–23

Machiavelli, 33–34
Maha Rajah Nundocumar, trial of, 101
Mansfield, Harvey, 33–34, 40
Marbury v. Madison, 149, 198
Maris, Judge Albert, 103–4

Marshall, Justice John, 95, 149

Marx, Karl, 43

material witnesses, 144–46, 155

Maxwell v. First National Bank of Maryland, 111

McCarthy era, 102, 224

Merit System Protection Board, 78

military tribunals, 125, 151–52, 218

Miller, Mark Crispin, 42

Mitchell, Attorney General William, 159

Montesquieu, 33, 196

Moody, Attorney General William, 96

Moschella, William, 189

Moss, Randolph, 114

mosaic theory, 17–18, 110–12, 133–34

Moynihan, Senator Daniel P., 47, 60

Mueller, Robert, 115

Murphy, Charles, 31

Muslims, 138

Nardone v. United States, 160, 164

National Center for Biomedical Research and
Training, 130

National Energy Policy Development Group,
116, 194, 208, 210

National Guard, 31–32

national security 2, 6, 45, 66, 69, 70, 73–75, 77,
84–85, 93, 108, 115, 120, 152, 157, 168, 170,
172, 205–7, 214; and electronic surveillance,
184; and foreign affairs, 15; and mosaic theory, 110; and *Reynolds* case, 20, 229n; and
warrantless surveillance, 156, 158. *See also*
Foreign Intelligence Surveillance Act

National Security Act, 53, 60, 71, 76, 82, 114

National Security Agency, 21, 52, 72, 87, 188–
90; and Homeland Security, 143

National Security Council, 2, 55–57, 71, 141

National Security League, 69

national security president, 8

national security state, 60

Navy, Department of the, 119

Navy, United States, 78, 97

Nelson, Lisa, 143

Neustadt, Richard, 12, 14, 19, 28–36, 42–44;
and persuasive power, 10; and presidential
honor, 12; and self-executing orders, 10–11

New Deal, 37, 162

New York Police Department, 137; and disappearance of cadet, 147

New York Times, 47, 188–89

9/11. *See* September 11 terror attacks

1984, election of, 13

Nixon, President Richard, 1, 17, 24, 75, 88, 115,
118, 156, 166, 168–69, 181, 188, 194, 198,
201, 210, 216; abuse of power by, 9, 13, 120;
and impoundment of funds, 26; presidential
records of, 207; secrecy claims of, 38; tape
recordings of, 193; and Watergate, 156–57

Nixon v. Administrator of General Services, 118

nuclear attack, defense against, 144

Occupational Safety and Health Act, 107

Office of Intelligence Policy and Reveiw, 177–
79, 182, 186–87

Office of Legal Counsel, 114

Office of Science and Technology Policy, 87

Office of Special Counsel, 78

Office of Strategic Information, 223

Olmstead v. United States, 159–60, 166

Olsen, Ted, 180–81, 184

Omnibus Crime Control Act, 126, 166, 172

Operaton Green Copper, 54

orders, self-executing, 31–32

organizational style, 142

overclassification, problem of, 119

Pakistan, nuclear weapons program, 112

Patriot Act, 136, 138, 147, 172, 175, 177–78, 182–
83, 220; extension of, 139; revisions to, 135

Pentagon Papers, 47

Plame, Valerie, 222

Pocock, J. G. A., 40

Poindexter, Admiral John, 46

political science, discipline of, 5

Polk, President James, 63–64

Pollock, Chief Barron, 102

Powell, Justice Lewis, 167

power: as influence, 31; as performative, 33

Powers, Richard G., 50

Prakash, Saikrishna, 197, 213

presidency: institutional, 4, 5; modern, 30; personal, 37, 44; plebiscitary, 29, 38, 44; teleological view of, 4; war orientation of, 28

president, as commander in chief, 70

presidential communications privilege, 199–
200

Presidential Records Act, 117, 206

Presidential Records Directive, 194
Privacy Act, 115
Privacy and Civil Liberties Oversight Board, 132
probable cause, standard of, 126
Project on Government Oversight, 78
Projects Minaret and Shamrock, 188

Quist, Arvin, 53, 60, 70

Ragsdale, Lyn, 12, 13, 157
Reagan, President Ronald, 9, 25, 33, 39, 43, 52,
    91, 119, 141, 157, 179, 198, 200, 207
records, business, 131
Red Scare, 15
Rehnquist, Chief Justice William, 97, 99, 151,
    179
Reno, Attorney General Janet, 115
Revolutionary War, 68
Reynolds v. U.S., 86, 94, 97–98, 102–7, 117,
    205
Rice, National Security Advisor Condoleeza,
    211–13
Ridenour, L. N., 53
Ridge, Tom, 139
Robb, Senator Charles, 114
Roberts, Chief Justice John, 153
Roberts, Justice Owen, 160
Roosevelt, President Franklin D., 13, 30, 36, 70,
    161–64
Rosenbergs, Julius and Ethel, 169
Rossiter, Clinton, 2
Rourke, Francis, 88
Rozell, Mark, 193–200, 203, 205, 207, 214, 219
rulemaking, 123
Rumsfeld, Secretary of Defense Donald, 1, 115,
    168

Scalia, Justice Antonin, 188, 202–3, 218
Schechter decision, 37
Scheindlin, Judge Shira, 145
Schlesinger, Arthur, 156
Scots law, 102
searches, "sneak and peek," 131
secrecy: abuse of, 6; and accountability, 5; and
    constitutionalism, 223; culture of, 222; and
    immigration, 133; and presidency, 2–12, 14,
    16, 22–23, 218; and tribunals, 154
Sedition Act, 151

Senate, U.S., 113, 123; Church committee of,
    165; Judiciary Committee of, 184, 186, 202
separation of powers, 8, 49, 85, 95, 142, 208,
    209
September 11 terror attacks, 8, 18, 22, 28, 33, 36,
    45, 57, 88, 108, 121–25, 127, 130–41, 143, 148,
    181, 183, 194, 218, 221; and Congressional
    response, 11, 15, 20, 158; detentions following,
    149; lawsuits following, 116; and meaning of
    "national security," 10; 9/11 Commission,
    211–13; warrantless surveillance following,
    21; wiretaps following, 175
shadow president, 122, 155
Shelby, Senator Richard, 141
Sherman, Roger, 61
Shulman, Mark, 69
Siegel, Johnathan, 203–4
Sierra Club v. Cheney, 208, 209
signing statements, 202
Silberman, Judge Laurence, 181
Silverstein, Gordon, 11, 163, 166
Sirica, Judge John, 105
Skowcroft, General Brent, 169
Skowronek, Stephen, 19, 28–30, 39–42, 44,
    218, 219
Smith v. Nixon, 158
Soviet Union, 52, 59, 77; communication inter-
    cepts by, 169; in Cuba, 157
Special Access Programs, 54
special prosecutor, 124
Speed, Attorney General James, 64, 96
Spicer, Michael, 142
State, Department of, 72, 83, 132; assessing
    alien releases, 148
state secrets privilege, 22, 42, 86, 87, 98, 100–
    111, 116–20, 193, 206–7, 212, 214, 218–19; as
    absolute, 93; and federal courts, 85, 88; and
    race/gender discrimination, 91
steel mills, seizure of, 31–32, 37, 225
Sterling v. Tenet, 108
Stevens, Justice John Paul, 153
Stone, General Charles P., 64
subpoena duces tecum, 95
Sullivan, Judge Emmet G., 116
Sulzberger, Jr., Arthur O., 188
Sundquist, James, 26–27, 220
Supreme Court, U.S., 6, 38, 77, 80, 123, 129,
    173, 181, 191, 198, 209, 214; and national

security, 215; as policymaker, 220; and presidential power to classify, 54
surveillance, 127, 136, 185, 189–90; electronic, 173–74, 178; minimization procedures in, 173; by phone, 127
Sutherland, Justice George, 94
Sylves, Richard, 143
Syria, 109, 149

Taft, Chief Justice William Howard, 159
Taguba report, 58
Tenet v. Doe, 96–98
terrorist: definition of, 132; forfeiture of citizenship by, 136. *See also* September 11 terror attacks
Theis, John, 157
Theoharis, Athan, 162, 222
Thetis submarine, 102
Thomas, Justice Clarence, 202–3
Tilden v. Tenet, 107–8
time: political, 29, 40, 219; secular, 29, 40, 42, 219; waning of, 43
Totten v. United States, 96–98
Truman, President Harry, 6, 13, 25, 31, 34, 38, 71–73, 157, 163–64
Tulis, Jeffrey, 4
Turley, Jonathan, 85
Tyler, President John, 63, 96

U.S. Court of Appeals: D.C. Circuit, 81, 110, 141, 152, 158, 170, 188, 199, 200, 211, 218; Federal Circuit, 78; Fifth Circuit, 100; Ninth Circuit, 97, 132; Second Circuit, 145; Third Circuit, 133
U.S. Customs Service, 83
U.S. Marshals Service, 82
U.S. Patent and Trademark Office, 74
Uniform Code of Military Justice, 154
unitary executive, 27
United Kingdom, 52; law of, 94
United States: citizens of, 18; danger to, 17, 89; foreign policy of, 127; protection of, 16, 66; security clearances granted in, 79
United States v. AT&T, 215

United States v. Awadallah, 145
United States v. Curtiss-Wright Export Corp., 6, 7
United States v. Nagler, 68
United States v. Nixon, 105–6, 195, 199, 203, 205, 209–10, 216
United States v. Progressive, 75
United States v. United States District Court (Keith case), 164, 165, 167, 170, 181
USS *Liberty,* Israeli attack on, 52

Vietnam, 7, 37, 38

Wald, Judge Patricia, 203–4
Walker, David, 140, 208
Walker v. Cheney, 208
"walls" between law enforcement and intelligence, 182–83
Walton, Judge Reggie, 116
war on terror, 142–43
War Powers Resolution, 37–38, 218
Washington, President George, 62, 98
Watergate, 9, 12, 34, 218, 221
Waxman, Representative Henry, 204, 222
Weber, Max, 47
Weinberger v. Catholic Action of Hawaii, 97
Westin, Alan, 161
Whistleblower Protection Act, 78–79, 113
White House, staff of, 33
Wilson, President Woodrow, 25, 89
wiretaps, illegal, 13
Woodward, Bob, 211–12
World Trade Center, destruction of, 146. *See also* September 11 terror attacks
World War I, 47, 65, 68, 70
World War II, 70, 104, 152; treatment of Japanese-Americans during, 151
Wright, Charles Alan, 88
Wright, J. Skelly, 170

Youngstown Sheet and Tube v. Sawyer, 6, 7

Zadvydas v. Davis, 123, 148
Zaid, Mark, 50, 108
Zweibon v. Mitchell, 170–71

Printed in the United States
93973LV00006B/12/A